"Most services are restricted in the number of sessions that they can give to help people with eating disorders. Until now, clinicians have had no guidance about which of the established cognitive behavioural therapy (CBT) techniques they should be delivering under such circumstances. This clear, focused book, written by experts in the field, guides clinicians through a 10-session CBT intervention. It brilliantly describes the key methods, alongside the rationale for their use, and provides clear examples and materials throughout. It addresses how to balance the use of the guide while ensuring flexibility to individual needs and responsiveness to weekly monitoring. It is essential reading for all clinicians working with eating disorders in the 21st Century".

—Professor Roz Shafran, UCL Great Ormond Street Institute of Child Health, UK

"This book makes a timely and significant contribution to the treatment of eating disorders. Firmly based on rigorous empirical research, it is innovative and clinically sophisticated. Cognitive behavioral therapy (CBT) is the most effective treatment for most eating disorders, but the reality is that a majority of patients do not receive quality evidence-based treatment. By providing a briefer, less costly, and more scalable form of CBT, this therapist-friendly treatment manual can help overcome the research-treatment gap. It is a must-read for professionals in the field of eating disorders".

—Professor G. Terence Wilson, Oscar K Buros Professor of Psychology at Rutgers, the State University of New Jersey, USA

Brief Cognitive Behavioural Therapy for Non-Underweight Patients

Most people with eating disorders struggle to find an effective therapy that they can access quickly. *Brief Cognitive Behavioural Therapy for Non-Underweight Patients: CBT-T for Eating Disorders* presents a new form of cognitive behavioural therapy (CBT) that is brief and effective, allowing more patients to get the help that they need.

CBT is a strongly supported therapy for all adults and many adolescents with eating disorders. This 10-session approach to CBT (CBT-T) is suitable for all eating disorder patients who are not severely underweight, helping adults and young adults to overcome their eating disorder. Using CBT-T with patients will allow clinicians to treat people in less time, shorten waiting lists, and see patients more quickly when they need help. It is a flexible protocol, which fits to the patient rather than making the patient fit to the therapy.

Brief Cognitive Behavioural Therapy for Non-Underweight Patients provides an evidence-based protocol that can be delivered by junior or senior clinicians, helping patients to recover and go on to live a healthy life. This book will appeal to clinical psychologists, psychiatrists, psychotherapists, dietitians, nurses, and other professionals working with eating disorders.

Glenn Waller is a Professor of Clinical Psychology at the University of Sheffield, UK. He has a particular focus on the real-world effectiveness of cognitive behavioural therapy for eating disorders. He served on the development group for the 2017 NICE eating disorder guideline. He is a past President of the Academy for Eating Disorders, and is an Associate Editor for the *International Journal of Eating Disorders*.

Hannah M. Turner is a Consultant Clinical Psychologist at the Southern Health NHS Foundation Trust Eating Disorders Service, UK. Her interests include treatment effectiveness in community settings. She is a British Association of Behavioural and Cognitive Psychotherapy (BABCP) accredited therapist and supervisor. She served on the development group for the 2017 NICE eating disorder guideline.

Madeleine Tatham is a Consultant Clinical Psychologist at the Norfolk Community Eating Disorders Service, UK. She is a British Association of Behavioural and Cognitive Psychotherapy (BABCP) accredited therapist and regularly contributes to Clinical Psychology Doctorate teaching programmes in the UK.

Victoria A. Mountford is a Principal Clinical Psychologist at the Eating Disorder Service, South London and Maudsley NHS Foundation Trust, UK. Her interests include early intervention, body image, and improving psychological treatment outcomes in the eating disorders. She is a British Association of Behavioural and Cognitive Psychotherapy (BABCP) accredited practitioner, supervisor, and trainer.

Tracey D. Wade is the Matthew Flinders Distinguished Professor of Psychology at Flinders University, Australia. She has served as President of the Eating Disorder Research Society (2017–2018) and is an Associate Editor for the *International Journal of Eating Disorders*. In 2016 she was made an Inaugural Honorary Fellow of the Australian Association for Cognitive and Behaviour Therapy.

Brief Cognitive Behavioural Therapy for Non-Underweight Patients

CBT-T for Eating Disorders

Glenn Waller, Hannah M. Turner, Madeleine Tatham, Victoria A. Mountford, and Tracey D. Wade

Routledge
Taylor & Francis Group

LONDON AND NEW YORK

First published 2019
by Routledge
2 Park Square, Milton Park, Abingdon, Oxon OX14 4RN

and by Routledge
52 Vanderbilt Avenue, New York, NY 10017

Routledge is an imprint of the Taylor & Francis Group, an informa business

British Library Cataloguing-in-Publication Data
A catalogue record for this book is available from the British Library

Library of Congress Cataloging-in-Publication Data
Names: Waller, Glenn, author. | Turner, Hannah M., author. | Tatham, Madeleine,
author. | Mountford, Victoria A., author. | Wade, Tracey D., author.
Title: Brief cognitive behavioural therapy for non-underweight patients:
CBT-T for eating disorders/Glenn Waller, Hannah M. Turner,
Madeleine Tatham, Victoria A. Mountford, Tracey D. Wade.
Description: Milton Park, Abingdon, Oxon; New York, NY: Routledge, 2019. |
Includes bibliographical references and index.
Identifiers: LCCN 2019003586 | ISBN 9780367192273 (hbk: alk. paper) |
ISBN 9780367192297 (pbk.: alk. paper) | ISBN 9780367192280 (ebk)
Subjects: | MESH: Cognitive Behavioral Therapy—methods | Feeding and
Eating Disorders—therapy | Psychotherapy, Brief | Body Weight | Body
Image—psychology
Classification: LCC RC489.B4 | NLM WM 425.5.C6 | DDC 616.89/142—dc23
LC record available at https://lccn.loc.gov/2019003586

ISBN: 978-0-367-19227-3 (hbk)
ISBN: 978-0-367-19229-7 (pbk)
ISBN: 978-0-367-19228-0 (ebk)

Typeset in Times New Roman
by Deanta Global Publishing Services, Chennai, India

[Companion website: cbt-t.shef.ac.uk]

Printed and bound in Great Britain by
TJ Books Limited, Padstow, Cornwall

Contents

Foreword

As with so many good ideas, this one took shape in a pub (over dinner, rather than drinks). Four of us (HT, VM, MT and GW) were passing post-conference time, mulling over the state of the field of cognitive behavioural therapy for eating disorders (CBT-ED). TW could not be with us in the pub but came on board when she heard about the plans.

Our experiences as clinicians and researchers were that many patients could do very well with CBT-ED – a point that was supported a few years later by the new NICE guidelines (2017) and several other reviews. However, a number of things were troubling us. The major issues will be addressed fully in Chapter 1, but they included the following:

- While the treatment of choice, CBT-ED, is clearly effective, it is very expensive to deliver, and becoming more so as the duration of the therapies gets longer (e.g. Fairburn et al., 2009).
- The first level of stepped care treatment is usually guided self-help (GSH), which is cheaper to deliver but has much poorer outcomes, suggesting a need for something between GSH and CBT-ED, ideally approaching the lower costs and greater accessibility of GSH while also approaching the better outcomes of CBT-ED.
- Services for other psychological disorders are increasingly constrained in the number of treatment sessions that they can offer.
- Psychotherapeutic interventions for other psychological disorders are being concentrated into fewer treatment sessions without any loss of benefit to patients (as exemplified by the UK's Improving Access to Psychological Therapies [IAPT] initiative, or Australia's Medicare scheme).
- Many clinicians discount the evidence of CBT-ED being effective, and offer unevidenced therapies instead (e.g. Tobin et al., 2007).
- Even when they do offer a form of CBT-ED, clinicians render it unlikely to be effective by failing to use key techniques (Waller et al., 2012), thereby supporting or leading to a belief that CBT-ED is ineffective.
- Many CBT clinicians continue to offer sessions over the recommended dose of therapy (e.g. giving an average of 45 sessions to a patient with bulimia

nervosa, rather than the recommended 20 – Cowdrey & Waller, 2015), suggesting to the client that they need long-term expert help, thereby undermining the self-efficacy that is critical for good outcome.

- Services for eating disorders often need to prioritise treating anorexia nervosa, due to concerns about risk management, meaning that the treatment waiting times for patients with non-underweight eating disorders are too often unacceptably long.

The upshot of all this is that many patients with non-underweight eating disorders do not get the treatment that is most likely to help them.

So, we wondered whether, as with other psychological disorders, a shorter CBT-ED might be effective and less expensive to deliver, thereby allowing more patients to be seen. We started by using our experience and the evidence base to work out what elements of existing CBT-ED treatment approaches we would retain and what we would discard to deliver this treatment in ten sessions (CBT-T). Of course, the treatment had to meet some key criteria:

- It had to have a protocol that could be followed easily by unqualified assistants, trainees, and experienced clinicians alike (with supervision, in all cases).
- It had to be suitable for delivery by clinicians who were relatively inexpensive (as with IAPT therapies), supported by expert case-focused supervision.
- We needed a measure of week-by-week progress, so that clinicians and patients could benefit from immediate feedback (hence, the development of the ED-15 – Tatham et al., 2015).
- It should be effective, and the reader of this manual should know that before implementing CBT-T.

In Chapter 1, we will address all these points in a way that should reassure you that CBT-T meets the criteria that we set ourselves at the outset of developing this therapy.

If there is a lesson to be learned from this story, it is that ideas generated in pubs are not always bad ones. No-one should pretend that any form of CBT-ED is perfect, but we should never see therapies as being 'gold standard' either. If we are complacent about what we have in our toolkit, then we stop pushing to get better. So, in the future, we need to keep working towards more effective and efficient therapies. For now, CBT-T is a step towards that goal, which we hope will mean that more patients get effective therapy, so that they can live happier lives, without the constraints that their eating disorder imposes on them and their loved ones.

How to use this book and the associated materials

This manual is intended for use by clinicians who wish to deliver this brief, evidence-based form of CBT to their patients with eating disorders. We recommend reading the manual all the way through before starting treatment with your first patient, so that you have an overview of what happens when and why.

Key tools are included as appendices, including the checklist that you will need to use with each patient, key measures, diaries, and some handouts. In particular, you will find a summary of the 'REAL Food Guide for CBT-T', kindly contributed by Susan Hart and Caitlin McMaster, to assist clinician and patient alike in the recovery process.

To assist in your use of these materials, they are all available for download and printing at cbt-t.shef.ac.uk, along with links to clinical research papers from our teams showing the evidence related to CBT-T and other tools that we find useful. The website also includes a downloadable 'therapy tracker', so that you can compile your own database of patient outcomes. Finally, the website will allow you to access a number of video clips of CBT-T skills being implemented, so that you can see how this is done in routine clinical practice.

Chapter 1

The background to CBT-T and its evidence base

Eating disorders carry substantial costs for the individual, their family and friends, and society more broadly. Those costs include the emotional, practical, developmental, and financial (e.g. Beat, 2015). Therefore, clinicians need to use treatments that are as effective as possible and ensure that those with eating disorders know there are such options.

Cognitive behaviour therapy (CBT) is a key tool in the armoury of psychological clinicians working with eating disorders. However, existing forms of effective CBT for eating disorders (CBT-ED) are relatively long and expensive compared to the treatment of other psychological disorders. For example, while CBT-ED is commonly 20–40 sessions long, 8–10 sessions of therapy is a more common duration for effective treatment of other disorders, such as anxiety and depression (e.g. Clark et al., 2018). Obviously, if this number of sessions is necessary to treat eating disorders, then that is what should be done. But what if we could get good outcomes with briefer treatment for a substantial group of such patients?

We developed CBT-T with just that question in mind. As clinicians, we know that it matters if we fail to treat patients efficiently – the lack of recovery for the individual, the ongoing emotional, practical, and financial costs of their eating disorder for them, the impact on their family and friends, the other patients waiting to get into treatment, and so on. Undertaking therapy is a substantial commitment for many, who may need to arrange time off work or childcare, and who, in some cases, travel considerable distances to the clinic. The cost to the patient of treatment is substantial in some settings (e.g. where the only option is private healthcare, or where there is little availability of publicly funded treatment for non-underweight patients). Therefore, it is reasonable to conclude that patients might also prefer a treatment that takes half the time, and where non-expert clinicians could deliver it (rather than having no access due to a lack of trained experts). So, we raised the question: what if we could reduce 20 sessions to 10? We would have the capacity to treat twice as many patients. But would there be a reduction in effectiveness that made that reduction unacceptable? This chapter answers that question.

This manual outlines the protocol for delivering CBT-T (the T stands for 10). The principles and processes of treatment begin in the next chapter. However, before describing the therapy, it is important to detail the context and the evidence for CBT-T. Therefore, this chapter will address:

- The context of CBT for eating disorders (CBT-ED).
- The evidence that existing forms of CBT-ED are effective.
- The problems of CBT-ED.
- The development of a ten-session form of CBT-ED – known as CBT-T.
- The evidence for CBT-T.
- What is needed to do CBT-T.

1.1 The context of CBT for eating disorders (CBT-ED)

Cognitive behaviour therapy (CBT) is a family of treatments that focus on the inter-action of behaviours, beliefs, emotions, and physiology, all in the context of the social environment. These therapies have their origins in behavioural therapies, and some of the most effective elements of CBT are the behavioural interventions that preceded the development of cognitive approaches. The cognitive behaviour therapies have added processes such as cognitive restructuring, which aim to test the validity of unhelpful/dysfunctional beliefs (cognitive content). This development includes more explicitly using behaviour change to weaken unhelpful cognitions and to strengthen alternative and helpful cognitions (behavioural experiments).

More recently, a so-called 'third wave' of CBT approaches has been devel-oped. While these are less cohesive than the behavioural (first wave) or cognitive-behavioural (second wave) therapies, their focus tends to be more on developing more adaptive cognitive processes. At present, the strongest evidence sits with the behavioural and cognitive-behavioural treatments, across most psychologi-cal disorders. That is also true of the evidence regarding eating disorders, where the evidence base is strongest for 'second-wave' CBT, where both behavioural and cognitive approaches are used. With the possible exception of dialectical behaviour therapy for binge-eating disorder, the 'third-wave' therapies remain in need of strong evidence before they can be recommended for eating disorders. At present, CBT has the strongest evidence base for a range of disorders (Roth & Fonagy, 2005), including anxiety and depression (both of which are most respon-sive to the behavioural elements, such as exposure and behavioural activation). As a result, the UK IAPT initiative uses CBT as its core therapeutic approach, offered to a very large number of patients who otherwise would have been unlikely to receive an effective therapy for their substantial problems.

Cognitive-behaviour therapy for eating disorders (CBT-ED) includes a range of CBT protocols that have an evidence base when used with such cases. The term CBT-ED was coined for the NICE (2017) guideline, to describe the collection of different versions of CBT that are supported by evidence and that address a number of key targets using the same therapeutic methods. An umbrella term was used to stress that none of the different versions of evidence-based protocols has a superior outcome (e.g. Linardon et al., 2017).

In CBT-ED, the target characteristics and methods include: collaborative weighing; healthy eating; weight gain where necessary (never intentional weight loss); addressing nutrition; addressing risk; monitoring diet, weight, thoughts, and feelings; cognitive restructuring through the use of behavioural experiments; mood regulation; body image concerns; reducing emphasis on control over weight, shape and eating for defining self-worth; and relapse prevention. The length of treatment and inclusion of any family members are dependent on the history and issues that the person brings to therapy. Consequently, while some forms of CBT can be considered to be CBT-ED (e.g. Fairburn et al., 1993; Fairburn, 2008; Waller et al., 2007), other forms cannot, as they lack key elements and/or an evidence base.

For most cases of eating disorders (i.e. the 80–85% who have non-underweight eating disorders, such as bulimia nervosa, binge-eating disorders, and most atypical cases), the recommended length of CBT-ED is approximately 20 sessions (NICE, 2017). However, there is no evidence to suggest that this is the 'right' number of sessions. Furthermore, it is clear that clinicians do not necessarily restrict themselves to this number, with many patients reporting that they are being given far more than 20 sessions (e.g. Cowdrey & Waller, 2015). On the other hand, some patients opt to cease therapy before 20 sessions elapse: are they 'dropping-out' before recovery or are they voting with their feet because they have enough tools on board to journey on alone on their recovery pathway?

1.2 The evidence for CBT-ED

Considering the evidence from randomised control trials, NICE (2017) identifies CBT-ED as the most effective approach for non-underweight adults with eating disorders; one of three effective treatments for adults with anorexia nervosa; and a second therapy for adolescents with eating disorders. More importantly, those results translate well to routine clinical settings. There is now substantial evidence that CBT-ED is equally effective in everyday clinical practice (Byrne et al., 2011; Knott et al., 2015; Raykos et al., 2013; Signorini et al., 2018; Turner et al., 2015; Waller et al., 2014), including out-, day- and in-patient settings. It is also effective with the so-called 'severe and enduring' eating disorders (e.g. Calugi et al., 2016; Raykos et al., 2018).

It is also important to note that the evidence indicates that therapies need to aim for early change, as their level of impact tails off by the tenth session – a finding that is true for a range of psychological disorders (e.g. depression and anxiety – Delgadillo et al., 2014) and therapies (e.g. Bell et al., 2017). In CBT-ED, therapy has its maximal effect by about the same point (Rose & Waller, 2017). Early therapeutic change (i.e. typically in the first 4–6 weeks or sessions of therapy) is the single best predictor of how well a patient will do in therapy for an eating disorder (Vall & Wade, 2015), and that finding is equally true of CBT-ED (e.g. Raykos et al., 2013; Turner et al., 2015). Lack of early change should be seen as an indicator that the therapy should be adapted, intensified, or discontinued.

Table 1.1 Evidence-based guidance for clinicians (drawn from NICE, 2017)

- For most adult cases of eating disorders, CBT-ED is the best therapy to use.
- CBT-ED works just as well in real-world clinical settings.
- Do not let comorbid conditions or the duration/severity of the patient's eating disorder get in the way of the plan to deliver CBT-ED.
- Press for early change as it predicts a better outcome for the patient; change is far less likely later in therapy.

Furthermore, CBT-ED has a substantial effect on the very prominent levels of comorbidity in the eating disorders. Despite not addressing these problems directly, CBT-ED reduces anxiety, depression, personality disorder characteristics, and alcohol misuse, while improving self-esteem and quality of life (e.g. Karačić et al., 2011; Linardon & Brennan, 2017; Raykos et al., 2013; Turner et al., 2015). In short, comorbidity is not a good clinical reason not to use CBT-ED in its existing forms. Rather, the rule of thumb should be to treat the eating disorder and re-assess for any residual comorbidity. These findings are summarised in Table 1.1.

1.3 The problems of CBT-ED

First, no therapy works for everybody, and CBT-ED is no different. Delivered well, CBT-ED has a better recovery rate than other psychological therapies for non-underweight adults (Linardon et al., 2017), around 50% recovery and another 25% improving substantially without full recovery. Its recovery rate is lower for anorexia nervosa among adults (c. 30%) but equivalent to the other NICE-supported therapies (Maudsley Model of Anorexia Nervosa Treatment for Adults; MANTRA and Specialised Supportive Clinical Management SSCM) for this group (NICE, 2017). It is effective with younger cases too, but Family Based Treatment has somewhat superior outcomes. Whatever the limits of CBT-ED's outcomes, overall it is the strongest therapy that we can use when treating people with eating disorders.

However, that takes us to the second problem with CBT-ED – clinicians routinely fail to deliver empirically supported treatments (Waller & Turner, 2016). For example, Tobin et al. (2007) have shown that fewer than one clinician in 10 delivers evidence-based therapies for eating disorders. The reasons for this are manifold, but include: clinicians who are untrained or whose training is not up to date (Institute of Medicine, 2001; Royal College of Psychiatrists, 2011; 2013); clinicians who have a preferred way of working; supervision that is not oriented towards patient outcomes (Simpson-Southward et al., 2018); and services that do not support evidence-based practice (e.g. do not train or recruit sufficient staff with the required skill set; set caseloads too high thus limiting quality; do not offer supervision of clinical practice).

The third problem with CBT-ED, which compounds the problems identified above, is when clinicians who claim to be delivering CBT-ED deliver a version that omits key techniques (e.g. exposure; body image work; dietary change). The evidence for such omissions is strong (Cowdrey & Waller, 2015; Mulkens et al., 2018; Waller et al., 2012), similar to what is found in other disorders (Waller & Turner, 2016). The reasons for those omissions are also clear – relatively few clinicians use manuals, despite evidence that they improve outcomes (Addis & Krasnow, 2000; Waller et al., 2013); clinician anxiety leads to the reduced use of key behavioural methods (Waller et al., 2012); and many clinicians see the therapeutic alliance as far more important than the therapy techniques in CBT-ED, despite strong evidence to the contrary (Graves et al., 2017). Unfortunately for our patients, this means that many clinicians do not use any agenda, and just let the patient talk without direction, structure, or expectation of change. While clinician competence has been recognised as an important obstacle (e.g. Fairburn & Cooper, 2011), efforts to roll out training via online methods have had relatively limited benefits to date. Therefore, if we are to rely on more traditional training and supervision to maintain and develop competence, it is important that both the training and ongoing supervision are effective, as demonstrated by strong patient outcomes.

The final problem with CBT-ED is that it has been getting longer, at a time when therapies in other areas are constrained economically and being shortened with no loss of effect (e.g. the 6–10 sessions offered for most disorders by clinicians working within the UK IAPT programme; the impact of brief and intensive therapies for anxiety disorders – Öst & Ollendick, 2017). There is little justification for extending the treatments that we offer, but there are many costs of doing so. When we realise that many patients are offered far more than the recommended treatment dose (Beintner & Jacobi, 2018; Cowdrey & Waller, 2016), it becomes clear that we run the risk of denying and slowing access to treatment for those who are on waiting lists or who are unable to access therapy because they are 'not underweight enough'.

All of the above leads to a simple question. Can CBT-ED be delivered more efficiently and cheaply without sacrificing its effects? We know from the above evidence that CBT-ED works, but that it is relatively expensive and that we fail to deliver it reliably to our patients. So, can CBT-ED be delivered more efficiently, and can clinicians deliver it competently with appropriate supervision?

1.4 Introducing the evidence for CBT-T: A brief intensive form of CBT-ED

The origins of 10-session CBT-ED (CBT-T) lay in the need to make this therapy more available. The twin goals were therefore to produce a shorter, stripped-down version of CBT-ED that could be delivered by relatively inexpensive clinicians. We wanted CBT-T to be easily disseminable (i.e. via this manual and the protocol checklist – Appendix 1), and easily delivered under appropriate supervision.

Thus, more patients could be seen, and waiting times reduced. Obviously, the initial aim was that the therapy should retain enough of CBT-ED's effect that it remained of value.

The context for developing CBT-T was the emergence of services and funding frameworks dedicated to such provision. In the UK, the relevant service was the IAPT framework, which had demonstrated (for other disorders) that treatment could be time-limited and delivered cheaply but could still be remarkably impressive (e.g. Clark, 2018; Clark et al., 2018). In Australia, the Access to Medicare funding was limited to 10 sessions annually. However, it was also noteworthy that there were often local service issues that were slowing treatment access. For example, many specialist eating disorders services were failing to see non-underweight patients quickly (or at all), as their efforts were directed towards risk management and monitoring of underweight patients. Similarly, while many eating disorders services were pushing for faster turnover of patients, their reluctance to discharge patients who were not doing well meant that access to treatment was very slow for most patients.

There are already shorter versions of CBT, in the form of guided and unguided self-help for eating disorders and groups for specific disorders (e.g. bulimia nervosa, binge-eating disorders). While guided self-help is effective (Linardon et al., 2017), there is a great variation in the protocols offered, which results in variable outcomes, and CBT-ED groups are not as effective overall as individual CBT-ED (though they are recommended for binge-eating disorder – NICE, 2017). The nearest to a comparably brief version of CBT was the one developed and tested by Bulik et al. (1998). However, the outcomes of that CBT-ED were not strong, possibly due to the content of the therapy.

1.5 The process of development of the final protocol

Developing CBT-T was an iterative process, informed by the evidence base and our substantial clinical and supervisory experience, to suggest what needed to be retained from CBT-ED and what could be removed across the whole course of CBT-ED. Then we considered the evidence and logical reasons for structuring the therapeutic elements that remained. On examining the result, we went through the same process repeatedly until we were satisfied that we had a protocol that had the best chance of combining effectiveness and efficiency. We then trialled the protocol with a small number of patients and collected the opinions of the clinicians and patients to determine some small final changes. The protocol for CBT-T that emerged is the one used to develop the following evidence and this manual.

Key differences to CBT-ED include the following:

- There is no period of motivational work, as there is little evidence that this is effective (e.g. Dray & Wade, 2012; Waller, 2012). Instead, positive reinforcement is used, in the form of praise for the patient upon successful implementation of CBT-T skills.

- The therapeutic alliance is not a target for development, given the evidence that early behavioural change promotes that alliance in CBT-ED, rather than the other way around (e.g. Graves et al., 2017).
- Behavioural and dietary change are stressed from the very outset of treatment, rather than being delayed.
- Individualised case formulation is rarely used, given the very poor evidence of clinical utility (e.g. Kuyken, 2006). Rather, there is an emphasis on the formulation of specific behaviours (e.g. the energy graph). Generic case formulation (e.g. Waller, 2016) can be used at assessment or early in the therapy to explain the development of the individual's problem and to outline the rationale for using core techniques such as addressing nutrition.
- Exposure with response prevention is conducted more intensively, using the inhibitory learning approach (e.g. Craske et al., 2014; Reilly et al., 2017).
- A stronger stress on supervision as a tool to enhance clinician adherence, rather than an assumption that clinician competence translates into best practice.
- A structured approach to body image work, where symptoms and interventions are linked explicitly.
- Weekly monitoring of attitudes and behaviours, to ensure that clinicians respond to change more quickly than if using existing measures, which are designed to be used monthly. This required the development of a weekly, brief measure of eating attitudes (the ED-15; Tatham et al., 2015) to map onto the measures used in the UK IAPT system and elsewhere for anxiety and depression.

Other features of CBT-ED remained in the CBT-T protocol, such as open weighing (present in all recent variants of CBT-ED), diary keeping, psychoeducation, relapse prevention, and the stress on nutritional and behavioural changes. No other techniques were incorporated (e.g. elements of third wave therapies, as these are not present in any variant of CBT-ED).

Having developed the final protocol, the remaining step was to demonstrate whether CBT-T works, prior to disseminating in the form of this manual. That way, one can be sure that CBT-T is evidence-based. The remainder of this chapter will detail the evidence to date showing whether CBT-T works, and how well.

1.6 The evidence for CBT-T

CBT-T has been tested in routine clinical settings, based on a three separate case series (Moore et al., under consideration; Pellizzer et al., in press; Waller et al., 2018), one with a waiting list control condition. In total, these studies include nearly 300 patients between two countries. Patient experience of the therapy has also been explored qualitatively (Hoskins et al., 2019). The patients have all been 16 years of age or older and have had a BMI of 17.5 or above, so the conclusions relate to older adolescents and adults who are within or above the normal weight range, and to those who might need a small amount of weight regain to return to the healthy weight range. However, as this is a substantial majority of patients presenting to services (e.g. Fairburn & Harrison, 2003), the findings are widely relevant. As will be addressed below, this means that some of the patients treated with CBT-T will be low in weight. Such patients need a strong focus on weight regain in the early part of therapy to ensure that other aspects of their eating disorders can be addressed effectively. The relevance to younger cases and significantly underweight patients will be established in future research.

The aim of the case series has been to demonstrate CBT-T's effectiveness with patients who most clinicians will work with in routine clinical practice, to show that the findings are replicable, and to confirm that CBT-T works in more than one clinical setting. Summarising the papers outlined above and comparing them to the findings from existing CBT-ED studies (e.g. Byrne et al. 2011, Fairburn et al., 1995; 2009; Knott et al., 2015; Signorini et al., 2018; Turner et al., 2015; Waller et al., 2014), key findings are detailed in Table 1.2.

Table 1.2 The evidence for CBT-T for non-underweight adults: Key outcomes

- CBT-T has a high suitability rate.
  - Very few patients excluded (usually on the basis of suicidality and/or significant levels of self-harm, where the life-threatening behaviours require urgent attention).
- It has a high acceptability rate.
  - Very low numbers declining to start CBT-T post-assessment, following the offer of the therapy.
- The attrition rate of CBT-T is somewhat lower than for CBT-ED in routine practice.
- CBT-ED randomised control trials have a slightly lower attrition rate than CBT-T.
- The outcomes of CBT-T are broadly comparable with those of 20-session CBT-ED, despite being half the length. The outcomes and the end of treatment at the three-month follow-up were similar in terms of:
  - Behavioural change.
  - Attitudinal change.
  - Remission and abstinence.
  - Reliable Change Index.
  - Clinically significant change.
- Comorbid psychological problems showed clinically significant reductions.
  - e.g. anxiety and depression.
- The therapeutic alliance starts at a high level at Session 1, improving further by the fourth session.
- As with CBT-ED, early change in eating pathology was the best predictor of outcome.
  - Early improvement in the therapeutic alliance and body image flexibility appear to be related to outcome.
- Patient experiences include themes and sub-themes reflecting CBT-T as:
  - "Firm but fair".
  - Requiring "personal effort".
  - "Challenging but beneficial".
  - Positive when "compared with previous therapies".

1.7 What is needed for CBT-T?

Assuming that the patient is safe to undertake treatment (see Chapter 4 onwards), then one needs access to the following, when seeing the patient:

- A copy of the protocol booklet (Appendix 1) per patient.
- Psychoeducation materials (see Chapter 5).
- A measure of cognitive and behavioural change (ED-15 questionnaire – see Appendix 3).
- Basic diary sheets (Appendix 2).
- Weighing scales, so that the patient and clinician can weigh the patient openly and discuss weight and its relationship to dietary intake, exercise, etc. (see Chapters 4 and 5).
- Pen and paper or a whiteboard/flipchart (for weight charts, energy graphs, etc. – see Chapter 4 onwards).
- Access to a full-length mirror for body image exposure work (see Chapter 9).
- Supervision that is patient-centred, and focused on the protocol.
- Medical review facilities, where necessary.
- Colleagues, supervisors, or peers who are willing to discuss patient progress by asking about change, and/or obstacles to change, in a manner that is open and non-threatening, to facilitate learning (whatever our career stage).
- Ability to tolerate our own uncertainty, to manage our own anxiety (which might be interfering with delivering therapy effectively).
- Courage in setting and reviewing our own therapeutic behavioural experiments, with the use of firm empathy.

Summary: The evidence behind CBT-T

CBT-ED has an important role to play in the treatment of eating disorders. However, it is expensive, compared to treatment of other disorders. NICE therefore recommended that briefer, less intensive therapies should be tested. CBT-T was developed to see whether such briefer therapies are effective. Clinicians should be aware that:

- CBT-T (10 sessions) is as effective as 20-session CBT-ED when delivered to non-underweight patients, with good suitability, acceptability, and clinical outcomes.
- As with all therapies, that benefit only emerges when the therapy is delivered to protocol.
- Clinicians who want to achieve the results that are possible with any protocol need to understand the principles of the therapy (the 'why') as well as its practical application (the 'how').
- A protocol of this sort should be adapted to the individual, rather than forcing the individual to stick to a rigid and impersonal treatment.
- The resources needed to deliver CBT-T are similar to those needed for CBT-ED, though the cost of delivery is substantially lower.

Chapter 2

Principles of CBT-T, and how to apply them in routine practice

While it is tempting to skip ahead to the 'how to do it' section, please do not underestimate the importance of this chapter's contents. As with any effective protocol-based therapy, CBT-T requires understanding the 'big picture' principles for delivering effective therapy (the 'why'), as well how to deliver it in practice (the 'how'). Subsequent chapters will address the 'how', but this chapter addresses the 'why' of CBT-T.

We assume that the most common principle is that we want to help as many people to improve and recover as possible. This is indeed a guiding principle of CBT-T: *what is best for the patient?* To provide the best outcomes for the patient requires that we hold the principles of CBT-T in mind, to maintain focus and work flexibly but effectively within the protocol. Of course, as with all principles, it is important that we should be able to articulate them, so that we can explain our thinking and actions to our patients, supervisees, supervisors, colleagues, and ourselves.

With the 'what is best for the patient' principle in mind, it should be stressed that a key benefit to CBT-T is that its shorter time frame allows us to treat patients more quickly, to treat more patients, and to reduce waiting times considerably. It is very common to hear just how distressing our patients find long waiting times, and to be able to reduce them enhances our chances of seeing the patient while they still have some of the motivation that led them to seek treatment in the first place.

2.1 Use a protocol to guide therapy

The first principle is to use a protocol – the outcomes for our patients are so much better when we do (Waller, 2016). That means more than just owning this book, as osmosis rarely works when it comes to books on shelves. We need to read, discuss, be familiar with, and experiment with the protocol, and regularly measure progress and review outcome in supervision. Reflecting upon the 'bigger picture' will assist our understanding in how to apply it flexibly, but without omitting the key elements. Even in the case of CBT-T, there are elements of the protocol that one can skip or amend for specific patients (see Table 2.1).

Table 2.1 Clinical example: Flexible application of protocols

- Sophie is a 20-year old patient with bulimia nervosa. On stabilising her on an adequate diet, her bingeing and purging behaviour cease completely.
- Emma is a 20-year-old patient with bulimia nervosa. On stabilising her on an adequate diet, most of her bingeing and purging behaviours cease, but she still binges and vomits a couple of times a week, when she feels stressed.

It is likely that the clinician can bypass focused work on emotional triggers to bulimic behaviours and emotional regulation strategies when working with Sophie, while needing to do that work with Emma.

Table 2.2 Supervision example: Identifying failures to deliver the protocol

SUPERVISOR: I notice that this is the second week in a row where you have not asked the patient to increase her carbohydrates across the day, and her binges don't appear to be improving? What is the problem here, do you think?

CLINICIAN: Well, I know that she is scared that her weight will shoot up, and that is worrying me too – what do I do if she is right, and she puts on lots of weight?

SUPERVISOR: Let's think this through – if the patient fails to get to a healthier diet, her binges will continue, and we can be pretty certain that she will not get better and she will probably gain weight. So your anxiety stops you pressing her to change, making it likely that the thing that she wants to avoid will happen, and you end up feeling like a lousy clinician. We also know that if she doesn't make these changes early in therapy, she is less likely to do so later in therapy. The alternative is that she tries a different approach, by following the protocol, making it less likely that she will gain the weight because the binges will decrease, but you have to tolerate your anxiety about what will happen to her. Which way do you think we should go? Which way is in the best interests of the patient?

A key benefit of a therapy protocol is that it allows the clinician and supervisor to discuss progress in a more concrete way. Being able to identify any gaps in the delivery of the protocol enables the supervisor and clinician to collaboratively explore the reasons for those gaps, and to work on developing the necessary skills (see Table 2.2).

2.2 Use a checklist to guide practice with the individual patient

As well as using a manualised protocol (such as the one included in this book), there is an equally powerful and complementary tool – the checklist. Checklists ensure that busy people who are multi-tasking in complex settings actually deliver the key tasks of therapy. The checklist approach is employed effectively across a range of complex and demanding jobs and professions, including flying aircraft, and ensuring that surgeons operate effectively (Gawande, 2011). Would it not be valuable in our clinical roles? If done well, therapy is an equally complex, demanding job, so it is not surprising that clinicians routinely omit key elements of that therapy.

That is why we have included a checklist of the tasks to be undertaken with each patient as one of the core tools to be used to implement CBT-T. We recommend that you print off a copy and use it to guide therapy on a session-by-session basis for each of your individual patients. You now have a tool for recording key clinical details and progress, and for noting what has been done. The key to using this checklist effectively is to ensure that you have covered all the relevant items for a session in whatever order is most clinically appropriate (e.g. if it is more natural to address an issue later, just leave it unticked to remind you that you need to come back to it). The checklist is also helpful in organising and using your clinical supervision time effectively.

2.3   CBT is a 'doing therapy', not a 'talking therapy'

We have all heard the term 'talking therapy' being applied to CBT in general. However, this ignores the key fact that the most effective elements of CBT are behavioural. CBT clinicians in general, and those delivering CBT-T in particular, need to be clear that we are advocating a 'doing therapy', and that if we treat therapy as being largely about talking (as many do – Cowdrey & Waller, 2015), we will substantially reduce its effectiveness. Behaviour change matters, whether it is in the form of exposure, behavioural experiments, nutritional change, body image work, etc. Such change drives: cognitive change (by reducing starvation and perfectionism; enhancing flexibility); emotional change (the availability of serotonin to stabilise mood; reinforcement of positive outcomes to reduce learned helplessness and enhance self-efficacy); and quality of life. The evidence across numerous eating disorder treatment studies, whether of bulimia nervosa or anorexia nervosa, or with children or adults, is clear: *the earlier the change, the better the outcome.*

Just as importantly, we need to transmit this message and convey the evidence transparently to inform the patient. Remember that cultural stereotypes and prior experience (i.e. previous unsuccessful treatments) might have taught the patient that: "Therapy is about talking about stuff, and if it doesn't work then I obviously was not talking enough or about the right stuff". How then can we frame therapy appropriately for the patient?

2.3.1   States of therapy

There are three 'states of therapy'. In the first, the patient is *'in therapy'*, which means being on the clinician's books, but not necessarily attending sessions. This state allows the patient to deflect demands (e.g. from family, friends and employers), by saying "But I am in therapy". In the second state of therapy, the patient is *'going to therapy'*, where they attend and engage during the session, but switch off until the next session, and don't undertake any meaningful homework tasks between sessions. In the third state of therapy, the patient is *'doing therapy'*, where they attend the session, then spend the rest of the week undertaking the key tasks of therapy. 'Doing therapy' results in engaging in therapy for 168 hours a week so it should be no surprise that it is the most effective state of therapy.

Both the 'in therapy' and 'going to therapy' states are therapy interfering behaviours (Linehan, 1993), whatever their origin (e.g. anxiety about change; unhelpful/counterproductive learning from previous therapies). Our task as CBT-T clinicians is to get the patient to move from being 'in therapy' and 'going to therapy' to the state of 'doing therapy'.

2.3.2 An unhelpful start to a CBT session?

Finally, remember that one of the most unhelpful things to say when the patient enters the therapy room is: "Hi, have a seat. How has your week been?". This approach is very welcoming but socialises and encourages the patient to think that therapy is about talking, and increases the likelihood that they will still be talking about their week half an hour later, rather than using the session to engage in the behavioural elements of therapy. We address more helpful approaches to structuring CBT-T sessions below.

2.4 Offer a limited number of sessions at the beginning

A key technique in CBT-T is that the patient is only offered four therapy sessions from the start of treatment, stressing that this can be extended to 10, dependent on whether they show substantial change over those first four sessions. This early requirement for change should be made absolutely clear, with the rationale explained to and understood by the patient from the beginning (see Table 2.3). If the clinician tries to bypass explaining this to the patient (usually because of their anxiety about potentially distressing or displeasing the patient), it should be addressed in supervision. The supervisor should re-emphasise that early change is in the best interests of the patient, however scary the clinician or patient might view it at the start of CBT-T.

In this context, an early lack of change needs to be raised with the patient (and supervisee) as a concern. Equally, useful or meaningful clinical change should be positively reinforced at every opportunity, with congratulations for a job well done. In cases where change has occurred by session four, a written letter to the patient at the end of the fourth session can be a powerful tool for reinforcing the importance of hard work and behavioural change. Where a patient does not make the necessary changes (e.g. in eating or completing diaries), we consider the use of abbreviated sessions to reinforce the point that the patient needs to be active during and between sessions for the therapy to be beneficial. Chapter 6 gives examples of some letters that can be used to reinforce change or explain ending therapy in a constructive manner if therapy is not going well.

Underpinning this approach is the need to ensure that both the patient and the clinician are clear that continuing therapy is dependent on the patient actively

Table 2.3 Example of setting boundaries for therapy length and change in the early sessions

Session 1

CLINICIAN: I will see you for four sessions. We can extend that up to 10, but I am only going to do that if you are progressing well by that point – and that means lots of change in your eating patterns, reduction in bingeing, and so on. All the evidence says that if you are not going to make that early change, you are not going to do well with this therapy, so I don't want to waste anyone's time by extending therapy when it is not going to work. So I suggest that we get active from the very start, and focus on early change. And just so that neither of us forgets that need for change, I am going to be counting down as the next few sessions go by, to check that we are heading in the right direction.

Session 2

CLINICIAN: Looking at how you are doing, I am concerned that you are not working on change between the sessions, as we discussed. You have not eaten as planned on four out of seven days, and your diaries are not complete for most days. I want you to remember that is it really important that we see change early on, or we will not be continuing therapy, to avoid wasting our time. Therefore, I am going to need you to make the changes that we agree over the coming week, to catch up. If you want to benefit from this therapy, then it is time to get going.

PATIENT: My other therapist never expected me to work this hard or this early. And she didn't care if I didn't do food diaries and never weighed me.

CLINICIAN: And what do we know about that other therapy? It didn't work. Otherwise, you wouldn't be here now. So yes, I am going to be 'firm', because I really want you to get better, and I know that is unlikely if I am nice but not firm. Just remember, I don't mind if you think I'm mean or too firm sometimes – as long as you are getting well, that is absolutely fine.

Session 3

PATIENT: All right, it was scary, but I did what we agreed, and my binges went down a lot. I still think you are a mean therapist, mind.

CLINICIAN: That is great. Well done. This tells us that you have more ability than you give yourself credit for. That is important to remember as we have plenty more to do, but that is a great step forward. Now let's look at what we need to do this time.

using the therapy to change, and that sessions will not be extended if there is no likelihood of change occurring. Numbering and counting off each session and linking them to the expected progress is a 'drip, drip' approach to remind both patient and clinician about the time available, and the need to attend to core tasks. Novice clinicians often find such reminders anxiety-provoking ("what if I upset the patient?") but in our experience, if the patient is clear about the rationale, it frequently allows patients to pull off achievements neither they nor the clinician were sure that they were capable of.

At Session 4, there is a review of progress against targets. This should be undertaken in a collaborative way, with the clinician also inviting the patient to reflect on what they feel is going well and what they could be doing better. If the patient is doing well, then the review can be brief and congratulatory. In contrast, if the patient is not progressing, then a discussion should take place about whether to terminate therapy. Services differ in their care pathways, according to clinical presentation – some will discharge if the patient is not engaging in the CBT-T, while others will transfer the patient to another therapy (though our experience is that such transfers are rarely associated with positive outcomes from the new therapy).

Obviously, the probability of sessions coming to an end should never come as a surprise to the patient, as it should have been raised and discussed as a possibility over the previous two sessions. It is possible for the clinician to offer an extension by one or even two sessions, if the patient really seems committed to change in the face of likely end of the CBT-T. However, the need for immediate and substantial change needs to be stressed, e.g.:

CLINICIAN: While I appreciate that you say that you want one last chance to show that you can change, you need to be clear that you would have to make a huge amount of change in one week – essentially making all the dietary changes in one week that you have avoided making over the past four weeks. Are you sure that you are ready for that? Because if not, then it would be better if you ended therapy now, remembered what you need to do in therapy in future, and came back when you are ready to commit fully to change, knowing what the demands will be.

It is important to stress that relatively few patients stop treatment as a result. However, without the explicit expectation from the outset to engage in 'doing' therapy, it is likely that fewer patients would make the early change that is so critical to positive outcomes across therapies – again, our focus is on what is best for the patient.

Where a patient is discharged at this stage, we do not know whether they could have benefited from CBT-T, because they have not really tried it. We understand that this could have been due to other commitments, or due to a hope that simply coming to therapy would be enough to recover. Either way, we do not treat this as the patient's fault, and we stress that we would like them to try again. We emphasise that we cannot conclude that they could not have done well – only that we know what happens when they are not able to engage in the recommended/required tasks (i.e. no change). In short, it is important that the patient should leave with the message that change is still possible in the future, but that they have learned that the next time they want to get away from their eating disorder, they will need to be more active in therapy.

2.5 Do not bring in unproven or ineffective elements to the therapy

Many clinicians routinely assume that they should or can introduce additional elements to CBT-ED, potentially reducing the effectiveness of their treatments and certainly reducing its efficiency. With CBT-T – a therapy that has many of those

elements deliberately taken out – that risk is even greater. Therefore, it is important to remember that the following techniques should *not* be used within CBT-T:

- Adaptations of motivational interviewing/motivation enhancement therapy
  (despite extensive research, these have no impact on outcome in eating disorders – e.g. Dray & Wade 2012; Waller, 2012). It is far more effective to offer
  positive reinforcement for change than to discuss the potential for change.
- Focus on developing the therapeutic alliance at the cost of progressing the
  tasks of therapy. It is important to remember that a good therapeutic alliance develops as a product of early change, rather than driving that change,
  and an approach of 'firm empathy' is more likely to be effective (Wilson et
  al., 1997). Putting it simply for clinician and patient alike, one cannot 'nice'
  someone better. Many clinicians believe that a good relationship with the
  patient is the same thing as a good therapeutic alliance. This is not the case,
  as the latter involves more of a tension between the attachment bond and
  the demands of therapy, which inevitably may involve necessary friction
  between the clinician and patient at times (which is why it is fine for the
  patient to be angry at the clinician sometimes – see Table 2.3). We routinely
  stress that such friction is normal, and that it is better for the patient to express
  their concerns rather than dropping out.
- 'Third wave' therapy elements such as mindfulness, compassion-focused therapy,
  etc. (which are still under development in the eating disorders more generally).

CBT-T is an effective therapy without those elements (see Chapter 1), and the
risk of incorporating such techniques is to reduce its effectiveness. In particular,
focusing on issues such as motivation and the therapeutic alliance in the first few
sessions will result in less emphasis on early behavioural change, which is proven
to be effective. It is also likely that other methods aimed at reducing anxiety levels
(e.g. mindfulness) will reduce the impact of therapeutic treatment methods that
require raised patient anxiety (e.g. exposure) to be effective. Thus, bringing these
methods into CBT-T or CBT-ED more generally could serve to weaken outcomes.

2.6 Session frequency

As with most forms of CBT-ED, CBT-T works on the basis of one session per
week. While Fairburn (2008) introduced the idea of two sessions a week in the
early stage, this double session pattern is frequently hard to implement in routine
practice. It also risks communicating to the patient that they are dependent on
the clinician when we are keen to promote the message that they are responsible
for making early change. As the two sessions a week model is not proven to add
benefit, CBT-T has a structure of one session per week for ten weeks (with two
follow-up sessions).

While it is emphasised at the outset that a weekly commitment to attending
therapy sessions is important, it is also very common that patients or clinicians

may need to miss a weekly meeting or two (e.g. pre-arranged commitments, illness, emergencies, etc.). In CBT-T, this is regarded as normal and acceptable, as long as the patient keeps implementing what they have learnt in therapy between sessions. In other words, as CBT-T is a 168-hour-a-week therapy, the patient simply has to keep implementing changes until the next session. If patients do not benefit from therapy and/or are not using the skills between sessions because of excessive breaks, they should be given the option of regular weekly attendance, or asked to consider whether their commitment to change is limited at that stage.

2.7 Monitor progress and outcomes

It is well-established that patients do better where their outcomes are measured and when the therapist is aware of those measures (Lambert et al., 2002; 2005). Therefore, CBT-T includes the monitoring of outcomes within the service and suggests that these should be regularly reviewed between clinician and supervisor. However, it is equally important for patient and clinician to monitor progress, as this allows them to set targets, monitor change, and revise those targets as appropriate. It can also be very helpful for both to see an objective measure of change (or not) over the course of therapy. Therefore, CBT-T requires the collection of weekly records of eating behaviours and attitudes (using a combination of diaries and the ED-15), as well as other, less frequently used measures.

2.8 Focusing on one disorder at a time

Comorbidity can be considered the norm in eating disorders. The great majority of people with eating disorders also have symptoms that could be signs of other disorders (e.g. anxiety disorders, depression, personality disorders, obsessive compulsive disorder, post-traumatic stress disorder, autistic spectrum disorders, alcohol and substance misuse). It is not always possible to decide which disorder is primary (if any), or whether symptoms are representative of other disorders or are the consequences of the starvation effects, impulsive behaviours, and safety behaviours that are symptomatic of the eating disorders themselves. It is certainly not uncommon for such patients to be moved from service to service, as each decides that they cannot tackle the complexity of the case and/or manage the associated risks.

The general rule in CBT is to treat problems sequentially. Address whatever appears to be the primary disorder according to the relevant protocol, see whether that approach also reduces any comorbidity, and then address any remaining comorbid problems. CBT-T takes the same approach – address the eating disorder using this CBT-T protocol, and then assess for any residual problems later and review the need for any additional self-help or clinician-led interventions. However, if the patient is using self-harm, then that can be detrimental to the CBT-T (i.e. a therapy interfering behaviour), as it can mean that the patient will use self-harm to reduce the anxiety caused by eating rather than experimenting with new and more self-respectful approaches to anxiety management and emotion regulation. Therefore, self-harm needs to be treated as a non-negotiable – where the patient stops using it during CBT-T, or (if it is more serious) where the self-harm is addressed prior to the CBT-T itself.

Common comorbidities are monitored as part of CBT-T, to determine their impact on issues such as depression and anxiety. As outlined in Chapter 1, both CBT-ED in general and CBT-T specifically result in substantial reductions in comorbidity, thus invalidating the assumption that 'the patient is too complicated for CBT or brief therapy'. Indeed, addressing the eating disorder might facilitate later treatment of any other issues that need further treatment (e.g. in the case of a patient with a history of severe trauma or neglect).

2.9 The role of supervision

Supervision for CBT-T is strongly focused on patient progress and outcomes. As such, it is structured around patient outcomes, and we aim to discuss every patient every week. It is usually delivered individually, to ensure that all cases can be addressed within each session. As a consequence of the focus on patient outcomes, the supervisor needs to address the clinician's own therapy-interfering behaviours (e.g. anxiety reduction – see below), in addition to such behaviours in patients. It can also be necessary to address supervision-interfering behaviours (e.g. the failure to be prepared with the information needed for supervision; not presenting specific cases). Again, a 'firm empathy' approach is useful here, as clinicians and supervisors need to be honest about the clinician's developmental needs. As with clinicians' work with patients, it can be equally tempting for the supervisor-supervisee relationship to focus on creating close bonds, which can make it hard to address clinician interfering behaviours or skill deficits.

As detailed in Chapter 1, many clinicians experience levels of anxiety that interfere with their delivery of CBT, CBT-ED, and CBT-T. This needs to be addressed in CBT-T, given the strong behavioural element to the therapy. The key problem for some clinicians is their own difficulty in tolerating uncertainty, which makes them reluctant to initiate behavioural change or to persist with it, because of uncertainty about the outcome and/or upsetting the patient (e.g. "But what if I ask the patient to add a snack and their prediction comes true – she really does gain 3 kg in a week?"). The combination of a nervous patient and nervous clinician can effectively stymie therapy, so the supervisor needs to encourage the clinician to recognise and manage their own anxiety, and to be prepared to tolerate their own uncertainty until they learn that therapy does not have the expected catastrophic effects and/or that the patient can tolerate a firmer approach. We usually speak of this in terms of a behavioural experiment for the clinician, just as they require their patient to do behavioural experiments to test anxious predictions. Pointing out that the clinician should treat themselves just as they do the client, using the attitude of "I don't know what will happen, but I do know a way of finding out", can be an effective motivator for the anxious clinician.

2.10 Define who is responsible for change

At the end of therapy (see Chapter 10), a key element in relapse prevention is to ensure that the patient attributes the benefits of therapy to their own work and change. This attribution work requires the patient to learn that they are responsible for change from the beginning. Therefore, the clinician needs to return repeatedly to this issue – the patient needs to learn to be their own therapist: the clinician's role is to be their coach.

This attribution to the patient can be done in that 'drip, drip' way. Sometimes, this is done by the clinician making frequent references to ways in which the patient has done a good job of initiating and maintaining changes. At other times, it can be assisted by not jumping in to tell the patient the best ways of achieving a task but taking a Socratic stance and letting the patient discover their own way of achieving it. However, more overt analogies can also be used to ensure that the patient understands their responsibilities in tasks such as homework (see an example in Table 2.4).

2.11 Food is a key factor in the eating disorder, and in its effective treatment

Many clinicians in the field buy into the common rhetoric that 'it's not about the food' (at least two books on eating disorders have titles that are based on this conjecture). There is little doubt that the eating disorders have many potential long-term antecedent factors, relating to a mixture of learning, genetics, social pressures, control issues, and more, varying across individuals. However, by the time that the patient reaches therapy, the eating disorders are very much about food, and the maintaining factors are far more important (a key tenet of CBT-ED). The lack of adequate eating is a key element, which will impede dealing with other issues, so the clinician should not underplay the role of nutrition. If we do and the patient remains in even a partial starvation state (e.g. not balancing carbohydrate intake), then we limit the patient's cognitive and emotional abilities to overcome the eating disorder.

Table 2.4 Focusing the patient on their responsibility to be their own therapist

---

CLINICIAN: I know that you have not changed your diet, as discussed. This is a problem, as I cannot do this stuff for you. Imagine if you were an athlete and I were your coach, and you told me that you had not done any of the training that we agreed you needed to do over the past week. How do you think a coach would react to that?

PATIENT: Well, I suppose they would probably ask me why I was here, as they could not do the training for me".

CLINICIAN: OK, so what do you think I am going to say to you? More importantly, what are you going to tell yourself?

2.12 Address any weight regain and other key nutritional needs from the beginning

A theme that recurs in CBT-T is the need to address core nutritional needs, and that issue is covered in several points in this manual. Those needs include ones that are about ensuring patient safety (e.g. potassium levels), cognitive flexibility, and emotional stability.

An early task in this domain relates to patients who start therapy at a low weight or with eating patterns that could cause nutritional deficiencies. For example, if the patient is at a relatively low weight (e.g. patchy menstrual function; biological or psychological starvation signs) then there needs to be an emphasis from the outset on getting the patient to at least a minimum functional weight. Similarly, if the patient adheres to a vegan diet, then their nutritional needs should be considered (e.g. ensuring an adequate protein intake).

2.13 Treatment targets in CBT-T

Do we know what we are targeting? Our goal needs to be twofold – to ensure the maximum recovery rate, and to prevent relapse. As a result, CBT-ED and CBT-T address the range of symptoms of eating disorders, with a particular focus on relapse risk factors. This means that CBT-T, as outlined in the coming chapters, pays attention to the following symptoms and risk factors:

- Eliminating dietary restriction.
- Ensuring that the patient does not end therapy underweight.
- Eliminating bingeing and purging behaviours completely.
- Normalising eating, weight and shape cognitions.
- Achieving body image acceptance.

Most importantly, CBT-T aims to address the two key cognitive patterns that underpin eating disorders:

- *The 'broken' cognitive link between eating and weight* (Waller & Mountford, 2015), which describes the way in which patients with eating disorders have lost the normal connection between their food intake/output and what happens to their weight. This connection is addressed particularly strongly in the early stage of CBT-T (using nutritional change, psychoeducation, exposure, behavioural experiments. and regular monitoring of weight).
- *Overvaluation of eating, shape and weight* (Fairburn, 2008), where patients judge their worth inappropriately powerfully in terms of their eating and body. This cognitive pattern is addressed more in the latter part of CBT-T, using psychoeducation, cognitive challenges, and body image work.

The structure and content of CBT-T is geared around modifying these cognitions, and addressing the clinical targets above. Each will be returned to over the course of the protocol, including explanations to patients, clinical targets and techniques, and supervision.

Summary: Principles to be considered in delivering CBT-T

- Use the protocol, adapting it for the individual patient's needs.
- Use the checklist provided, because we are human and we miss or forget things.
- Stress CBT-T as a 'doing therapy', rather than a 'talking therapy'.
- Do not start out by offering a full course of CBT-T.
  - Make continuation dependent on the patient starting well.
- Stick to the protocol, rather than adding in unproven techniques.
  - Especially if we are only adding those bits in because we are used to them or like them.
- Hold sessions weekly.
  - Some gaps are acceptable (e.g. for leave), as long as the patient keeps doing the work in the interim.
- Outcomes should be monitored, but so should progress.
  - Use evidence of progress to encourage the patient and to set targets as CBT-T progresses.
- Treat one disorder at a time, using the best protocol that you have.
  - Other problems can be treated subsequently, if they persist.
- Supervision needs to be active and focused on patient progress/outcomes (see Chapter 12).
- Stress that responsibility for change rests with the patient, to facilitate relapse prevention.
  - The patient is the therapist: the clinician is the coach.
- Effective therapy depends on normalising food intake, and needs the low-weight patient to get up to a normal weight as a priority.
- CBT-T aims to eliminate key maintaining symptoms and behaviours, and to overcome two core cognitive distortions.
  - Key targets for the end of treatment are: eliminate restriction; not being underweight; not using bingeing; purging, or compensatory behaviours; normalising eating attitudes; and body image acceptance.
  - The first cognitive target is reducing the belief that weight will rise out of control if eating normally.
  - The second cognitive target is the reduction in overvaluation of eating, weight, and shape.

Chapter 3

The CBT-T protocol checklist, and how to employ it

As outlined above, clinicians have substantially better clinical outcomes if they use evidence-based manualised protocols (e.g. Addis & Waltz, 2002; Cukrowicz, Timmons, Sawyer, Caron, Gummelt, & Joiner Jr, 2011). However, despite that evidence, few clinicians use manuals to guide their practice when working either with eating disorders or with other disorders (e.g. Addis & Krasnow, 2000; Waller et al., 2014). This apparent conundrum can be explained in a number of ways, including:

- Clinicians preferring to use their clinical judgement, even though the use of protocols is far more effective, regardless of the length of time one has worked in a field (Grove et al., 2000).
- Clinicians assuming that simply owning a manual (but never opening it) ensures that they become a better clinician, via some osmotic process.
- Clinicians having negative attitudes to manuals, despite often not having used them (Addis & Krasnow, 2000).
- A belief that manuals constrain the clinician's 'artistry' (remember, not all artists are *good* artists).

None of these apparent explanations is a true justification for failing to do the best for our patients. Therefore, we recommend that clinicians read this manual fully, so that you can get the best possible outcomes for your patients when using CBT-T.

3.1 How to use this manual: Guidelines for clinicians

If you want to get the results that CBT-T can deliver, then follow this manual and the protocol within it. If you are familiar with CBT-ED manuals (e.g. Fairburn, 2008; Waller et al., 2007) then many of the methods will be familiar to you already, but the overall protocol will be more intensive than you are used to. Some of the changes may take a while to get used to (e.g. not focusing on an individualised formulation; stressing early change rather than motivational enhancement work). However, as with all evidence-based CBT manuals, one should not be unduly rigid.

Thus, the first rule is to remember that any protocol should be treated flexibly, to match the individual's needs and presentation. However, this is not an excuse for drifting off protocol. If a patient does not engage in purging behaviours, then the clinician should bypass the relevant parts of the protocol. In contrast, if the clinician feels uncomfortable addressing purging behaviours, that is no justification for not addressing them. Some patients, particularly those with a past history of anorexia nervosa who have gained some weight, may not be binge eating or purging, and more time may be spent on psychoeducation about healthy weight and experimenting with expanding nutrition, eating flexibly, and testing specific nutritional beliefs in order to ensure the necessary weight gain for stability. For patients who are of a low weight, an initial focus on weight gain will be important in order to ensure that the patient's body is biologically stable and not in a state of constant starvation. For those who regularly purge or engage in 'clean eating' but who do not regularly binge eat, the protocol can to be used flexibly to ensure that the patient's treatment goals remain the focus of the therapy. In addition, there are some techniques that need to be delivered in a specific way at specific points in the session or in therapy (e.g. the weighing of patients – see the next two chapters).

The second rule is that clinicians are prone to forgetting and postponing tasks, thinking that they will address them at some unspecified point in the future. A classic example of this is the way that many clinicians bypass exposure or weighing patients, even though these tasks are vital to the protocol being effective. Consequently, starting with the next chapter, this manual presents the protocol in the form of a checklist. Literally – check off elements as you go. The checklist is to ensure that key tasks are carried out (or consciously bypassed if they are not needed for the individual).

3.2 The structure of CBT-T

Table 3.1 shows the five phases of CBT-T, as detailed in subsequent chapters, along with the two key sessions (1 and 4) that are addressed in separate chapters in this manual. Managing assessment (pre-therapy opportunities) is outlined in the next chapter.

Figure 3.1 shows the sequence of targets and methods across the phases. It also indicates the non-specific elements of therapy that underpin the use of the techniques (e.g. maintaining a working relationship; psychoeducation; maintaining motivation; managing risk; addressing therapy-interfering behaviours) and that run alongside any therapy for eating disorders. Each phase is labelled with the range of sessions where these techniques are most likely to be employed (see subsequent chapters).

It will be noted that the phases are presented as overlapping, demonstrating what needs to happen first, but allowing for the fact that different patients will traverse each phase at different speeds and that some tasks can overlap in their function (e.g. addressing emotionally driven binges while conducting an experiment to reduce body checking). As a result, most of the following chapters detail

Table 3.1 Phases of CBT-T

Session 1 Laying down the basics and the non-negotiables, and getting therapy started.

Phase 1 *(Sessions 1–4)*: Early dietary change and exposure.

 o Targets – education; change in biology; reduction in anxiety; reduction in binge/purge behaviour.

Session 4 Formal review; decision about continuing or ending therapy.

Phase 2 *(Sessions 3–6)*: Behavioural experiments relating to food.

 o Target – cognitive change.

Phase 3 *(Sessions 5–7)*: Exposure and cognitive restructuring relating to emotions.

 o Target – reduction in emotionally driven bulimic behaviours.

Phase 4 *(Sessions 5–9)*: Body image work, using surveys, exposure, behavioural experiments.

 o Targets – reduction in maintaining behaviours; enhanced body image acceptance.

Phase 5 *(Sessions 9–10)*: Relapse prevention and implementing the therapy blueprint.

 o Targets – maintain changes; plan follow-up; cement patient's attributional shifts.

Follow-up sessions (one and three months post-therapy)

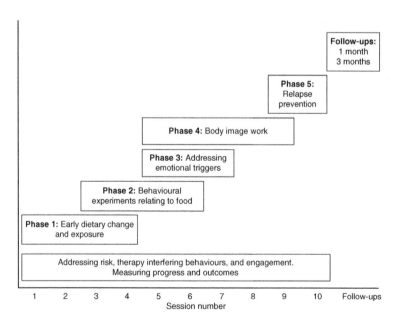

Figure 3.1 The structure of CBT-T.

the tasks needed in each phase, rather than being laid out session by session. There is no hard and fast rule about how many sessions should be taken to complete each phase, though one should normally aim for rapid rather than slow change wherever possible, to keep up the patient's momentum towards recovery. The phrase "well, maybe next time" should be treated as potentially negative, whether expressed by the patient or the clinician.

3.2.1 The logic of sequencing the phases of CBT-T

The rationale for the sequencing of the phases is that the early ones facilitate the later ones. For example, nutrition and exposure (**Phase 1**) are needed to stabilise the patient's mood and reduce anxiety. This reduction in anxiety allows the patient to undertake the behavioural experiments (**Phase 2**) that are needed to change cognitions without anxiety getting in the way (e.g. the patient panicking and exercising to compensate for dietary changes), but the nutritional stabilisation also allows for the identification and tackling of emotionally driven bingeing and compensatory behaviours (**Phase 3**) where starvation is not responsible. Each of these phases is necessary before body image can be addressed (**Phase 4**), and that work is naturally followed by relapse prevention work (**Phase 5**). However, remember that it is possible that whole phases might not be necessary (e.g. there might be no emotionally driven binges; body image issues might resolve during the earlier phases, or might not have been present from the beginning). Indeed, it is noticeable that approximately 10–15% of CBT-T patients do not need the full ten sessions to achieve recovery, and discharge (with follow-up) can be negotiated early.

3.3 Using the checklist in practice: The structure of this CBT-T manual

The checklist in Appendix 1 can be downloaded (see 'How to use this manual'), and is designed to be printed off and used – one per patient, to collate key clinical information, symptoms, behavioural progress, and core clinical notes. It is laid out session by session, though it is made clear that material that is irrelevant can by bypassed. With some indicated exceptions (e.g. where patient agenda items are addressed; the ordering of reviewing diaries and weighing the patient), items in the checklist can be addressed and ticked off in any order that is natural in the clinical context.

The coming chapters address the protocol in the order outlined in Table 3.1. Two key sessions (1 and 4) require special attention, so are addressed in separate chapters. The remaining chapters address the five phases of treatment and the follow-up sessions. You will find that the protocol is relatively full for early sessions, but that there is less specific material on later pages, as the protocol needs more individualisation to the specific patient. In each chapter, themes will be identified (e.g. addressing anxiety) before details are given about how to address them.

Finally, before you start on the protocol itself, a word of caution. While it is possible to learn as one goes along, reading just one chapter ahead of the patient's progress through CBT-T, we do not advise it. The flexible and patient-centred application of any protocol such as this one will benefit from being aware of the 'big picture' and what that entails. For example, it is common that one can predict the targets and techniques for body image work from Session 1 if one is aware of what is coming in this manual. So we advise reading the whole manual through before starting CBT-T, and discussing it with your supervisor.

Summary: Using the CBT-T manual

- Using a manual is far more effective than when clinicians rely on their judgement, regardless of their experience, profession, etc.
- Protocols need to be delivered flexibly, but without omitting the key elements completely.
- CBT-T is structured in phases, which patients can pass through at different rates.
- Those phases are in a logical order, relating to the way in which the eating disorder can best be addressed.
- It is a good idea to read the manual fully before starting to treat patients, to ensure that you have an overview of what is coming.

Chapter 4

The critical first session

The first session is where the principles outlined in Chapter 2 and the techniques of CBT-ED are used to drive CBT-T from the outset, focusing on early behavioural change to get the maximum benefit for the patient. The checklist and symptom record for this session are presented in Appendix 1.

As noted above, the checklists for this and other early sessions are relatively detailed, though they can easily be delivered within 50 minutes, even where the patient has a fairly complex presentation (see Videos). The detail reflects the need for patient and clinician to undertake a lot of key tasks over several sessions, where those tasks relate to almost all of these patients' needs. Later sessions have lower levels of prescribed detail, reflecting the different individual needs of the patients following their progress so far. In addition, many of the tasks from the early sessions (e.g. risk monitoring, weighing) will be repeated across the 10 sessions, so more detail on their implementation is given early on.

4.1 Pre-therapy opportunities

Services and clinicians differ in how they engage patients in therapy. Some will start with Session 1, as the initial assessment (e.g. diagnosis, comorbidity, risk) has been conducted elsewhere. For those services, starting from scratch with the material outlined in the checklist is appropriate. Other services will do their own assessments. In that case, many of the key issues might already have been explored during the assessment, though they should still be addressed fully in Session 1. Repetition of these key concepts is helpful. Particular topics to foreshadow in this way are non-negotiables (as detailed below, but including ensuring safety, self-harm as a non-negotiable, attendance, completion of homework, weighing, etc.). Thus, any pre-treatment assessment can be used to get the patient into active treatment as immediately as possible to capitalise on existing readiness to engage in change.

4.1.1 Preparing the patient for Session 1

A key element of the therapy at this stage is to ask the patient to complete a week's worth of food diaries (e.g. Appendix 2) in advance of Session 1, so that the role of dietary intake and normalisation can be stressed from the beginning.

The patient can be given key tips on diary-keeping (record in real time everything eaten and drunk; include alcohol, etc.). It can also be useful to send the patient a copy of the ED-15 (Appendix 3) in advance of the first session, so that core cognitions and behaviours can be discussed at that session. Alternatively, the ED-15 can be completed at the beginning of the session (see below). We also provide an information sheet about CBT-T (see Appendix 4).

4.2 Themes in Session 1

The core themes for Session 1 are given in Table 4.1. Each should be addressed explicitly with the patient in this session, so that the patient knows what to expect, and so that the themes can be revisited if there is any sign of slippage over forthcoming sessions.

An important clinical observation here is that patients are often far less resistant to these themes and the related tasks than clinicians might expect, especially when the evidence-based rationale is presented along with the principle of doing the best by the patient. We need to keep in mind the goal of patient recovery and the evidence that this approach is effective. Our own anxiety about pushing for change is understandable, but usually misplaced.

4.3 Specific tasks in Session 1

In Session 1, the following should be completed. The 'crib sheet' here is not a substitute for the checklist (see Appendix 1), but provides an overview. As noted above, many of these tasks are repeated in later sessions, where they will be dealt with in less detail (Table 4.2).

4.3.1 Completing background information and current symptoms and problems

These two sheets (see Appendix 1) should be completed in the first session, based on information from any recent assessment and using material that arises during

---

Table 4.1 Themes to be introduced and used to direct Session 1 (and subsequent sessions)

- Engaging the patient, and setting expectations, e.g.:
  - Expressing 'realistic optimism'.
  - Change from the beginning.
  - Differences relative to previous therapies.
- Establishing the non-negotiables.
- Firm empathetic stance.
- Beginning behavioural change, dietary change, and psychoeducation.
  - Educating the patient about how the body works, to enable them to take risks in relation to behavioural change.

Table 4.2 Outline of specific tasks in Session 1 of CBT-T

- Complete the cover sheet and the Session Record sheet for Session 1 (see Appendix 1).
  - o Using information gained in this session and from any prior assessment.
- Address any life-threatening or therapy-interfering behaviours, e.g.:
  - o Physically risky behaviours, such as frequent vomiting and self-harm.
  - o Non-completion of core tasks, such as homework.
- Complete the ED-15 and discuss it with the patient.
- Review past therapies.
- Establish rules for this therapy.
  - o Probably counter to the rules of past therapies.
- Explain the model.
  - o Introducing energy graphs.
- Explain the structure of the therapy.
- Review current eating.
  - o Using energy graphs.
- Determine and record symptoms (bulimic behaviours, weighing, etc.).
- Select psychoeducation material on the basis of the individual patient's symptoms.
- Start the healthy eating process.
- Homework based on individual need (education, eating changes, diary) plus monitoring measures.

Session 1. The same applies in later sessions, of course, as each has its own session record.

Supervision and our own clinical work has shown us that clinicians do not have perfect memories for key information (e.g. how much has the patient's bingeing reduced over the course of the first few weeks; the patient's own goals). To minimise time spent on flicking back and forth in the notes during the session, the protocol has a cover sheet, which includes a simple table of changes in key symptoms, to share with the patient regularly (*Clinician*: "If you look at this table, you can see how far you have come in just three sessions – you have almost completely stopped bingeing and vomiting, and your weight has not changed"). Another point that should be noted is that the cover sheet includes the patient's diagnosis. We stress the importance of diagnosis, given the evidence that services using diagnoses/problem descriptors get better outcomes in treating some common disorders (Clark et al., 2018).

As well as the cover sheet, there is a record sheet opposite the protocol checklist for each session. This sheet (see Appendix 1) is used to assist in keeping notes that will prove useful in supervision. While there are such record sheets for each session, the sheet for Session 1 has two specific questions to ask the patient at the outset of treatment (see below) – how confident the patient is about this approach, and how suitable they feel it is for them. These are questions that are similar to those used in a number of forms of CBT. Each of these ratings can help the clinician to understand how well the patient has understood the potential of CBT-T, particularly in their case, and can guide us to address any specific concerns that the patient might have. In the case of low confidence, it can be helpful to guide the patient to remember past instances where they have successfully tackled difficult tasks and perhaps surprised themselves in the process of doing so.

4.3.2 Addressing risk and therapy-interfering behaviours

A variety of factors can disrupt therapy. While some relate to physical and psychological risks that will require support before CBT-T can be undertaken at all, others are factors that can be considered 'therapy-interfering behaviours' (Linehan, 1993).

4.3.2.1 Risk

Obviously, it is vital to ensure that any risks to health or life are addressed as a priority. Key risk factors are:

- Very low mood and active suicidality (though these are comparatively rare, in our experience).
- Risk events relating to childbirth/parenting.
- Self-harming behaviours to manage mood.
- Electrolyte imbalance (particularly low potassium levels, due to purging behaviours).
- Exacerbation of other conditions, such as diabetes.

Each of these must be attended to as an absolute priority, using appropriate social, medical, or other support. As Linehan (1993) has indicated, it is important not to attempt to deliver therapy when one is dealing with such priorities. Therefore, we recommend agreeing to suspend therapy until the risk has been dealt with and/or managed safely (Table 4.3).

Table 4.3 Prioritising risk factors

CLINICIAN: I know that you are keen to get on with therapy for your eating disorder, but right now we have an additional issue, which takes priority. You have told me that your husband is being violent toward you, and we have to make sure that you are somewhere safe before we can think of therapy. So can we plan how to get your family on board to support you, or to contact social services for their help? Then we can get that under way, and we can come back and start therapy from this point.

Or:

CLINICIAN: Before we can get started on your eating disorder, we need to address one issue – your cutting your arms. Self-harm is something that you use to manage your anxiety, and as long as you are doing that then you will not be able to focus on learning that your eating changes are OK, even though they make you anxious. So, we can start CBT-T if you are willing to hold back and not self-harm. I know that will worry you, but I hope you are happy to agree to that, as it is a non-negotiable – we have to have that agreement, or we cannot help you to change your eating.

4.3.2.2 Patients' therapy-interfering behaviours

These are behaviours that all clinicians are likely to have seen in the field of psychotherapies – action or inaction that interferes with the possibility of effective therapy. Examples includes the patient who:

- Is repeatedly late to therapy, so that there is less time for the key techniques to be implemented, and even more time is spent on discussing the lateness and how to avoid it in future.
- Does not understand the necessary structure of therapy sessions, and who repeatedly comes back to talking about current or past life events.
- Is reluctant to be weighed, and expresses distress or threatens to leave.
- Does not complete key homework, such as food diaries.

It should not be assumed that the patient is being deliberately difficult in any of these ways of behaving. If we have not explained to the patient the guidelines of effective therapy (see below), then it is likely that the patient has no idea that these are important issues to overcome. Indeed, it is perfectly possible that the patient was coached in these behaviours and attitudes from previous, unsuccessful therapy experiences (see below).

Many patients will return to the protocol if we make it clear that it matters. However, sometimes their anxiety or their beliefs about therapy can get in the way of their participation. In such cases, there are three potential reactions by the clinician:

1. In the first, the clinician stresses their empathic side in isolation:
   CLINICIAN: I understand that it is very hard for you to make the time to fill in the food diaries, given how much you have going on at home. Maybe we could spend a while now here in the session, writing out the diaries that you would have done over the last week, and then look at how we could make it easier for you next week?
   o Note that the result will be that it will take most of the session to produce the diary, that it is highly unlikely to be accurate, that it will not have served the function of getting the patient to be aware of what they ate at the time that they ate it, that there will not be time to discuss it adequately, that other tasks of therapy are not carried out, and that the patient will learn that homework is not necessary because it all gets done in the therapy session anyway. By reacting in this way, we have taught the patient that therapy is done in one hour a week, rather than taking all 168 hours in the week.

2. In the second possible response, the clinician is firm (but authoritarian):
   CLINICIAN: What you have to understand is that therapy is what I say it is, and you need to do everything that I tell you to do. If you don't, then it won't work.

     o   In this situation, the likelihood of the patient engaging actively in the treatment is reduced, as the encounters with the clinician are seen as unengaging and the non-negotiables of therapy are not explained (Geller & Srikameswaran, 2006).

3. Therefore, in CBT-T (as in CBT-ED generally), it is important for the clinician to combine firmness and empathy (Wilson et al., 1997) in their response:

CLINICIAN: I know that completing the diary is hard, because it makes you think about food, and you have been trying for years not to think about food. In fact, that is quite likely to be why you end up binge-eating and starving yourself. However, if you want to get rid of this eating disorder, you will need to learn that what you do or don't eat is what pushes you to binge. And you will also need to learn that you can eat very differently and be much happier. To do that, you will need to do the diary – so that you can learn and change. If you don't, then we know how things will be – the bingeing stays as it is. So when I'm firm about the need for you to do the diary, it is because I want you to get rid of the eating disorder. Remember, you won't have to keep them forever, but for now the diaries are very important. Are you going to give it a try?

PATIENT: Yes, I get it, I know I hate having to think about what I've eaten, but I can see how I need to do this.

CLINICIAN: That's great, I'm really pleased that you're committed to doing this. Are there any obstacles that we need to problem solve?

     o   Here, the non-negotiables have been explained, in a way that indicates that we would not be pushing the patient in this way if we were not interested in their long-term recovery. Our experience is that this approach is most likely to get the patient to take the risk of experiencing the anxiety that they have been trying to avoid.

However, sometimes the patient does not respond by doing the task (e.g. a homework task, such as diary-keeping; an in-session task such as being weighed), even when the rationale has been given. In such cases, the CBT-T clinician should respond by highlighting the importance of the work again, and then stopping the session immediately (the 'five-minute session' – Waller et al., 2007), stressing that therapy cannot continue meaningfully, but expressing certainty that the patient will have it done by the following week. This approach is almost always successful in getting the patient to understand that we are serious, and to do the task. The use of the five-minute session is described to the patient before it actually happens, so it can be seen as part of a strategy, rather than an act of frustration on the part of the clinician.

Of course, this approach to therapy-interfering behaviours is needed all the way through therapy, and in some ways is more likely to be an issue after the first session of CBT-T (when there has been more opportunity to perform/fail to perform key therapy tasks). However, it is stressed here because the first session has some tasks that need to be addressed from the very beginning. The example of diary-keeping has been used, but the other CBT-T task that has to be carried out in Session 1 is weighing the patient openly (where the patient knows their weight). Methods for weighing the patient are detailed later in this chapter and in Chapter 5 (see also Waller & Mountford, 2015). It should be noted that far fewer eating-disordered patients seem to object to being weighed than clinicians commonly assume. However, if the patient declines (or asks to be weighed another time, or tells you their weight was read at home before they came so they do not need to be weighed again), it is important to address that immediately here in Session 1. First, it can be explained that weighing is vital for safety purposes, but mainly so that the patient can learn for themselves that their eating does not make their weight climb hugely (Waller & Mountford, 2015). If the patient continues to say 'no', then it is our experience that the most effective approach is to reply along the lines of:

CLINICIAN: Of course you have the right to say 'no' to being weighed. However, that means that I cannot pretend that we are going to be doing an effective therapy. If that is your decision, then we can stop now, and you can return to therapy sometime in the future when you are ready to actively take part in the elements of treatment that we know are important in helping you to recover. So, are we finishing here, or are we going to weigh you? Absolutely your choice.

To date, we have never had a patient decline to be weighed at that point, and none have later declined in future sessions. Indeed, several patients have commented on how that one experience of a firm stance in Session 1 made them realise that this was going to be a whole new experience compared to their previous (unsuccessful) therapies.

4.3.2.3 Other therapy-interfering behaviours

We should also remember that therapy-interfering behaviours are not all driven by patients. We also see clinicians impeding therapy, either because they drift off track (e.g. letting the patient talk without imposing structure in the form of an agenda) or because they consciously or unconsciously take decisions that prevent therapy being effective. For example, many clinicians allow their own anxiety to prevent them asking patients to undertake behavioural change. Others opt not to use a protocol or checklist to guide treatment, justifying their choice because they do not want any constraint on their clinical judgement.[1]

Of course, patients' therapy-interfering behaviours (e.g. not wanting to be weighed in-session, to reduce anxiety) can become locked in with clinicians' own therapy-interfering behaviours (e.g. not wanting to upset the patient, so agreeing not to weigh them). This results in a pattern of 'accommodation', where nothing can progress as both parties get more and more anxious about breaking the stalemate. Supervision needs to address any sign of such mutual therapy-interfering behaviours and push the clinician to break the pattern of accommodation as early as possible.

Finally, there are also patterns of supervision-interfering behaviour, undertaken by clinicians and supervisors. Supervision is an area where there is little consistency across models, except in one rather disappointing respect – there is very limited focus on patient outcomes (Simpson-Southward et al., 2018). The risk is that supervision focuses more on process and the supervisor-supervisee relationship than it does on patient recovery. Therefore, it is important that supervisors should emphasise the need for all patients to be presented weekly, using structured progress notes, and addressing any apparent therapy-interfering behaviours used by the clinician as soon as they become visible. Where this is a repeated pattern and the clinician fails to respond to guidance on preparing for supervision, it is even possible to use the technique of a 'five-minute supervision' (see above for the parallel situation in the therapy session itself), where the supervisor ends the supervision session early because the clinician has come ill-prepared.

4.4 Completion and review of ED-15 scores

Where possible, the patient should have been given or sent a copy of the ED-15 (see Appendix 3) in advance of Session 1 (e.g. posted with diaries, handed over at

Table 4.4 Using the ED-15 to start planning with the patient in Session 1

CLINICIAN: Looking at the questionnaire, I can see how much of a problem for you those eating behaviours are – bingeing and vomiting about four times a week. It is going to be really vital to get rid of those completely. Your beliefs about your eating and your weight and shape are just as important, as they are likely to drive the behaviours. From what I can see here, while you score pretty high on lots of the items you are extremely preoccupied by food, and fearful of losing control of your eating. My best guess is that you feel more and more like that as you go longer and longer without food. Is that right?

PATIENT: Well, yes. But I am always worrying that if I start eating then I won't be able to stop, so I spend all day getting hungrier and hungrier and more and more scared that I will binge. In the end, it just gets easier to give in and binge.

CLINICIAN: Well, that all makes perfect sense, when you start off the day without eating – we will talk more about that in a minute or two, when we talk about something called an 'energy graph'. But I am also interested in some of your other answers, where you say that you are very likely to check your body and worry what other people think about your appearance. Those are classic things that mess up your body image, and make you feel worse about it. It is going to be very important to look at that too. However, we will do that later in the therapy. I will explain more shortly, when we talk about the structure of the therapy.

PATIENT: I really hate my body – can't we do that first?

CLINICIAN: I can tell that from your questionnaire, and it is really important that we get you to that place. However, we know that it has to be 'eating first, body image second' if you are going to get rid of the eating disorder.

---

any assessment). However, if not, then it should be completed early in Session 1 (it usually takes only two minutes), so that it can be discussed in the session.

The ED-15 is designed to be used weekly (unlike other measures, which are intended to reflect the past 28 days), so that it can be used for weekly monitoring of change in eating disorder cognitions/attitudes and behaviours. It is important that the ED-15 is looked at jointly in every session, so that clinician and patient can identify the strongest maintaining beliefs and behaviours and begin to plan how and when to target them. This should start from Session 1 (Table 4.4).

4.5 Review the patient's past therapy experiences

We ask patients about their experiences of other treatments, partly to understand what might be effective for that individual, but also to help that patient to engage in CBT-T itself. While we are not cynical about the chances of therapy working for our patients, we frequently find that most therapy previously offered to adults with eating disorders was not evidence-based or delivered fully (see Chapter 1).

When asking about previous therapies, it is useful to ask the patient what they found helpful and why, as this provides an opportunity to understand the expectations and hopes they may bring to treatment and to discuss any evident differences with the rationale. It can be useful to stress the positives of those treatments, though emphasising that they were not adequate (Table 4.5).

At other times, the therapy patients describe is clearly not evidence-based for eating disorders.[2] The patient should be told that the previous therapy had little chance of being effective. The reason for being clear about this point is to help the patient to overcome any sense of learned helplessness or hopelessness, so that they go into CBT-T with a sense of realistic optimism (Table 4.6).

Table 4.5 Using previous therapy experience to point to possible benefits of CBT-T

CLINICIAN: So, you were on 80mg of that antidepressant (fluoxetine) for six months and your mood got better and you binged less. That is what we would hope for, as the drug increases your level of something called serotonin, which stabilises your mood. However, when you stopped taking the drug, what happened?

PATIENT: I felt really lousy for days, and then the bingeing slowly came back.

CLINICIAN: That is pretty much what we would expect. Maybe this time we could try getting your serotonin back in a more natural, maintainable way – getting you to eat carbohydrates in your diet routinely. Same thing that they were trying for before, but in a way that you can learn to do permanently.

PATIENT: That is a really scary way to do it. Carbohydrates are just not my thing. Are you sure it will work?

CLINICIAN: Any clinician who gives you a 100% guarantee of an outcome is misleading you. However, I know what your chances are of recovering using CBT-T, and we already know that the drugs alone don't do it. So it looks like a much better bet to do it this way, to me. But the truth is that we will have to try CBT-T and see.

Table 4.6 Addressing learned helplessness based on patient's previous therapy experiences

CLINICIAN: Well, what you have just described sounds fascinating – one therapy where the main objective seemed to be to talk about whatever was on your mind while the clinician kept quiet, and one where the main approach seemed to be so patient-centred that you only talked about changing things you felt comfortable to change. However, I have no idea how either was meant to help you with an eating disorder. Neither sounds likely to be an effective therapy to me, which is probably why you are back to looking for help, though it has taken you a few years to return.

PATIENT: Well, last time, the therapist said that she could not work out why the therapy wasn't working, because it normally works in her experience. So I figured that she was the expert, so it must be me, and there was no point in trying again. After all, I saw her every week for a year, so it couldn't be that the therapy did not have a chance to work – I thought I must be doing it wrong or that I was just too broken to get better.

CLINICIAN: I can't guarantee that CBT-T will work for you, but I can tell you that it has a better chance than something like those previous therapies. I can also tell you that we will know within a few sessions whether it is on track to help you – no need to spend a year.

This discussion can be used to support the relapse prevention process, where we work to attribute change to the patient themselves, rather than as a product of the clinician's work (see Chapter 10).

4.6 Establish the non-negotiables for this therapy

Here, we stress that CBT-T is going to be different from other therapies – shorter than the patient might be used to, and very different in content to most other therapies that they might have experienced (see Section 4.5). The non-negotiables outlined here are largely things that we have already addressed for the reader, but which should be explicitly communicated to the patient. It is likely that they might well be counter to what patients have heard from previous clinicians in other therapies, so clearly explaining the rationale for any non-negotiables that are new to the patient (Geller & Srikameswaran, 2006) should be an important aim when it comes to CBT-T. We list the most important ones in Table 4.7.

In our experience, few clinicians address this topic with their patients. Some clinicians prefer to maintain an air of 'I am the expert, so the tools for change are known to me but should not be known to you'. However, the more common justification that clinicians give for not outlining these rules to the patient is that we are concerned that the patient will be too fragile or too reluctant to cope with them. This assumption on the part of clinicians is akin to Meehl's (1973) notion of the 'spun glass theory of the mind' – the clinician who sees the patient as being too fragile to be pressured in any way, and so who does not get the patient to change at all. Clinicians may also feel under pressure to keep patients engaged or 'on the

Table 4.7 Non-negotiables of CBT-T to communicate to the patient

Firm empathetic stance

CLINICIAN: I want to help you get well, but you need to know that this will be hard work, because there is no simple solution.

CLINICIAN: Anxiety is an inevitable part of this treatment, as it is for any effective treatment. Especially early on. But you have tried other therapies that do not make you anxious, and you know how that worked out.

All tasks are core tasks – food, weighing, diaries, staying safe, homework, etc.

CLINICIAN: The tasks that I am going to ask you to do will not be optional. They are ones that you are going to have to sign up for and do, with my help. Looking at what I know about you so far, that will include eating, being weighed by me, changing your eating pattern, working on reducing your body avoidance, and more.

PATIENT: Well, that is not how it has been in my other therapies. No-one ever weighed me in the session before.

CLINICIAN: And yet, here you are … think it might be time to try something different?'

We do not need the patient to like us

PATIENT: Well, if you are going to ask me to do all that, I am going to find it really hard, and I will predict that I am going to shout at you sometimes.

CLINICIAN: Oh, that is OK. It really does not matter if you see me as a pain. In fact, it is perfectly possible that you won't like what I have to say sometimes, but as long as you are getting better, I am fine with that. I don't need you to like me – just to get rid of the eating disorder.

Patient as therapist: Clinician as coach

CLINICIAN: Therapy needs to happen all the time – 168 hours a week. You come here for me to guide you in how to make it happen. That means that you have to learn to be your own therapist, and I have to be your coach. Of course, that means that I will have to be strict as a coach too, if you are not doing the work.

CBT-T as a brief, focused, time-limited therapy

CLINICIAN: We will start with four sessions, then extend that to a maximum of ten. However, we will only do that if you are making lots of very clear changes in those first four sessions. So you are going to have to be an active therapist for yourself from early on, and I am going to have to make that a focus of my coaching of you. Early change is our best predictor of doing well, so it really matters. I just don't want to waste your time or mine if you are not going to get going with that change. I think I warned you that you might not like what I had to say sometimes–this might be one of those times.

books' (e.g. fear of a complaint being made). However, our experience has been that there are very few times when patients protest about these non-negotiables of therapy when given the rationale. It could be argued that many patients know that change is difficult, and that we do no favours to those patients when we downplay the hard work involved.

4.7 Explaining the CBT-ED model of therapy and how it relates to the eating disorder

The patient's previous experiences of therapy might help here, but they can inter-fere with their understanding of CBT-T. For example:

PATIENT: I don't get it. I have had CBT before, and no-one ever insisted on weigh-ing me or wanted me to do food diaries before.

Any such misunderstanding needs to be addressed immediately, so that the patient is more receptive to the new requirements from the beginning:

CLINICIAN: I am a bit taken aback by that, because what you are describing doesn't sound like any evidence-based therapy to me. I am going to suggest that we stick to this version of CBT, as we know that the previous version of 'CBT' did not work.

The core points to communicate to the patient are detailed in Table 4.8.

The other element of CBT-T that should be mentioned here is the construct of the 'energy graph' (Waller et al., 2007) as a means of understanding why the patient's eating might be problematic. At this stage, it is useful to draw out a nor-mal energy graph (based on someone who eats normally), which you will return to when reviewing the patient's eating in order to understand starvation and bulimic behaviours (see Section 4.9.1).

Table 4.8 Explaining the CBT-T model

- CBT-T (like other forms of CBT-ED) is strongly focused on the here and now. It addresses the maintenance of the eating disorder far more than its history (which can be many years ago, and poorly remembered)
- Behavioural and nutritional chance are key, because they address the patient's emotional and cognitive problems, as well as their behavioural and biological needs.
  CLINICIAN: I know that you have spent many years assuming that food is your enemy and to be beaten. However, we are going to have to turn that on its head. Given all that you are going to learn here, you need to think of food as your way out of the eating disorder. As Fairburn puts it: "There's a medicine for that – it's called food." We are going to keep coming back to that.
- A key piece of learning is that the best single predictor of their weight is what the patient eats (rather than what they feel or believe). Hence, it will be critical to know what the patient eaten and to be able to weigh them.
- The non-negotiables really are not options (we should be prepared to explain them all, of course – Geller & Srikameswaran, 2006), and include:
  o Staying safe.
  o Attendance on time.
  o Completing diaries and other tasks of therapy and homework.
  o No dieting for weight loss during the therapy (as that is likely to trigger binges).
  o Being weighed (for safety, learning about links to eating, etc.).

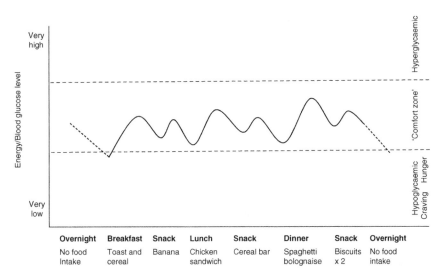

Figure 4.1 An example of an energy graph, showing carbohydrate levels for an individual who eats complex carbohydrate regularly throughout the day.

An example of a normal energy graph is provided in Figure 4.1, showing how regular eating of complex carbohydrates ensures that the body has sufficient fuel to function at all times without entering into hypoglycaemic states, where the craving for food results in binge-eating. This is a useful explanation to provide before discussing the patient's own unhealthy eating pattern in the first session and thereafter. We stress that: complex carbohydrates are more effective at producing sustained energy levels than simple carbohydrates, but they have to be taken regularly; that hunger is a normal state, which is the body's way of telling us that we should top up that level; that people go into a state of craving if their carbohydrate level drops too low; and that craving is less controllable than hunger, and is more likely to be addressed quickly through use of simple carbohydrates.

4.8 Explaining the structure and phases of CBT-T to the patient

The overall structure and the content of the phases of CBT were detailed above for the reader (Section 3.2). However, it is important to detail and explain that structure to the patient, so that they know what is to come and why. To reiterate, the core elements of the structure of CBT-T are outlined in Table 4.9.

Table 4.9 Explaining the structure and phases of CBT-T to the patient during Session 1

Phase 1 *(Sessions 1–4)*: Learning and changing eating.

- o Nutrition.
- o Psychoeducation.
- o Exposure with response prevention.

Session 4 Formal review to decide whether to continue or end therapy.

Phase 2 *(Sessions 3–6)*: Challenging beliefs about eating, food, and weight.

- o Behavioural experiments.
- o Cognitive restructuring.

Phase 3 *(Sessions 5–7)*: Addressing emotional triggers.

- o Exposure.
- o Cognitive restructuring.

Phase 4 *(Sessions 5–9)*: Body image work.

- o Surveys.
- o Behavioural experiments.
- o Exposure.
- o Imagery rescripting.

Phase 5 *(Sessions 9–10)*: Relapse prevention.

- o Therapy blueprint.

Follow-up sessions

4.9 Review current eating

It is best if the patient has provided food diaries for the past week (see Appendix 2). However, if not, then one can focus on the past 24 hours, or the last day where a binge occurred. If the patient has good eating days, one of those should also be reviewed. The clinician should highlight the positive aspects of the patient's eating pattern, exploring the reasons why a binge did not occur. While our patients usually complete paper diaries, completing them on their phone or online is viable as long as they are completed at the time that they were eating and are presented in a way that the clinician can make sense of them. We encourage the patient to complete diaries for a full week for this first session, but if they are not complete then we can still use them, as long as there is enough information to work with.

The aim is to demonstrate to the patient that the majority of their bulimic behaviours occur in the context of starvation, where their beliefs drive them to try to restrict food, but their bodies respond to the consequent craving by overeating. Once the eating has begun, issues such as abstinence violation and emotional consequences can result in the binge being maintained and followed by purging behaviours. Obviously, emotional factors play a greater role in some cases (see Chapter 8), but it is rare to encounter a patient's eating pattern where there is no need to work on normalising that eating. All of this needs to be explained to the individual, to explain their eating pattern and make clear the rationale for treatment tasks.

When reviewing eating, it is important to explain that the patient is undertaking any restrictive behaviour (even over a brief period) as a safety behaviour in an effort to manage immediate anxiety. However, it is also necessary to explain to the patient that, like all safety behaviours, this results in more problems soon after and in the longer term. The inevitability of the longer-term negative outcomes has to be set against that initial positive, as outlined in Table 4.10.

4.9.1 Developing a personalised energy graph

Reviewing the food diary should be carried out by building one or more energy graphs, to demonstrate key aspects of the patient's eating cycle. The aim is to teach the patient to be able to draw these themselves, and to be able to chart their food intake across the course of the day to identify risks (e.g. not eating lunch) before they manifest as problems such as bingeing. We stress that this is not a precise graph, requiring detailed knowledge of the individual's metabolism and carbohydrate levels. Rather, we stress that it is a heuristic, to help the patient to understand how their dietary intake can explain their patterns of hunger, craving and bingeing. Our experience is that patients only very rarely ask for more precision in understanding levels of carbohydrates, and understand that obsessing

Table 4.10 Explaining the negative effects of restriction

CLINICIAN: I can see why you don't feel safe starting to eat in the morning, because you are afraid of losing control over your eating and that will lead to losing control over your weight. The problem is that your head might be saying that you should not eat and winning for a while, but your body is saying that you need to eat. As we can see from your diary, your body will win that particular battle after a while, and you end up bingeing at the end of the day or the next day. The problems get worse, though, because your body tells you that you need high calorie, high carbohydrate foods when you start to binge, and you start to believe that it is those foods that are dangerous. However, as we can see from your energy graph, your body craves those foods because you are starving yourself – not because the foods themselves are dangerous. So you end up managing not to eat for about eight hours, but then eating huge amounts, which you cannot get rid of completely, and feeling scared of the foods themselves, and then gaining weight because you could not get rid of all of the food when you were sick. That sounds like a pretty poor deal to me. What do you think?

---

about precise amounts of food intake is unhelpful. We can model this lack of obsessional striving in our education of the patient. For example, in Section 4.12, we recommend Hart and McMaster's REAL Food Guide (Appendix 5) and the St George's guide (Waller et al., 2007), because they do not advocate precise weighing or counting of portions. Rather, almost all of our patients are very positive about how their energy graph lets them understand and change their bulimic behaviours, rather than treating those behaviours as random and uncontrollable.

Figure 4.2 is an example of an energy graph worked out with a patient who restrains most of the day and then binges later on due to starvation.

Of course, people differ in their patterns of eating and their reasons for doing so. For example, it is important to consider the following when drawing out the energy graph:

• If Karen were to binge every two or three days, the energy graph might show that her carbohydrate levels were drifting down more slowly, as she was eating some carbohydrates but not enough, so that her craving only took over after a couple of days. Figure 4.3 shows an energy graph that reflects such a risky day of eating, where restriction (e.g. small meals; minimal carbohydrates in snacks) results in a particularly low energy level going into the next day, so that eventually bingeing occurs on the second or third day.

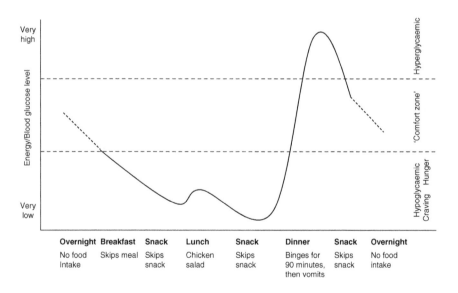

Figure 4.2 Karen's energy graph from Session 1.

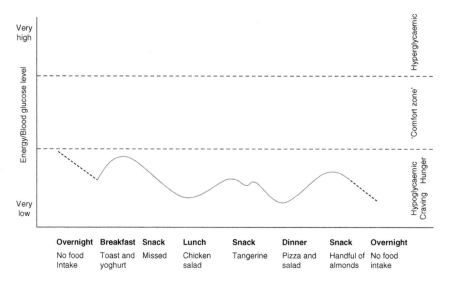

Figure 4.3 Energy graph on a day where intake is restricted but there is no binge eating episode.

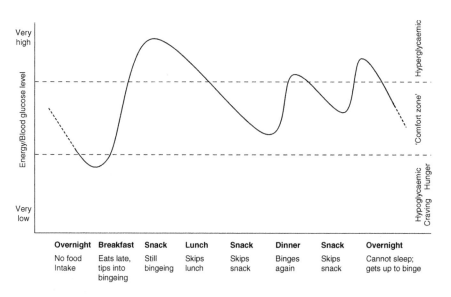

Figure 4.4 Energy graph on a day where there is no restriction but where binges are driven by emotional triggers.

- Purging is commonly followed by bingeing again. This is the result of a number of potential mechanisms, such as abstinence violation, further cravings, desire to reduce emotional states caused by having binged, and physiological mechanisms (particularly cravings due to the release of insulin during the initial binge, causing additional cravings when a lot of the carbohydrates ingested are purged).
- The binges might be more frequent, still distressing, but lower in quantity eaten (subjective binges). Such a presentation suggests that the inadequate intake can be addressed through changing eating patterns, and through normalising the patient's views of the amounts eaten.
- If the binges are happening despite a normal food intake, then it is likely that this indicates that we will be working with emotional triggers later in CBT-T. This pattern is shown in Figure 4.4, and is commonly found in binge-eating disorder cases.

Table 4.11 provides a summary of the aims of using energy graphs in this way. These aims are useful in discussion with patients, and explaining them might explain why patients report finding them to be a key step in understanding their eating disorders.

4.10 Review current eating

The majority of this work has been done while going over the diaries, but it is important to identify broader patterns and to discuss them with the patient. Such awareness can be useful in identifying both weaknesses and strengths. Obviously, this work should be done collaboratively with the patient, inviting them to spot patterns too (Table 4.12).

Table 4.11 Aims of using energy graphs with the patient

- Explain that the binges and purging behaviours are understandable and predictable and are not uncontrollable or a sign of the patient being 'broken'.
- Identify the trigger points for bingeing and purging behaviour.
  CLINICIAN: So, looking at your energy graph, when do you think yesterday's binge began?
  KAREN: Well, at about 5.30 in the afternoon, when I got to my car after shopping in the supermarket, opened those biscuits, and started to eat them.
  CLINICIAN: Now there I am going to disagree with you ... I would say that your binge really began at about 7.30 that morning, when you decided not to eat breakfast. Your starvation really started then, and the binge just became more and more inevitable from then on. Can you see why that might be important?
  KAREN: I am guessing that you are going to say that I should eat breakfast.
  CLINICIAN: And the rest ... the sooner you get eating a normal diet throughout the day, the sooner your body and head stop fighting, and you stop needing to binge.
- Identify risk at the time, by getting the patient used to drawing out their own energy graphs during the day (initially on paper, later mentally).

Table 4.12 Themes and patterns to look out for when reviewing current eating

- Specific dietary choices or regimes.
  - There are few dietary choices that need to prevent the patient having an adequate intake. For example, we routinely work with patients who opt for vegan or vegetarian diets.
  - Similarly, dietary regimes prescribed for medical reasons are rarely a problem (e.g. the need to avoid gluten does not equate to a need to avoid carbohydrates).
  - Of course, there are some individuals who use a dietary regime as a 'mask' for dietary restriction (e.g. *Patient*: Well, I am vegan, but I don't like all those foods on your list with things like fat or carbohydrate in them, so I don't want to eat those). Such constraints should be treated as therapy-interfering behaviours (see Section 4.3.2.2).
- Patterns of eating and bulimic behaviours that vary with circumstances. For example:
  - Some patients binge only on weekdays, while others binge only at weekends, due to when they can get time alone.
  - Link to disinhibitory behaviours (e.g. drinking alcohol; taking drugs).
- Never eating food that the patient has not prepared themselves.
- Irrational reasons for eating, such as the patient who starts to eat, but feels that their stomach is very full immediately. In such cases, the patient is usually reacting to their abdomen feeling tense (an anxiety reaction) rather than to their stomach itself being full (asking the patient to point to their stomach usually resolves this confusion easily, as they misplace their stomach being far lower than it actually is).
- Labelling of small amounts of food as 'binges'. Where the patient labels intake in this way, we immediately address it, by stressing that we see any sense of loss of control as important, but that we need to distinguish 'subjective' from 'objective' binges (small versus large amounts). We explain that we are going to focus on getting their eating straight so that the objective binges stop, and their sense of control increases and they understand that the subjective binges are just normal reactions to normal hunger.
- Patterns of bingeing on foods that the patient usually strives to avoid, e.g.:
  - Learning that the avoidance triggers the binges – not the specific food.
- Repeated binges (e.g. due to abstinence violation).

4.11 Determine and record symptoms, including weighing the patient

Again, much of this has already been done, using the ED-15 and the food diaries. The clinician should ensure that these are recorded on the Protocol cover sheet and Session 1 record sheet (see Appendix 1), so that they can be revisited weekly in order to make progress transparent. However, there is one key piece of information to gather – the patient's weight.

Weighing the patient *needs to follow the review of the patient's eating and bulimic behaviours*. This task is less elaborate in Session 1 than in later sessions (see below). However, as in those later sessions, it is important to raise the patient's anxiety about their weight, to ensure that they make predictions about their weight that are higher than they would be if they were not thinking about their recent eating. Those higher predictions are even more likely to be incorrect, making the patient more likely to learn that their beliefs are inaccurate.

If the patient is reluctant to be weighed or to know their weight, this needs to be treated as a therapy-interfering behaviour and addressed as outlined above. Similarly, if the patient weighs themselves at home or elsewhere, this also should be addressed and discouraged from the beginning (e.g. *Clinician*: You need to get rid of the scales at home, or you will get caught up on using them to reassure yourself, and you won't learn what you need to). Again, this could become something that has to be treated as a therapy-interfering behaviour, if the patient fails to comply.

4.12 Psychoeducation

Throughout this stage, the clinician is likely to be able to identify a range of key areas where psychoeducation is likely to be useful for the patient. These will differ from patient to patient, but a number are relatively common across cases.

While these areas can be discussed during the session, it is better not to enter into debate with the patient, but to give them time to consider the necessary information in a non-confrontational way. We also advise that they do not seek for this material in the form of random internet searches, as this is not a reliable source of information (patients usually understand that point immediately). Therefore, it is necessary to provide the patient with information that they can consider separately.

You should have a range of key psychoeducational handouts, including those outlined in Table 4.13.

Handouts relating to these key materials are available from a number of reliable sources, including the websites for the Centre for Clinical Interventions (CCI), Beat and CREDO, and texts (e.g. Waller et al., 2007, 2010). We include a version of the REAL Food Guide in Appendix 5, courtesy of the authors (Susan Hart and Caitlin McMaster), as this is a very useful and accessible tool for clinicians to use, allowing psychological therapists to access dietitian expertise about normal eating. It also clarifies when to seek more comprehensive support from a dietitian, to address complex dietary needs (e.g. patients who are pregnant or who have diabetes).

Table 4.13 Psychoeducation handouts to have on hand to pass to patients in Session 1

- The effects of starvation (based on the Minnesota study).
- A healthy eating plan (e.g. REAL Food Guide; St George's Healthy Eating Plan), showing the importance of a balanced diet, which includes carbohydrates.
- Calorie needs of the average person.
- Calorie content of alcohol (because many patients assume that alcohol has negligible calorie content, and so they do not factor it in when trying to understand their weight).
- Does purging work? (showing that vomiting usually results in the body retaining over 1000 kcal; showing that laxative use has almost no effect).
- The risks of binge-eating.
- The risks of purging behaviours and exercise (e.g. potassium depletion, damage to gastro-intestinal tract).

4.13 Planning initial dietary change, and getting the patient to predict weight change

This is the first element of CBT-T where exposure with response prevention comes into play. The reason for this use of exposure therapy is that anxiety and safety behaviours are key factors driving eating behaviours and cognitions.

4.13.1 Exposure principles: Inhibitory learning

As a reminder (see Section 1.5), the principles of inhibitory learning are used to guide how to use exposure (e.g. Reilly et al., 2017). That means that we do not use graded exposure, systematic desensitisation, or hierarchies. Instead, we aim for the maximum amount of anxiety that the patient can tolerate at that point, we do not rely on anxiety reducing in-session, and we aim to get the patient to generalise their learning by trying the exposure in a wide variety of settings. This approach allows the patient to overcome anxiety far more quickly, more generally, and more robustly than other methods that have traditionally been used. Therefore, rather than aiming for gentle changes in eating, the approach from the beginning is to push for the largest changes that the patient can cope with. This often means that we start with a very strong suggestion about the amount of food to be added or modified each week.

While clinicians are often reluctant to push the patient to make meaningful levels of change, this is commonly the result of the clinician's own anxiety about the patient's reaction, rather than the patient's ability to make the change. Our experience is that most patients make very substantial eating changes in the first few sessions, understand why they need to do this, and tolerate the anxiety well. They also show very substantial cognitive and emotional improvement as a result. Remember, as we aim to do our best by the patient, we should not let our anxiety or lack of confidence in their ability to change get in the way of allowing the patient to experience rapid change, and the buzz that this gives them as it starts to radically challenge their view of themselves and the intractability of the eating disorder.

4.13.2 Adding structure and content to the patient's eating

The food diary and energy graph will demonstrate clearly what needs to change in the patient's eating. Two changes are usually key – introducing structure (e.g. eating something at all meal and snack times), and adding content and variety (eating enough food in those regular slots to overcome starvation and craving effects, and to increase weight if necessary). We discuss this with the patient from the outset, stating that we need to:

- Get the structure in place immediately.
- Get the content in place simultaneously or very soon afterwards.
- Normalise eating as much as possible by Session 3 or 4 (using a healthy eating guide to indicate normality).

We then plan what the patient will need to eat to achieve this between Session 1 and Session 2. The usual approach is to suggest that the patient should either:

- Make sure that they are eating to the structure by the second week, where the amount eaten does not matter except at breakfast, where a full dose of complex carbohydrate should be taken; *or*
- Add to content across the day, by moving towards the full carbohydrate dose for each meal and snack over the coming two weeks.

If both are viable, then aim for the second of these options. Again, the rule is to maximise the anxiety generated to influence weight change predictions. We also stress that we cannot know true weight immediately, because of natural weight fluctuations (particularly if the patient was using laxatives and has the potential for additional fluid-related weight changes in the short term).

4.13.3 Getting the patient to predict the impact of this change in eating on their weight

Our goal here is to ensure that the patient's schema (uncontrollable weight gain) is challenged by the data (no weight gain or controlled weight gain – depending on whether the patient starts at a normal/high weight or a low weight). Therefore, we aim to demonstrate the patient's schema regarding weight gain, so that we can test it.

The patient is asked for their prediction following weighing and planning dietary change for the coming week, to maximise the patient's anxiety about what might happen to their weight. Again, this anxiety drives more extreme predictions of weight gain, which are even less likely to happen, allowing the patient to realise that their weight is not out of control and their anxieties and fears are exaggerated.

Following the establishment of eating plans, the patient is asked to predict their weight change over the coming week and to rate the certainty of this happening (e.g. out of 100), which the clinician should note. If the weight gain predicted is minimal or the patient is not worried about it, then it is important to return to the previous stage and increase the proposed increase in the amount eaten. However, given that weight fluctuates, it is possible (though highly unlikely) that the predicted weight increase will occur. Therefore, stress the need to 'give it a couple of weeks' before one can be sure what is happening to the patient's weight, as illustrated in Table 4.14. This prediction will be revisited (and reviewed) in Session 2, and weekly thereafter.

When monitoring predicted weight gain and actual weight gain, it is important to note that the weight charts will look different in terms of the actual weight element according to whether the patient starts at a normal/higher weight (see Figure 4.5) or at a relatively low weight (see Figure 4.6). However, as the following two weight charts show, the pattern of cumulative weight predictions looks very similar across both groups, reflecting the central 'broken' cognitive link of uncontrollability of weight gain, which gradually lowers as therapy progresses. The 'repair' of that link is shown where the two lines in a chart run parallel, indicating that weight predictions have become relatively accurate.

Table 4.14 Predicting weight change following developing eating plans in Session 1

CLINICIAN: So, you are all sorted with what you are going to do about your eating over the coming week. Now, you sounded a bit worried about the effect on your weight and your bingeing. How much do you think your weight will go up from your current weight of 55 kg?

PATIENT: At least 2 kg ... maybe 3 kg?

CLINICIAN: How certain are you about that – that you will gain at least 3 kg – on a 0 to 100% scale?

PATIENT: Probably only about 30–40%?

CLINICIAN: And what about at least 2 kg?

PATIENT: Oh, that is pretty certain – about 80–90%

CLINICIAN: So let's go with that very certain 2 kg gain. You reckon that you will gain 2 kg. Now that is possible, but the books would say it is unlikely if you eat that amount, especially if you binge less as a result. However, there is only one way to find out, and that is to give it a try. So let's see if you are right, and then we can see if we need to adjust your eating up or down to get your weight stable. However, you need to remember that weight fluctuates, so whatever happens next week, we cannot be sure that is the true story – we will have to give it a bit longer than one week to understand how your weight operates when you eat differently. For example, if your weight goes up or down next week, that might be a random blip, so we won't be able to reach conclusions immediately.

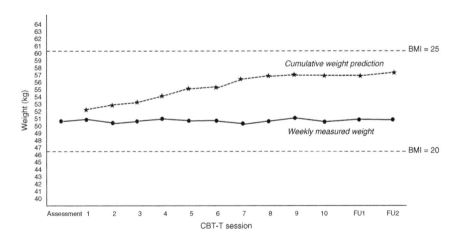

Figure 4.5 Weight chart for a patient starting therapy at a normal weight, showing weekly measured weight and cumulative weight predictions across CBT-T, comparing actual weight stability (data) with the patient's fears of uncontrollable weight gain over time (schema).

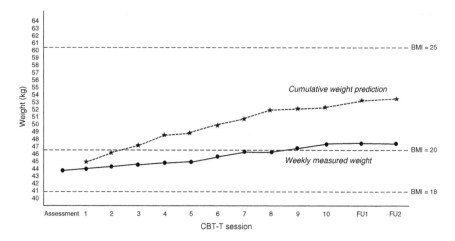

Figure 4.6 Weight chart for a patient starting therapy at a low weight, showing weekly measured weight and cumulative weight predictions across CBT-T, comparing planned weight regain (data) with the patient's fears of uncontrollable weight gain over time (schema).

4.14 Ending the session and preparing for next week

Having obtained the patient's weight prediction at this late stage in the session (enhancing the likelihood that the anxiety-based prediction will be remembered), we now wind down the session by reminding the patient to:

- Read the relevant psychoeducation handouts provided.
- Complete the diary in real time (rather than after the event), including all that is eaten and drunk (at this stage, beliefs and emotions are an optional addition).
- Make the planned dietary changes.
- Think about whether there are any items that they would like to put on the agenda for next time.

Summary: Setting the scene in Session 1

- If offering a preliminary assessment, use it to foreshadow key elements of CBT-T (particularly the non-negotiables), to prepare the patient for active treatment.
- Ask the patient to complete food diaries and the ED-15 before Session 1.
- Use the protocol checklist.
- Engage the patient ('realistic optimism') and set expectations for therapy (early change; active role as own therapist).
- Clarify the non-negotiables of CBT-T.
- Be empathic but firm about the need for change.
- Start change in eating and diary recording.
- Start using exposure.
- Psychoeducation for the patient (including core information and use of energy graphs).

Notes

1   It should be remembered that Grove et al. (2000) have shown clinical judgement to be a weak basis for clinical actions compared to more protocol-based methods.
2   The examples given are relatively mild demonstrations of some of the more extremely odd things that we have heard of, done in the name of 'therapy'. The rule of thumb in CBT-T is not to be surprised by some of what one hears, but to use it to our advantage in persuading the patient that they are not 'broken' or 'helpless', but have had a therapy that never stood a chance of working.

Chapter 5

Phase 1 – Exposure, nutrition, and repairing the 'broken' cognitive link

This initial phase usually takes approximately three sessions (2–4), though it can take less or a little more. As with all CBT-ED, this initial phase in CBT-T is where very substantial amounts of behavioural, cognitive, and emotional improvement can be achieved, and where that change is very powerful in determining longer term outcome. It is important to get this phase under way and completed as quickly as possible, to allow more time for cognitive restructuring and body image work. Therefore, we need to keep up the 'drip-drip' approach of reminding patients (and clinicians) about the number of sessions available and the core tasks to be completed.

Given that patients differ in their progress and the nature of the problems that they present with, the specifics of what we address in each session will differ from patient to patient. However, there are core themes in the treatment during CBT-T, and specific tasks that are critical. Some themes and skills have already been outlined in Session 1. Other themes and tasks/techniques will be focused on in this section of the therapy and are addressed here (as well as being carried into later stages of CBT-T).

The protocol checklists for Sessions 2–4 can be found in Appendix 1. Again, each checklist should be used to ensure that core tasks are completed (or discounted if not relevant to that individual). The sequencing of the tasks should be as appropriate to that patient, though there are some general rules that should always be observed – particularly the need to place the patient's agenda later in the session (to avoid distraction), and the sequencing of diary discussions/weighing the patient (see below).

It has already been stated that some patients will not need all the phases of CBT-T, as they might relate to symptoms that some patients do not experience at all or are irrelevant by that stage in therapy (e.g. emotionally driven binges; body image disturbance). However, this phase is one that applies to all patients with eating disorders.

5.1 Themes during the first phase of CBT-T (Sessions 2–4)

The three themes in Table 5.1 are naturally intertwined, each facilitating and being dependent on the others, so they need to be addressed in parallel. They also

Table 5.1 Themes during Phase I

- Address starvation and bulimic behaviours (nutritional imbalance).
  - ○ Structure, then content.
- Address anxiety (exposure).
  - ○ Use inhibitory learning approach.
- Address 'broken cognition' regarding weight.
  - ○ Eating to an appropriate level for weight stability (or gain, if necessary).
  - ○ Open weighing at every session.
  - ○ Linked to dietary monitoring.

---

need to be explained to the patient fully, of course, to enhance engagement and collaboration.

5.1.1 Changing eating patterns and content to address nutritional imbalance

Encouraging the patient to eat differently is key, as it addresses starvation effects (which can occur regardless of weight). Changing eating to a healthy pattern can:

- Reduce cognitive inflexibility.
- Help with mood stability (through enhancing functional levels of serotonin).
- Reduce binge-purge behaviour substantially (totally in most cases), allowing emotional triggers of binges to be identified and tackled later in therapy (see Chapter 8).

These effects are in addition to those brought about by the exposure element (see below).

Of course, healthy eating has to be addressed as a psychoeducation topic (usually in Session 1). While some patients understand that a healthy intake will be made up of an appropriate balance of foodstuffs, others believe that 'healthy' eating can be defined by the consumption of a limited range of food (e.g. omitting carbohydrates and fats), or by the eating of specific foods (e.g. a particular vegetable). This does not mean that one cannot use CBT-T to treat patients with specific diets (e.g. veganism; gluten-free), as these are not prohibitory of whole food groups. However, if that diet is used as a justification for omitting key nutrients then the clinician needs to treat this as a therapy-interfering behaviour and address it immediately, e.g.:

PATIENT: I am gluten intolerant, so that means that I cannot eat carbs.
CLINICIAN: Fortunately, there are lots of gluten-free options that will give you all the carbs that you need, so let's list those out for you. Unless you are really saying that you do not want to eat carbs at all?

In this phase, for many patients, eating needs to begin with implementation of *structure* (three meals plus two or three snacks, avoiding long gaps). We then move as quickly as possible (sometimes simultaneously) to adding in adequate *content*, where the patient is eating a diet with a balance of nutrients (e.g. see REAL Food Guide – Appendix 5) with enough calorie content to stabilise weight. The only exception would be where the patient is below a maintenance weight, in which case we explain to the patient that the calorie content is higher in the short term to ensure longer term stability at a healthy weight. It should be stressed to the patient that while the content will need to be adequate during this phase, we will still be changing content (in terms of diversity and facing specific feared foods) during the behavioural experiments in Phase 2 (see Chapter 7).

5.1.2 Addressing anxiety using exposure with response prevention

The key element of exposure at this stage is changing the patient's eating towards a normal pattern (usually for weight stability, unless the patient needs to gain some weight to be in the healthy range). For our patients, this means planning to eat more regularly and in greater quantities at meal and snack times (rather than eating in the form of binges). The aim is to provoke anxiety by reducing the use of restriction and other compensatory behaviours. Thus, we ask the patient to eat differently, generating anxiety in the short term but letting the patient learn that eating normally has greater positive benefits, and the anxiety fades.

Exposure to anxiety triggers is a key therapeutic process in different phases in CBT-T, but most critically here. Restrictive eating (along with many purging behaviours and body-related behaviours) is an avoidant/safety behaviour aimed at either preventing weight gain or producing weight loss, which reduces anxiety in the short term, while amplifying anxiety in the long-term. Therefore, it is inevitable that the exposure element of changing from restrictive to normal eating patterns (see Table 5.1) will make patients anxious in the short-term, as we are asking the patient to give up their safety behaviour. However, when we use exposure appropriately, that anxiety can be reduced as the patient learns that the feared outcome (e.g. uncontrollable weight gain) does not happen.

The issue of what constitutes the best use of exposure therapy is one that has been reviewed in a range of disorders over the past decade. It has become clear that traditional approaches to in vivo exposure (e.g. use of hierarchies, systematic desensitization, graded exposure, flooding) are slow and limited in their effectiveness (e.g. Becker & Waller, 2016; Reilly et al., 2017). Instead, and as with treatment of anxiety disorders (e.g. Craske et al., 2014), we use an inhibitory learning approach to exposure in CBT-T. This approach is based on aiming for maximal tolerable anxiety, without the expectation or need for anxiety to reduce within the session. It is also important that the patient develops the skill in diverse settings, where predictability is minimised (e.g. eating a new food in a new café; trying unknown and feared foods routinely). Our experience is that our patients understand that this is going to be scary, and that it is not helpful if their clinician is anxious about change as well. We find that very often it is not only patients who underestimate their ability to withstand the anxiety, but clinicians commonly underestimate the patient's ability as well. Our patients and clinicians alike have found it very helpful to focus on the following 'mantra': "You are stronger than you know". When used in conjunction with validation ("It is normal to feel anxious when changing long-term patterns"), this often works well to help patients face the challenges of the coming week. Patients tend to show very rapid reduction in anxiety, as the inhibitory learning approach would suggest, allowing for improved self-efficacy and rapid progression to behavioural experiments for cognitive change (Chapter 7).

5.1.3 Addressing the 'broken' cognitive link between eating/food and weight

The other related theme (tied to addressing eating and anxiety) is the reduction of the central belief that: "Whatever I eat, I will gain weight". This theme continues beyond this phase, as it is also tested by the behavioural experiments in Phase 2 (Chapter 7). It requires the clinician to help the patient to learn that food does not have the effects on weight that they predict and fear. So, three tasks are critical throughout the course of CBT-T:

- Changing eating patterns to enhance structure and content, aiming to achieve normal eating and (where the patient starts off below the optimum weight) a functional weight.
- Weighing the patient openly (so that the patient sees their weight).
- Linking their weight to what they eat (i.e. completing food diaries).

Without those three tasks being completed, CBT-T has little chance of teaching patients that their central belief is wrong. The first phase uses exposure to a range of previously avoided behaviours – weekly weighing, food monitoring, regular eating, and regular intake of carbohydrates – to challenge the central belief of the patient that these will make their eating worse and increase their weight (unless of course they are underweight and one of the aims of therapy is to assist in weight gain).

As above, it should be recognised that some patients use diaries and weighing as safety behaviours to reduce anxiety in the short term – failing to record what they eat or recording obsessively; avoiding knowing their weight or weighing themselves multiple times in a day. Either approach has the inevitable outcome of the safety behaviour – making the patient feel worse in the long term. Therefore, the clinician's job is to regularise both behaviours (weighing just once a week and making the patient aware of their weight; appropriate food diaries) so that the patient can learn in the longer term. This will make some patients anxious in the short term, but failure to address these tasks from the beginning means that CBT-T is unlikely to be effective in the short or long term. Addressing patient reluctance is addressed below (Section 5.2.4), but clinician reluctance to push for open weighing or diary-keeping is a clinician therapy-interfering behaviour that needs to be discussed and addressed as a priority in supervision.

5.2 Specific tasks in this phase

The tasks for these three sessions are detailed in Appendix 1 and are summarised in the following text box. As some of those techniques across the sessions are already detailed in Session 1 (Chapter 4), only the new or changed ones are outlined in this section of the manual. These are detailed in Table 5.2, in **bold**.

In general, all of these techniques need to be used in every session, as appropriate to the patient's needs and progress. Which tasks require more focus in each of the sessions during this phase depends on how quickly the patient starts to make key changes, especially around the implementation of regular eating. In turn, that

Table 5.2 Specific tasks in Phase 2 of CBT-T (Sessions 2–4)

Tasks in bold are new ones in this phase and are detailed below. Others have been addressed previously (see previous chapters).

- **Review learning from last time and homework.**
  - ○ **Questionnaires from last week.**
- Address any life-threatening or therapy-interfering behaviours.
- **Review changes in eating:**
  - ○ **Food intake.**
  - ○ **Contemporaneous diaries.**
- **Diaries and weighing to address the 'broken' cognitive link.**
- Review current eating.
  - ○ Using energy graphs.
- **Review behavioural changes and problems (especially bulimic behaviours).**
  - ○ **Clarify what makes a binge, and chart such behaviours.**
  - ○ **Stress ineffectiveness of purging behaviours.**
- Determine and record symptoms (bulimic behaviours, weighing, etc.).
- Re-explain the model if necessary as you use energy graphs to summarise the patient's risky behaviours and outcomes.
- **Response to performance to date.**
  - ○ **Positive reinforcement for helpful changes.**
  - ○ **Clear feedback on chances of recovery if not engaging with treatment tasks.**
  - ○ **Session 4 only – formally review progress (see Chapter 6).**
- **Review cognitive change in ED-15 and other problems from questionnaires.**
- Discuss the ED-15 with the patient.
- **Address the patient's agenda items (if any).**
- Select any additional psychoeducation material.
- Homework.
  - ○ education, eating changes, diary, monitoring measures.
  - ○ **Session 2 – prepare a list of 'feared' and 'safe' foods.**
  - ○ **Session 4 – start behavioural experiment process (earlier if possible) – see Chapter 7.**

---

is influenced by our willingness to push the patient to make early, wide-reaching changes, so that the inhibitory learning process is under way. The clinician's role requires patient-centred responsiveness, while maintaining the overall drive towards recovery (i.e. firm empathy). If a patient changes eating quickly, their starvation effects and bulimic behaviours are likely to be reduced substantially. Similarly, their anxiety reduces, allowing the clinician to move on to behavioural experimentation to encourage the patient to test and modify specific cognitions (see Chapter 7 for details of that process).

It is important to reduce the patient's anxiety before we try to implement cognitive change and behavioural experiments, so that the patient can learn from those cognitive methods. If we introduce behavioural experimentation too quickly, the patient is likely to be too anxious to make the change without trying to compensate (e.g. when the patient eats an extra biscuit per day to see whether their weight would stay stable or go up by 2 kg, but then exercises more to cope with their anxiety, they cannot learn from the behavioural change). So, we use exposure-based change to help the patient to reduce anxiety before undertaking behavioural experimentation and cognitive restructuring.

Table 5.2 shows the specific tasks that are new in this phase. Remember, the order of presentation of the tasks is not fixed. You can use them in whatever order makes sense within the individual session, as long as all the relevant tasks are completed.

5.2.1 Review learning from last time and homework

This will be a key task each week from this point on, as it stresses the opportunities that the patient has had to learn both in and out of sessions. Obviously, the content will change as therapy progresses. For example, in Session 2, one will be addressing learning about the reasons for regular eating, and the consequences of restriction (e.g. binges, emotional instability), as well as the structure and rationale of CBT-T. In contrast, in Session 3, one will review whether the patient has identified feared foods. A particular focus throughout should be reviewing the questionnaires and diaries that the patient has been asked to complete (detailed below). As outlined above, we should be looking for the patient to be eating more regularly, with a much more balanced intake. In particular, we usually find that we need to press the patient to increase their planned intake of carbohydrates, fat, and protein. We emphasise regular intake of carbohydrates over the day (see the REAL Food Guide – Appendix 5) because patients commonly avoid these but end up bingeing on them. We frame this as:

CLINICIAN: Your head is telling you to avoid carbohydrates because you hate your lack of control, but your body is trying to be a friend to you and telling you that it needs them regularly. When the cravings get too much, your body is taking over and you end up bingeing – your energy graph shows that really clearly. The bingeing leaves you feeling terrible, and the cycle begins again. So, we are going to have to get you eating normally, to overcome those binges and to help you feel better about yourself again. That means that carbohydrates are going to the top of your eating, if you want to get better, and then you will learn that the anxiety goes away quickly and your weight does not go out of control. And later, we will get you to start experimenting with eating your scariest foods, so that you can see that your weight still does not go out of control.

5.2.2 Review changes in eating

In this first phase, it is imperative that clinicians should stress the importance of dietary change and food diaries at every session, to address the 'broken' cognitive link, to reduce nutritional deficits and to overcome anxiety levels. Food diaries and eating patterns will be reviewed more fully later in the session. However, the patient should be asked early in the session whether they kept the necessary contemporaneous diaries and whether they changed the structure and/or content of their food intake as planned in the previous session.

Remember that sessions in this phase are unlikely to be effective if the patient has not completed the necessary diaries and changes in eating, as there will be no real opportunity to address the key beliefs, nutritional needs, and anxiety. Therefore, if the patient has not completed these tasks (at least partially between Sessions 1 and 2 and completely thereafter), this should be treated as a therapy-interfering behaviour. In such circumstances, it is important to stress to the patient that therapy is unlikely to be effective and cannot proceed unless they are able to actively engage in all elements of the therapy. On the first occasion, the session should be shortened considerably, and any subsequent omission of these core tasks should result in the session being ended very quickly ('five-minute session'). For example:

CLINICIAN: Here we are at Session 2. I know that we addressed this in Session 1, but you have only completed the diaries for about one and a half days this week, and you tell me that your eating has not really changed on other days. Of course, that means that we have very little to discuss today, so I'm going to make this a shorter session. We'll review the changes we agreed last session – the diaries and structured eating plan – so that they are clear in your mind for the coming week. In order to keep you on track we'll also cover the other changes that you need to be making by Session 4. That will mean the diaries, getting in the structure we agreed last week, and implementing the other changes we have agreed. OK – let's cover what we can do usefully and then I am going to end the session for this week and send you off to get on track for Session 3 next time. But I need to stress we will have little to talk about next time if you do not do the diary and eating changes.

Or:

CLINICIAN: OK – here we are at Session 3. How did you get on with the diaries and your changed eating?

PATIENT: 'Well, I was going to do the diary/bring in the diary, but unfortunately I left it at home/I was at work and could not get it done with all those people about/I didn't think I needed it/hated how it made me feel (etc.), so I did not bring it. I ate according to the healthy eating plans a couple of times but not the rest of the time, because…'

CLINICIAN: 'I am going to stop you there. I think what you are saying is that you did not do the diary and/or change your eating. Is that right? Unfortunately, this means that we have nothing to work with this week, as I explained to you last time. Therefore, let's take a weight recording, make sure you understand what the tasks are to focus on, and then we will end the session for this week. You will need to get back on track by next time otherwise I'm concerned that you won't get anything useful out of these sessions. As we've previously discussed, making changes can make you feel more anxious in the short term, but I would strongly encourage you to take the risk as the more changes you make, the more you'll find out about the relationship between your weight and your food intake.'

Our experience is that such shortening of sessions stresses to the patient that therapy is what goes on outside the room (see Session 1), and it has never been necessary to do more than one five-minute session for any individual patient. However, where there is no such stress (usually because the clinician does not want to challenge the patient), the patient cannot learn that these are key tasks, and instead learns that homework is, effectively, optional. Note that we treat each short session as one of the 10 sessions that the patient has, emphasising it by numbering the sessions explicitly. This is to avoid the position where the patient assumes that the number of sessions is not really limited, or where they assume that by not doing the therapy the number of sessions will be increased ad infinitum. Remember, that repeated extension might well have been their experience in previous therapies (e.g. Cowdrey & Waller, 2015), so it is important to be explicit.

Another consideration is that the nature of the diary keeping should be considered from a functional perspective – did the patient keep the records contemporaneously, to ensure awareness of eating at the time? This is far more important than the question of what method the patient uses to record their intake (e.g. completes a paper diary; records on their smartphone). Many patients find it easier to keep the diary on their phone or online at work, because they look like they are texting, and that attracts less attention. That approach is fine. However, we ask the patient to write out or print out what they have typed ahead of the session, so that the diary can easily be shared and discussed later (see Section 5.2.4.1).

Finally, remember that this review should be a small part of each of session if it goes well, but a critical part if the work has not been completed. All of the above is simply how to deal with the 'did you make the changes?' question at the outset of the sessions. We will return to scrutinising the diary fully and its implications for weight change later in the session (see below).

5.2.3 Review behavioural changes and problems (especially bulimic behaviours)

Using the diary and questionnaires, the number of bulimic behaviours should be noted, and compared to previous weeks. We focus on objective binges and teach the patient the difference between objective binges (sense of loss of control plus eating a very large amount) and subjective binges (sense of loss of control, without the large amount eaten). We record both but tell the patient that we usually find that addressing the objective binges will take away the sense of loss of control across the board. The frequency of these behaviours per week should be transferred to the cover sheet of the protocol checklist, so that progress can be shared with the patient simply, and benefits of therapy or roadblocks to progress are easily identified.

Where the patient binges, we review the patient's learning from the previous sessions (e.g. energy graph as an explanation of bingeing), we address psychoeducation about the ways in which bingeing is problematic (health risks), and we review how it results in far more calories being absorbed than is assumed (over 1000 kcal per binge/vomit episode). Where the patient uses purging or compensatory behaviours, we stress their physical dangers (potassium depletion; dental damage), their ineffectiveness (e.g. of vomiting, laxatives), and the way that behaviours that the patient initially saw as solutions to problems (e.g. exercise) have become a problem (e.g. injury, lack of opportunity for a social life, turning something enjoyable into something driven).

5.2.4 Diaries and weighing to address the 'broken cognition'

At this point, we change the pattern of weighing the patient from what was used in Session 1, in order to address the 'broken cognition'. In Session 1, the patient was asked to estimate their weight and was then weighed (openly) by the clinician and their weight discussed and recorded in the protocol and on a weight chart. The chart includes the actual weight and the anticipated weight gain as two separate lines (in CBT terms – the data and the schema, which are presented together to allow the patient to challenge their belief system).

Now, we aim to make the process more powerful in terms of anxiety induction, so that the patient can learn quickly that eating normally does not result in uncontrollable weight gain. Underpinning this approach is the inhibitory learning approach to exposure therapy. So that the patient does not reduce their anxiety (and hence the impact of the exposure), it is important that we should already have agreed with the patient not to weigh themselves between sessions. This weighing process is detailed in Waller and Mountford (2015), but Table 5.3 summarizes the process.

It is important to note that the actual weighing is only a very small part of the weighing process – 95% of the work and learning impact of weighing the patient happens when they are off the weighing scales.

Table 5.3 The process of weighing in CBT-T

- Review food diaries with the patient.
- Get the patient's weight change prediction (and certainty rating) and chart the predicted change.
- Prepare the patient regarding time needed to be sure.
- Weigh the patient openly and chart actual weight.
- Discuss discrepancy, to keep possibilities open.

5.2.4.1 Reviewing the food diaries with the patient

Before starting this process, it is important to remind ourselves that our patients' anxiety about weight gain is very high, and leads them to anticipate that their weight will go up by far more than is likely, given what they have eaten (e.g. non-under-weight patients in CBT-ED will routinely state that they are absolutely certain that their weight will have gone up by at least a kilogram over the past week, even though their eating has barely changed). We have to remember the implausibility of these predictions, in the same way that a clinician working with a patient with a spider phobia has to remember that the patient is highly unlikely to be harmed by a spider, or that a patient with OCD is highly unlikely to harm a relative if they do not count the railings on the way to work. This is not to discount the patient's fears as trivial, as they clearly are not, but to remind ourselves that they are usually incorrect. However, it must be remembered that an anxious clinician is more likely to be concerned that the patient might be right, and hence will push less for change.

The reason for reminding ourselves of these points is that the inhibitory learning model of exposure requires us to maximise anxiety at all stages in the exposure process. Therefore, we begin the weighing process by using the diaries to enhance patient anxiety, to maximise their predicted weight gain and certainty. To do this, we aim to generate 'hot' cognitions about the patient's food intake by focusing on specific elements, reminding the patient of the experience of eating the food and considering the potential impact on their weight of eating those foods. For example:

CLINICIAN: OK – looking at the first day of your diary, you have clearly increased the amount that you ate over this past week. As agreed, you have had three meals and three snacks, and you have added carbohydrates in nearly every time, as per the meal plan. It's great to see you taking these risks, especially as you have eaten *lots* more than you did in the week before we started therapy, and you have added in a lot of what you see as 'risky' foods, like bread and cheese. Let's talk about a few examples so that you can tell me how it felt and what you thought when you were eating so differently.

5.2.4.2 Getting the patient's weight change prediction

Immediately after refreshing the patient's cognitions about their eating and elevating their anxiety, we ask them to make a prediction about their weight change from the previous session, and to give a certainty rating for that prediction. Of course, we had asked the patient to make a weight prediction in the previous week, based on what they agreed to eat over the follow week. However, there are two reasons for getting a fresh prediction now – first, the patient's eating is unlikely to be precisely what they estimated a week previously; second, the prediction after discussing the eating that has actually taken place (the 'hot' cognitions) is usually higher than was predicted when the eating was only a plan.

Note that the emphasis at this stage is not on the specifics of the cognitions – the food changes are not precise, and there is no effort to consider alternative cognitions that might be supported. That is because this stage is based on exposure, rather than behavioural experimentation. The precision of food changes and alternative predictions using behavioural experiments comes in Phase 2. A common interaction in the session might be:

CLINICIAN: So, given all that you have told me that you ate last week, what is your best prediction about how much weight you have put on or lost since last time?

PATIENT: It is certainly a lot more than I was eating before, if you don't count the binges. I think I must have put on about 2 kg. I could feel it on me when we were talking about my diary just now.

CLINICIAN: OK – how certain are you about that, on that 0-100% scale.

PATIENT: Say 90%? Yes, about that.

CLINICIAN: OK – let's find out.

The patient will sometimes suggest very high levels of weight gain that they see as relatively unlikely, e.g.:

CLINICIAN: So, given all that you have told me that you ate last week, what is your best prediction about how much weight you have put on or lost since last time?

PATIENT: Oh, well, it sounds like a huge amount to eat now that I look at it … maybe I will have put on about 5 kg?

CLINICIAN: OK – how certain are you about that, on that 0–100% scale.

PATIENT: Oh – only about 20%.

A key skill here is to get the patient to suggest the maximum weight gain that has a strong level of probability, e.g.:

CLINICIAN: So you reckon that it *could* be 5 kg, but you sound pretty unsure about that. What sort of weight gain would be less unlikely? For example, how certain would you be that you had gained at least 3 kg? 2 kg?

PATIENT: Hmm – for 3 kg, about 50% certain, but I can't have put on less than 2 kg, so I will go 100% on that one.

CLINICIAN: 'Right. It sounds like you are pretty certain that you must have gained at least 2 kg, so how about if we put that down as the minimum, because you are so certain?'

Remember, a weight gain of 2 kg in a week is, in reality, very improbable (requiring approximately an *additional* 2000 kcal a day for the average woman). Therefore, it is very unlikely that reducing the prediction in this way will result in the patient achieving their predicted gain. The finding that one was wrong with a 100% certain prediction has far more potential impact on beliefs about weight uncontrollability than finding one was wrong with a 20% or 50% certain prediction. That final prediction is then charted (see Figure 4.5). Remember that the cumulative weight prediction line is always based on adding this week's prediction to the previous week's prediction point (hence, *cumulative* weight prediction) rather than to the previous week's actual weight, thus showing the schema regarding uncontrollable weight gain.

Finally, if the patient predicts little or no weight gain or is not worried about whether they have gained weight or not, there are four possible reasons. (1) In the early part of therapy, this can mean that we have not pushed the patient out of their comfort zone when setting eating targets the week before, and we need to push the patient into greater levels of anxiety (usually meaning that we have to be willing to be firmer). (2) In the latter part of therapy, it is more likely that we have achieved our goal of helping the patient to understand that their weight gain is not uncontrollable, as they had once feared. (3) It is also possible that the patient is experiencing a variant of ARFID, where the issues about eating are driven by broader emotional states, rather than by fear of weight gain. Such patients can be transitioned quickly to Phase 3 of CBT-T. (4) Finally, one should consider the possibility that the patient is telling us that they are going to change their eating, but have no intention of doing so in reality. Obviously, this final possibility should be challenged as a therapy-interfering behaviour.

5.2.4.3 Preparing the patient for the time taken to be sure about weight changes

Of course, human weight fluctuates naturally, and one cannot be sure whether any single reading is accurate or directly comparable with the previous week. Therefore, before the actual weighing, the clinician needs to address that point with the patient:

CLINICIAN: Right, so you are predicting a 2 kg weight gain, at least. Let's find out if you are right. However, remember that weight fluctuates naturally, so it is possible that your weight might have gone up, down or nowhere, and that is not a real change but a fluctuation. So, while we are going to weigh you and record it now, remember that we cannot really rely on this single weighing, and we will need to look at how your weight goes over the next week or so before we can get to a conclusion.

5.2.4.4 Weigh the patient openly and chart actual weight

At this point, we weigh the patient openly, so that both clinician and patient can and do see the reading on the scales. This is usually done with the patient in light clothing, without shoes, on well-calibrated scales (which have a high upper limit, to accommodate obese patients). The patient's weight is then charted by the clinician, so that both the clinician and the patient have copies.

5.2.4.5 Discuss discrepancy between prediction and actual weights

This is the point where we aim to keep the patient open to possibilities long enough to not jump to conclusions about their weight. However, this also requires us to keep our minds open to the possibility that we might be wrong (that simple Socratic approach again – "You might be right, you might not be – let's think about how to find out"). Whether the patient is right or wrong in their prediction in any one session, the response needs to be similar, e.g.:

CLINICIAN: You predicted that your weight would go up by 2 kg, and you were 100% certain about that. Actually, it has not changed from last week. However, as I said before you got on the scales, we cannot really tell based on this one weighing, so all I can say today is that your belief might be right or it might be wrong – it will take us another week or so to be sure.

Or:

CLINICIAN: You predicted that your weight would go up by 2 kg, and you were 100% certain about that. Actually, it has gone *down* by 0.5 kg since last week. However, as I said before you got on the scales, we cannot really tell based on this one weighing, so all I can say today is that your belief might be right or it might be wrong – it will take us another week or so to be sure.

Or (and this is by far the least common of these scripts to be needed):

CLINICIAN: You predicted that your weight would go up by 2 kg, and you were 100% certain about that. Today's reading matches that prediction. However, as I said before you got on the scales, we cannot really tell based on this one weighing, so all I can say today is that your belief might be right or it might be wrong – it will take us another week or so to be sure.

Remember, the Socratic principle of openness in testing beliefs matters when addressing the 'broken' cognitive link. If the patient is incorrect one week and we use that as an opportunity to tell them that their belief system is wrong, our jumping to that conclusion means that they will be justified in concluding that one really *can* tell after only one session. Then, if their prediction of an increase in weight is supported in a subsequent week, they are highly likely to trust that one reading and to dismiss any alternative possibilities – after all, we did the same thing ourselves.

Whichever is the appropriate response to the circumstances, we should be preparing to ensure that the patient maintains or adds to their food intake over the coming week, as part of their homework. In Session 2, we also use this part of the process to start to identify some 'safe' and 'feared' foods, to be expanded on for homework and addressed later as part of Phase 2, when planning behavioural experiments.

Finally, what conclusion can we reach if the patient is eating at what appears to be a normal level, is not reporting bingeing or overeating, and is gaining weight? This is a matter that occasionally comes up in supervision. Five options should be considered:

- First, the patient might be failing to report binges that are taking place.
- It is possible that this patient needs less food than we expect. Remember that 1950–2000 kcal a day for a normal-weight woman and 2500 kcal a day for a normal-weight man are means, and some people will need less while some need more. We need to work with the patient in front of us – not a textbook 'average' case.
- Activity levels might need to be increased (e.g. if the patient has been told that all exercise should be stopped when they were experiencing a much lower weight).
- Some patients believe that they should be at a relatively low normal weight for their height (e.g. BMI 19–20), while their body's 'set point' is higher (e.g. BMI = 23). In these circumstances, we have to remind the patient that "your head is saying one thing, but your body is saying another, and your body will always win in that case".
- In some cases, the patient needs time for their metabolism to re-establish a normal level, after years of being disrupted by the eating disorder behaviours.

In all of these cases, we explain to the patient that their slow rate of weight gain is far lower than their beliefs lead them to predict, so that they cannot use it as evidence that their fears about uncontrollable weight gain are coming true.

5.2.5 Response to performance to date

A critical stance in CBT-T is that we use positive reinforcement for helpful changes, to emphasise the patient's agency in making change (i.e. the patient as the therapist) and motivate them to make further changes. Do not be surprised if the patient is taken aback the first time that you do this – remember that patients with eating disorders often see themselves as helpless, and that previous therapies might not have resulted in any real change that they could attribute to themselves, e.g.:

CLINICIAN: Right – this is our third session, and I have to say that I am really impressed with how well you have been working to get your eating sorted and learning what happens when you do. You have nearly stopped all those binges, which is impressive after ten years of bulimia nervosa. Good job. Now, we just have to get that last binge out of the way and make sure you don't slip up on your morning snack again, and you will be ready to start the next phase. I am pretty confident that you will make it through the review next time and we can start working on those beliefs about food and your body image.

In a similar vein, we should be honest with patients who do not engage with the tasks of CBT-T, stressing that there is no miracle cure but that their chances of recovery go up enormously if they actually actively engage in the therapy. That means that we need to be realistic, rather than pessimistic, e.g.:

CLINICIAN: Right – this is our third session, and I am still worried that you are not changing your eating enough to stop those binges, as we discussed last week and the week before. This is not me saying that you cannot make it – I am absolutely sure that if you were to implement the changes then you would have the chance to pull it back and get through that review next time. However, if you don't make those changes it is looking clearer and clearer that things will not suddenly get better on their own. It is like I said in Session 1 – being 'in therapy' is not likely to sort you on its own – just like in your last therapy. You need to actually *do* the therapy. So let's plan for this week as your last chance to get out of this trap that you have been in for years.

Over this first phase of therapy, each session should be used as a 'countdown' to Session 4, when the review will take place (see Chapter 6).

5.2.6 Review cognitive change in ED-15 and other problems from questionnaires

We always review the measures that the patient brings in and ensure that they are completed fully. This should be done with the patient each time, to get the maximum benefit from all the patient's work. At the beginning, this is done to ensure that we understand the patient as well as possible. As therapy progresses, we use the measures to monitor and feedback on progress (both to the patient and in supervision). It is also useful for clinicians to monitor their individual outcomes and to use these in supervision.

The ED-15 (Appendix 3) was designed to be used on a weekly basis in this way. We ask the patient to complete it immediately before starting the session (in the waiting room). It is necessary to keep previous completed measures to hand when talking with the patient, to be able to point to session-by-session changes in eating attitudes. The Therapy Tracker (available on website) automatically creates a graph, which can also be shared with your patient. We also stress the linkage between the targets that we have been addressing and what is changing now –

again, stressing to the patient that they can create real change and that they are not failing if only part of their symptoms is changing at this stage, e.g.:

CLINICIAN: Now, let's look at your ED-15 for this week, compared to last week … that is impressive – your beliefs about what will happen to you if you eat more normally are really coming down. If you look at this week, most have shifted down a point or two since last week, which is just what they did last time. As I said at the start of treatment, just changing your eating is helping you to change your beliefs. Well done. You are nearly at the normal level now, which is great. But before we get complacent, let's remember that some of your other beliefs don't look like they are shifting yet – the ones about how you and others see your body. So remember what I said at the start – we do all this work with your eating, emotions and food-related beliefs first, and *then* we work on your body image.

After Session 4, we also recommend reviewing key comorbid states. In particular, you can use the same measures of anxiety and depression that were used in Session 1 - the GAD-7 and the PHQ-9 (which are used in the UK's IAPT service as standardised measure of anxiety and depression, respectively) or the DASS. Again, changes on these measures are discussed directly with the patient, using them to emphasise that the treatment of their eating can result in improvements in their wider problems.

The recommended schedule of measures is provided in Appendix 6. There is no reason that other elements of psychopathology could not be assessed locally, but the use of the ED-15 and the measures of anxiety and depression is key to this protocol.

5.2.7 Address the patient's agenda items (if any)

This is usually done during the second half of the session, though not too close to the end of the session, where it might push out the homework planning. The nature of what is to be covered depends entirely on what the patient brings. It is a noteworthy point that the early acculturation of the patient to CBT-T (through explaining principles and techniques clearly) means that patients are relatively focused on the core of the therapy, and many say that they really do not have any other issues to raise at this point. Obviously, some patients do have agenda items (e.g. issues with family, partner or children). However, if we make it clear that the time to discuss those issues is limited (e.g. *Clinician:* We have 10 or 15 minutes to talk about anything else that might be on your mind before we talk about the tasks for next week), then the patient is generally very good at focusing their concerns (rather than filling an unspecified gap in the session).

It is always useful to remember that many problems will be addressed by the early changes in nutrition and consequent reductions in mood instability, impulsivity, anxiety, rigid thinking, social isolation, physical risk, etc. (see Waller, Evans, & Pugh, 2013). That means that one can return to Fairburn's phrase:

"There's a medicine for that – it's called food". We find that this is a useful thing to say to our patients, saying that we will address other points later in CBT-T if they remain problematic.

5.2.8 Homework

The session is finished with a review of how far the patient has come, and what homework is needed to move therapy forward. Some previously addressed homework tasks should be included in this phase, particularly:

- Give the patient the ED-15 for completion just before the next session.
- Provision of any additional psychoeducation that might be needed.
- Set further nutritional changes, aiming to maintain relatively high levels of anxiety to ensure maximum learning through exposure.
- Predicted outcomes of eating differently (e.g. weight gain? more or less bingeing?).

Three other homework tasks are important in preparing the patient for Phase 2:

- Following Session 2, prepare a list of 'feared' and 'safe' foods, using known avoided food, examination of what others eat, exploring foods available in supermarkets, etc.
- Following Session 3 or 4 (depending on speed of engagement in the exposure element of Phase 1 and if therapy is to continue – see next Chapter), start the behavioural experiment process.
- Following Session 4, review progress in terms of anxiety, depression, and other comorbidities.

Summary: Overview of new tasks in Phase 1

- Changing eating is essential in this phase.
- Change the structure of eating if necessary, but move to changing the amount of food quickly.
    - o Reducing starvation.
    - o Improving cognitive and emotional functioning.
- Elevating anxiety so that the patient can learn that the anxiety reduces.
    - o Inhibitory learning approach.
    - o Aim for maximum tolerable anxiety to improve that learning.
- Use diaries and weighing strategically, to challenge cognitions regarding uncontrollable weight gain.
    - o The sequencing of these must be precise, to allow the patient to learn.
- Remind the patient that progress is being monitored to determine whether treatment should continue.
    - o If tasks are not completed, use shorter sessions to remind the patient that therapy is dependent on the work being done at home, rather than in the session.

Chapter 6

Session 4 – Reviewing progress and deciding whether to continue

This chapter deals with a specific aspect of Session 4, which was discussed earlier – the decision of whether to continue therapy past this point. The rationale for this decision point is clear – if the patient is not progressing substantially by this point then they are unlikely to do so thereafter. This is not a factor just for CBT-T or even for CBT-ED, but for therapy in general for eating disorders (e.g., Vall & Wade, 2015). Where therapies have monitored progress, the lack of change in this early part of therapy has been shown to be a strong predictor of the patient doing poorly.

However, despite this evidence, we know that clinicians tend to 'do more of the same' and offer more therapy than is justified in such cases (e.g., Cowdrey & Waller, 2015). Such extended therapy is often given because we are concerned that we are 'abandoning' our patients, and we hope that if we just keep seeing the patient then they will recover. It is also worth considering that our own anxiety about the fragility of our patients makes us more concerned about ending therapy (Turner et al., 2014).

Supervision is clearly important in the run-up to this session and for Session 4 itself. It helps us to consider the likelihood that the patient who is not engaging in change will suddenly change at some later point versus the likelihood that the patient will not change and eventually conclude that they are not able to recover after a full course of therapy. In short, if we feel that we are 'abandoning' our patients, we need a supervisor who can point out that not only is the non-engaged patient unlikely to change, but other patients who are on the waiting list are not getting access to treatment as a result. Again, this is not just a matter for CBT-T, but for all therapies.

For most patients, our use of Session 4 as a review point has been effective well before Session 4, as they have used the prospect of an early review to inspire them to change from the beginning. Indeed, in our experience only 5% of patients need to be discharged at this point. However, if we are not honest with the patient from the beginning about the risk of ending therapy at this point, we cannot expect the patient to take it seriously. Our goal is not to be excessively firm or authoritarian with the patient in the run-up to this session, but to avoid being excessively empathic or protective, thereby letting the patient 'drift' into a therapy that is costly for them (e.g. "I am broken and can never get better") and for others who could benefit (e.g. "How long will I be on this waiting list?").

6.1 The formal review of progress

This usually occurs early or around the midpoint of Session 4, as it follows directly from monitoring eating changes and their results. In the majority of cases, it is a straightforward opportunity to positively reinforce the patient for changes that have already been made, e.g.:

CLINICIAN: Well, we agreed that we would make this the session where we reviewed how you are doing. I think that the easiest thing to say is that you have been doing really well since the start, taking risks, coping with your fears about what would happen, and seeing your symptoms and your negative beliefs falling fast. I don't mean to make that sound easy, because if it were easy then you would never have needed therapy. I am just really pleased that you have shown that you are willing to make the changes, because there are more to do, and I suggest we get started on those other changes now.

Or:

CLINICIAN: We said from the start that this would be the point where we reviewed your progress. I know that you were slow to get going, not making much change in the first couple of sessions, and I know that I had to chase you to get you to see how important it was. I even had to remind you that we would have to conclude that now was not the right time for you to do the key tasks of therapy that you needed to do to help you. However, you got started after that, and I am happy to see how quickly you have worked to catch up. I am also pleased to see how you have realised that your symptoms started changing for the better after that. I know that you have not got rid of all your binges yet, but I think that we should continue, as another week of regularising your eating could let you catch up, then we can move on to all the other changes that we need to work on, such as your body image.

6.2 When the patient is not progressing adequately but wants one last try

When the patient has reached Session 4 with only minimal change, it is not uncommon for the patient to ask for "one more go" at undertaking CBT-T. We have had patients who have asked for this and who have gone on to complete the therapy successfully, so we do not treat such requests as doomed to fail. However, we have to stress to the patient that this is their last opportunity during this course of therapy, and that we would need to see almost total catch-up over the coming week if the patient is to have the opportunity to move on to other key issues (particularly the behavioural experiments of Phase 2, which could already have started, and the body image work of Phase 4), e.g.:

CLINICIAN: As I said from the start, this review is necessary to decide whether you should carry on in therapy. Unfortunately, while you have made small changes to your eating, they have not been substantial enough or consistent.

The result is that we have reached this session and I am coming to the conclusion that we should draw therapy to a close at this point. It would be better to stop now, so that we can say that we have no idea whether this treatment could work for you, because you have not been doing CBT-T. That way, you could come back to treatment another time, knowing that it did not work when you simply *came to* therapy, and that next time you need to actually *do* the therapy. What do you think?

PATIENT: OK, I get it – not taking risks early on just meant that I am stuck here, a month later. However, I get it, and I really want to change. Can I *please* give it a go now? One last try?

CLINICIAN: Look, while that is tempting, you have to realise what you are suggesting. You would have to be prepared to put into practise all the changes we have discussed over the past three weeks, and I would not be prepared to continue if you had not caught up by next time. If I did, we would never have a chance to work on your body image, which I know really distresses you. So, I would be wasting your time. OK – I could offer you one more session to catch up. That would mean normalising your eating so that you were no longer starving or emotionally unstable. However, it would be your last chance, and following this, I would be expecting you to be consistently making changes each week after that. What do you think about that?

PATIENT: I will show you that I can do it. I know it has been a pain so far to get me to take risks, but I really get it now. What would I need to have changed by next time for you to think we could carry on?

Thus, we offer the patient the opportunity to consider whether it is realistic that they should commit to such rapid change. We emphasise once again that this "last chance" can work well for some patients, in that they do catch up and then go on to do well.

If it is not realistic or the patient is not really committed to change, then we conclude that they should stop therapy now and return to it in the future. Then they will know what the terms of CBT-T are, and (more importantly) they will know what happens if they do not undertake the tasks of therapy, e.g.:

PATIENT: I would love that extra time in therapy. The only issue is that I would need more time to get into changing. I have a holiday coming up, so I want to lose some weight and cannot really make any changes until that is done. And I am still really not sure about carbohydrates, so I want to try without eating them.

CLINICIAN: It sounds like there are a number of things that are stopping therapy being your priority right now. So let's stick with the plan to end it now, and then when you are ready to do the therapy fully in future, you can come back and start again. However, remember that we will both know that you need to get started with major changes from Session 1 – delaying doesn't work for you any more than it does for anyone else.

6.3 Helping the clinician to cope with ending therapy at this point

Many clinicians fear that ending therapy at this stage will be seen negatively, as stated above. There is the concern that our patients will see us as abandoning them, but there is also the concern that others (e.g., colleagues, supervisors, family members, other professionals) will see us as failing the patient and the service, or will see us as being unnecessarily harsh and punitive. This latter concern is likely to be worse in some specialist eating disorder services, where there is a perception that the eating disorders service is the last line of treatment, and where other services would rather not work with eating disorder patients, passing them on to 'the specialists'.

If we are to end therapy in an appropriate way at this point, we need to make sure that the clinician does not let their habitual reactions ('just keep seeing the patient until something good happens') or their anxiety (how others see them; feared risk to the patient) stop this process. Clinicians need to remind themselves and to be reminded by their supervisors that keeping the patient coming to therapy is not productive and is likely to be counterproductive in the longer term. The worry that 'my patient might not get better if I don't keep seeing them' is a common reason that clinicians cite for keeping the patient on their books, but many do not process the fact that simply seeing the patient occasionally does not actually make the patient any better. It is also common to hear that knowing that the patient is 'in therapy' can mean that other clinicians do not attend to the patient's risk factors, even where they are better placed to monitor those risks (e.g., *Family Doctor*: Well, at least I don't have to keep seeing that patient who vomits all the time, because they are being seen by the eating disorder service).

Disengagement is a topic that should be considered routinely in supervision. The clinician should be encouraged to explore their concerns about being seen as a failure and their beliefs about the pros and cons of discharging the patient or keeping them in therapy. The supervisor can also encourage the clinician to remember that not all people get well with any specific therapy, so any clinician who expects perfect outcomes is not being fair to themselves.

6.4 Summary of ways of using disengagement constructively

On the relatively uncommon occasions where we need to disengage from therapy, we should aim to avoid making the patient feel like a failure, e.g.:

CLINICIAN: I don't know if you could succeed … I just know that you cannot do so like this. By ending now, you know that you might be able to succeed if you come back and do the therapy fully in the future. Now you know what the rules are, and you will know what you are getting into when you enter an evidence-based therapy in future – which I hope you will do.

We should also stress that the patient has learned some things, but not others, so that they know what they are going to need to do differently, e.g.:

CLINICIAN: What is good is that you learned some of the things that you will need to do next time. You got good at keeping the diaries, and you put most of the structure into your diet – you just did not add in those essential carbs. That means that next time you could move onto getting your eating straight much more quickly.

We also detail routes back into treatment, along with this information about what the patient would need to do differently. Finally, if the patient does not attend for the final session (due to knowing what is likely to be coming), then a letter or email to the patient is a useful way of communicating this key information.

6.5 Writing to patients

The use of letter writing to patients is not a uniform procedure across services or clinicians, but we encourage clinicians to consider reserving time in their practice for the routine writing of letters to patients at this stage in CBT-T. This practice can range from therapeutic letter writing (e.g. Allen et al., 2016) to simply summarising the state of play, and using validation and encouragement. It is worth remembering that our patients' recall of what was said in sessions is sometimes incomplete or inaccurate, given that it is perceived through a lens of attentional or interpretation bias. Therefore, it is important to provide a written summary. We recommend writing letters to CBT-T patients at the end of the assessment, after the Session 4 review, at the end of therapy, and then after any subsequent follow-up session. The following letters are provided as examples of how to engage effectively with the patient at the critical fourth session.

An example of an end of Session 4 review letter to a patient who is progressing well in therapy is provided in Box 6.1. Box 6.2 gives another example of an end of Session 4 review letter, where the patient has started well in therapy, showing a wider range of change. In contrast, Box 6.3 gives an example of a review letter written to a patient who agreed to cease therapy after a collaborative discussion about lack of progress.

Box 6.1 Example of a letter sent to a patient who is doing well after Session 4 (1)

Dear Tom,

I would like to congratulate you on the progress you made over the course of therapy so far. The progress in the first few sessions sets you up well for a good outcome.

Prior to starting treatment, you reported having one or more objective binges and several subjective binges per week. You were also exercising in a driven, obsessive way on six days per week and restricting your food intake such that you often did not eat carbohydrates or eat regularly throughout the day. You were extremely dissatisfied with your weight and shape, which created constant preoccupation with food, weight, and shape throughout the day and made you feel exhausted. This preoccupation combined with fear of weight gain, constant checking, and negatively comparing yourself to others was extremely distressing for you, as was your current binge and restriction cycle.

Since starting treatment, you have reduced the frequency of the subjective binges to two per week. You have also succeeded in eliminating the objective binges and driven exercise. You now have a clearer idea of the triggers that lead to bingeing and you understand the importance of regular eating and increasing carbohydrate intake. You have worked hard during the past four weeks to decrease the influence of the disordered eating in your life, and your efforts are paying off.

Continuing to work on and extending the gains that you have made during treatment thus far will be essential in order for you to achieve freedom from the eating disorder and its grip on your life. As we have discussed, the binge eating often occurs after periods of semi-starvation when snacks are missed or carbohydrate intake is low, so continuing to focus on regular eating across all the food groups will be essential to help you to eliminate the bingeing. Bingeing has also occurred in response to feeling tired or bored, so increasing your use of alternative strategies (e.g. playing piano) and seeking support from people will be an important part of this process.

I congratulate you on your hard work and look forward to our future sessions.

Kindest regards

Box 6.2 Example of a letter sent to a patient who is doing well after Session 4 (2)

Dear Jasmine,

I would like to congratulate you on the progress you have made over the course of therapy so far. You may remember me saying that the progress in the first few sessions sets you up well for a good outcome.

When you started treatment, you were bingeing 1–5 times a week and regularly engaged in both fasting and restriction of your food intake to a limited range of 'safe' foods. You were engaging in occasional self-induced vomiting and laxative use, and, of most concern to you, had developed a habit of chewing and spitting food. You described regularly feeling guilty after having eaten and you were experiencing a high degree of concern regarding your weight and shape. You described previously engaging in driven exercise but had stopped this in the month prior to treatment in favour of yoga and netball. The bingeing and over-evaluation of your appearance were distressing for you, and you expressed a wish to feel more comfortable and confident with both food and your body.

Since starting treatment, you have succeeded in both eating a greater variety of foods more frequently and reducing the frequency of your bingeing to almost zero, such that in the past fortnight you have had only one minor binge episode. Over this last week, you have also successfully managed any urges to engage in either self-induced vomiting or chewing and spitting, and you have been committed to identifying and combating the desire to restrict your food intake. You are now striving to gain more balance in how you evaluate yourself, and to place less emphasis on how your weight and shape influence how you judge yourself. You have worked hard during the past four weeks to decrease the influence of the disordered eating in your life, and your efforts are paying off.

Continuing to work on and extending the gains that you have made during treatment thus far will be essential in order for you to achieve freedom from the eating disorder and its grip on your life. Moving forward, it will be helpful for you to continue to focus on your reasons for change and your desire to have 'food freedom'. As we have discussed, continuing to build on the changes you have already made and addressing your underlying unhelpful thoughts related to eating, weight, and shape will play an important role in replacing the old, habitual program that has been with you for the past 10 years.

I congratulate you on your work so far and look forward to our future sessions.

Best wishes

Box 6.3 Example of a letter sent to a patient who has agreed to cease CBT-T after a discussion about lack of progress

Dear Julie,

Thank you for your interest in the 10-session Cognitive Behavioural Therapy (CBT-T) for eating disorders and for attending the baseline assessment and five treatment sessions. Taking these first steps to change has required a lot of courage and I want to commend you for the commitment you made to restoring regular eating.

Thank you also for being open and honest with us about the challenges you are currently experiencing. I appreciate that making changes to your eating and monitoring your weight is anxiety provoking. You have made significant improvement to the structure and content of your eating, particularly by eating more regularly and increasing your intake of complex carbohydrates. I am sorry to hear that you have been self-critical since suspending treatment and that you have not made much progress with restoring regular eating. The break in treatment was designed to allow you to experiment with methods of change, to assist you in deciding whether you would like to continue the CBT-T. In terms of changes in your weight, your weight has fluctuated within a 2 kg range since commencing treatment and we consider this fluctuation to be normal (e.g., not indicative of weight gain). I understand that weight loss is one of your long-term goals. However, it is unlikely that you will be able to achieve weight maintenance, or weight loss, unless you first eliminate your binge eating. Even though it seems counterintuitive, in order to eliminate the binge eating you will need to reduce dietary restriction, by eating regularly (three meals and three snacks per day) and having regular complex carbohydrate intake. By removing restriction, you will 'inoculate' yourself against binges.

I am pleased to hear that you have the continued support of your psychiatrist and the dietitian to further work on your eating, and I wish you well with your recovery. However, if you feel as if you are ready and willing to recommit to treatment for your eating disorder, you are more than welcome to contact us again to re-engage with CBT-T. Should you decide to re-engage with treatment, we would start treatment afresh, as the nature of the treatment program does not allow for intermittent attendance.

If you wish to seek further treatment options for your eating disorder, you may wish to visit [RELEVANT WEBSITE], which provides a directory of eating disorder services.

Please also remember that you are welcome to contact us again if you are willing to commit to the treatment and would like to re-enter treatment at [NAME OF SERVICE], or if we can assist you to find alternative treatment options.

Kind regards

6.6 Other clinician responsibilities

Obviously, it is good practice to let the referrer and other involved parties know that the patient has been discharged. We also stress the importance of informing the referrer about the reasons for the discharge, and about the best way to encourage the patient to be more prepared for treatment next time (e.g. a summary of what the patient did well and of what they did not do). That allows the referrer to check that the patient is really ready for treatment next time, and helps any future clinician to be aware of what to look out for from the beginning of therapy.

In the event of discharge, it is also vital to ensure that any necessary medical monitoring and treatment is undertaken. The clinician should indicate the likely risks that the patient faces (e.g. low potassium, dental problems, weight gain), so that these can be monitored. Such monitoring obviously gives the referrer more material to work on with the patient to encourage a return to therapy. We may also suggest attention be focused on issues that created therapy interfering behaviours, such as lack of stable accommodation, acute relationship problems, or substance abuse, which when dealt with can then enable the patient to focus their efforts more fully on therapy.

Summary: Overview of Session 4

- This review should have been flagged from the outset of CBT-T, and mentioned each week thereafter.
- Where the patient is on track with the therapy, this review should be used as an opportunity to reinforce the patient for their hard work and resultant progress.
- We should remember that if the patient is not progressing but we continue therapy, it has potential costs for the patient and for others (e.g., on the waiting list).
- If we extend therapy, it should be on a strictly limited basis, and dependent on rapid progress over the coming week.
- Clinicians and supervisors need to ensure that we consider the interpersonal issues involved in discharging the patient from therapy, and ensure that the patient does not feel blamed.
- Letters to the patient after this session can be very helpful in ensuring that the patient learns from the experience, whatever the outcome at this point in therapy.
- Ensure that post-discharge care is in place, if needed at this stage.

Chapter 7

Phase 2 – Addressing cognitions regarding food, eating, and weight, using behavioural experiments and cognitive restructuring

This phase in CBT-T is where we move our central focus away from the anxiety that drives many of our patients' safety behaviours and towards the cognitions – particularly the 'broken' cognitive link between food intake and weight. Working with cognitions requires some precision, as will be seen below. Without that precision, beliefs are less likely to change. For example, learning from making a specific change in eating will not be so strong if one has made other changes that block that learning (e.g. exercising more) or if thinking is too rigid (e.g. due to starvation). Therefore, we need to ensure that the patient's anxiety and nutritional state are normalised in the previous phase, so that we can move to this part of therapy and obtain the best results.

This means that Phase 2 begins when Phase 1 has been completed adequately, such that the patient's anxiety is more manageable (without recourse to safety behaviours), their thinking is more flexible, and their mood is more stable. Depending on the pace of Phase 1, this can mean that behavioural experiments and cognitive work regarding eating and food begin around Session 3 to 5. We would recommend that most of these should be completed by Session 6 or 7 at the latest (apart from the behavioural experiments relating to body image – see Phase 4), to allow time for body image work. That does not mean that the patient is not encouraged to continue developing their eating beyond that point. Patients are encouraged to continue experimentation throughout the remaining sessions and into the follow-up period, so these sessions should be treated as being about teaching patients the skills needed to develop their own healthier cognitions.

Phase 2 is all about changing cognitions – particularly the 'broken' cognitive link between eating, food, and weight. Given their effectiveness, we use behavioural experiments far more than other methods of cognitive restructuring, maintaining our focus on what is best for the patient by using behavioural methods rather than talking-based methods where appropriate.

As already indicated, this happens when anxiety about the effects of eating is lowered, and where bingeing and purging behaviours are largely reduced (though there might be residual emotional triggers to those behaviours that need to be addressed in Phase 3). This allows the patient to maintain a stable, healthy core intake of food (whether maintaining or working to increase their weight), so that the impact of changes in food intake (the experimental manipulation) can be understood. Of course, we aim to focus dietary changes on the patient's list of feared foods (usually collected following Session 2 – see above). As with Phase 1, the time taken for this task will vary from person to person, dependent on how rapidly the feared foods are tackled. As with the earlier exposure work, we do not aim to get the patient to address feared foods in any sort of hierarchy – rather, we aim to get the patient to maximise their learning by aiming to modify their eating in a less structured or predictable (and potentially calming) way.

The specifics of these sessions are outlined in the protocol checklists (see Appendix 1). However, it is not uncommon for patients to maintain some experimentation into later sessions and into the follow-up period (see above).

In short, in Phase 2 we aim to address beliefs about restriction, eating, and weight, using behavioural change methods as far as possible. Our target is to teach our patients that what they eat has a clear, predictable link to what happens to their weight, rather than food and eating being seen as linked to uncontrollable weight gain.

7.1 Themes in Phase 2

This phase has a more limited set of themes than in Phase 1, as its focus is more specific (Table 7.1).

7.1.1 Addressing the 'broken' cognitive link between eating and weight gain

In this phase, we aim to teach the patient that eating and weight are closely linked. That means one of two things, depending on whether or not the patient is below an optimum weight at this stage:

- Eating a moderate amount means no weight gain.
- Eating a controlled amount more means controllable weight gain, if the patient is underweight.

Table 7.1 Themes during Phase 2

- Address 'broken' cognition regarding uncontrollable weight gain.
  - o Open weighing at every session.
  - o Dietary experimentation (not just dietary change).
- Behavioural experiments to modify cognitions regarding eating and weight.
  - o Address beliefs linked to dietary experimentation.
  - o Use changes in eating to demonstrate the discrepancy between anticipated and actual weight change.
- Cognitive restructuring to modify cognitions.
  - o Addressing beliefs regarding eating and weight.
- Planning for Phases 3 and 4.

Our target is never weight loss during therapy, as restriction is likely to result in overeating. While some patients whose overweight status was maintained by their binges find that they lose weight as a result of the stability of this stage and the lack of those binge episodes, we do not encourage any active efforts at weight loss. Indeed, any deliberate attempt to lose weight is discussed as a therapy-interfering behaviour. Naturally, we maintain diary-keeping and open weighing during this phase, as the aim is for the patient to learn from what they eat and whether it has any effect on their weight.

As mentioned above, the aim is to allow the patient to establish that weight is inherently related to dietary balance (energy taken in/energy expended). Therefore, we now move from dietary change to dietary experimentation. It is important that clinicians should understand the key elements of an experimental approach to modifying beliefs in this way.

7.1.2 Behavioural experiments to change cognitions regarding eating and weight

Key to any behavioural experiment is the need to use behavioural change to test beliefs within a framework where other potential factors are held constant. In other words, if we want to know whether eating an extra biscuit has the feared outcome of weight gain, we can only learn that if we do not change anything else to compensate for it (e.g. no additional exercise). While such experiments can be used to test a belief in isolation or without planning (Bennett-Levy et al., 2004), we use the more powerful method of testing alternative beliefs, where an existing belief (e.g. "If I eat an extra biscuit a day, I will gain 2–3 kg in a week") and its alternative (e.g. "If I eat an extra biscuit a day, it won't have any real effect on my weight") are tested in competition with each other. We always agree time frames with the patient. We also ask the patient to rate their certainty in their beliefs, because an early shift in certainty is a good sign of likely change in the content of such cognitions.

A point to note in CBT-T is that we do not aim for small, less meaningful changes in intake. Rather, we aim to make the quantity and type of food challenging, so that the patient can learn more rapidly that their weight does not increase as expected. Thus, behavioural experiments can take 1–2 weeks, rather than the longer period taken with slower approaches to introducing new foods.

The outcome (weight stability/loss/gain) is compared to the prediction that was previously made, to demonstrate the patient's systematic overestimation of weight gain due to eating specific foods. Details and examples are given below (Section 7.2.3).

7.1.3 Cognitive restructuring to modify beliefs and attitudes

The majority of cognitive restructuring in CBT-T is a product of the early nutrition, exposure and psychoeducation (as evidenced by the early cognitive changes that are seen during Phase 1). While behavioural experimentation is the strongest method for making further cognitive change in Phase 2 (as outlined above), it is also useful to employ some further cognitive restructuring methods in some case. This often includes addressing the origins of negative beliefs about eating, weight, and shape (e.g. family 'rules'; teasing) and their pertinence in the here and now. Examples are given below (Section 7.2.4).

7.1.4 Planning for Phase 3 (emotional triggers)
and Phase 4 (body image)

It is also important to attend to the patient's remaining symptoms, to begin planning the individualised approach that will be needed for working with the patient over the remaining part of CBT-T – particularly in relation to emotional triggers and body image. It is not necessary to do this in the first few sessions (Phase 1), because many emotions and body image features resolve in that early part of therapy. As Phase 2 progresses, clinicians should consider evidence of the following, from the patient's self-report, behaviours, and psychometric measures:

- Emotional triggers to bingeing, purging, and exercise.
- Body image issues, focusing on the maintaining safety behaviours.

In some cases, these will not be present, allowing therapy to focus on behavioural experiments for longer. However, where they are present, the clinician can stress to the patient the importance of completing the behavioural experiments so that they develop the skills required to devise further experiments independently, thus allowing for time in sessions to focus on Phases 3 and/or 4.

7.2 Specific tasks in this phase

Table 7.2 details the specific techniques that are employed in this phase of CBT-T. As before, the new tasks are in bold, and are addressed below in detail. The remainder are techniques that have been addressed in previous chapters and are not repeated here (e.g. risk assessment; the use of diaries and weighing). Note that these techniques might be employed in the same sessions as the techniques outlined in Phase 3, so Table 7.2 is not a definitive list of what might be delivered in that phase.

The protocol checklists show the full set of techniques used across the sessions of Phase 2 (and 3). However, as before, the order in which we use those methods is not fixed (apart from the processes of using diaries and weighing the patient to challenge the 'broken' cognitive process). Use all relevant techniques, in whatever order makes sense within the individual session.

7.2.1 Review of learning so far

In Session 5, we focus on changes in cognitions and mood since the start of treatment, using the measures completed by the patient at the end of Session 4. We highlight the progress, which usually includes substantial positive change in

Table 7.2 Specific tasks in Phase 2 of CBT-T (Sessions 3–7)

Tasks in bold are new ones in this phase, and are detailed below. Others have been addressed previously (see previous chapters).

- Review learning from last time and homework.
  - o Questionnaires from last week, **focusing on changes in eating and weight cognitions since start of therapy and over past week.**
- Address any life-threatening or therapy-interfering behaviours.
- **Session 5 only: Ask the patient about their experience of the review in Session 4.**
  - o **Review any catch-up if the patient had committed to that.**
  - o **Discontinue CBT-T if the patient has not made those changes.**
- Review changes in eating.
  - o Food intake.
  - o Contemporaneous diaries.
- Review current eating and changes in cognitions, bulimic, and restrictive behaviours.
- Positive reinforcement for changes made, and problem-solve remaining problems.
- Diaries and weighing to address the broken cognition.
- **Behavioural experimentation.**
  - o **Select foods to use to challenge beliefs.**
  - o **Set maximum tolerable change.**
  - o **Set up the experimental conditions.**
  - o **Evaluate cognitions as a result.**
- **Additional cognitive restructuring.**
  - o **Remaining concerns re eating and weight.**
  - o **Historical review.**
  - o **Current evidence.**
- Address the patient's agenda items (if any).
- **Identify emotional triggers for residual bulimic behaviours (Phase 3).**
  - o (Treatment methods to be addressed in the following chapter).
- **Session 6: Identify maintaining behaviours for the individual's negative body image (Phase 4).**
- Homework.
  - o Diary, monitoring measures.
  - o **Behavioural experimentation.**
  - o **Collating photos for surveys (Phase 4).**

eating and weight cognitions and in mood/anxiety. However, we also stress that those changes are not yet enough, and that there is still further to go (particularly in terms of body image and shape cognitions). This review also allows us to let the patient know that we are not giving up on them because they have made just some of the changes needed and reminds them that it is important that they do not drop out at this stage in the hope that all will be well from now on.

From this point on, we continue to look at ED-15 scores on a weekly basis, to show how the behavioural experiments (and later, body image work) are driving change. We also use those scores to identify remaining beliefs that need to be addressed (i.e. highly scored ED-15 items).

7.2.2 Review the patient's experience of Session 4, and any issues of engagement

In Session 5, we always ask the patient about their experience of the review in Session 4. If the review was an easy one, where the patient and clinician were agreed that progress was positive, then the aim is to build on the motivation that has been demonstrated and to stress that more work is to come. If it was agreed that progress had been limited and the review concluded that any further therapy sessions should be dependent on a very substantial behavioural change between Sessions 4 and 5, then there are two possible outcomes. The first is to congratulate the patient if they have made that change. You should also stress that you believe that they can make the remainder of the changes needed thereafter, and that they will be able to carry on learning skills and changing during the follow-up period. The second is to conclude that the patient is still not engaging in adequate change, and that now is not the time for them to undertake therapy for their eating disorder (see Chapter 6), and to discontinue CBT-T until they are ready to try again. Examples of these possible conversations as detailed in Table 7.3.

7.2.3 Behavioural experimentation to link food and eating with weight

In the behavioural experiments that we use in this phase of CBT-T, we focus on repairing the 'broken' cognitive link between food eaten and weight change/stability. The beliefs to be addressed using this method are specific ones (in contrast to the more general beliefs that will be tackled in Section 7.2.4).

The patient needs to understand the context and process of a behavioural experiment. First, we explain the need to hold other variables constant, to understand the link between the change introduced and the outcome of that change. Specifically, for the individual to learn from such a behavioural experiment (e.g. determining the impact on weight of eating a food that they have avoided for years), they need to hold other factors stable (e.g. not reducing intake elsewhere; not exercising more). We remind the patient that this context means that we could not have started these experiments until their anxiety was reduced (in Phase 1).

In terms of process, we explain that the steps that we will be following are as detailed in Table 7.4. We stress that we need to push the patient to make changes that would test their beliefs strongly (though we do not know whether they will be proven right or wrong), so that they can learn the outcomes very quickly. To assist in the process of planning behavioural experiments, we use the diagram in Figure 7.1 to remind ourselves of the tasks needed and the sequence that we need to use. As an example, we might introduce the plan for behavioural experimentation towards the end of Session 3 (see Table 7.5). With that preparation, the patient is ready for the first experiment, set up in

Table 7.3 Session 5: Reviewing Session 4 and its sequelae

CLINICIAN: OK – last time, we reviewed your progress so far, as agreed at the start. We looked at how well you have committed yourself to changing, and the outcomes so far. How did you find that review?

PATIENT: Well, I was worried that you might say we should stop, because I still have lots of those worries about my eating and my body, but I was happy when you reminded me about how far I have come.

CLINICIAN: I was very impressed by how far you have come so quickly. It gives you a really strong chance of recovering fully. There is still lots to do, of course – we need to get your beliefs about food and weight sorted, and we want your body image to be much more acceptable, but the fact that you have already done so much means that we have even more time to dedicate to those parts of your eating disorder.

Or

CLINICIAN: OK – last time, we reviewed your progress so far, as agreed at the start. We looked at how well you have committed yourself to changing, and your limited progress and outcomes so far. How did you find that review?

PATIENT: I think I knew that it was going to be tough. When we started, I didn't think that you could be serious about ending so early, but I think I was slowly realising that you might mean it, and last week was a wake-up call. That is why I have had a really scary, uncomfortable week, eating like I should have from the start.

CLINICIAN: Well, I'm sure it *was* scary. No wonder – you have taken a lot of risks with your eating, and managed to make a huge amount of progress in just one week. You are not quite there yet, so I have to keep pushing you to change over the coming weeks, but I think you have proven to me and to you that you could make this therapy work. Good job.

Or

CLINICIAN: OK – last time, we reviewed your progress so far, as agreed at the start. We agreed that you had not made much progress, and that you would need to make lots of changes over the past week. Unfortunately, you haven't really changed your eating since then, and your other symptoms are just as bad. What are your thoughts on that?

PATIENT: Well, I meant to do the work, but lots of stuff got in the way – work, visiting my father, my partner being around in the evenings. So I never got around to it. It felt unfair that I should have to do all that, or that therapy would be stopped.

CLINICIAN: Unfortunately, I think we are out of therapy options, here. I think we were right to give you that one last go at doing this therapy, as it means that we can be sure that this is not the right time for you. So, this will be our last session. However, when you are ready to come back to therapy, you will know what to do from the start, and why.

Session 4 (see Table 7.6). Then we revisit the behavioural experiment over the next week or two (see Table 7.7).

Usually, we find that the patient learns rapidly from this process, particularly because the level of challenge is pitched at a relatively strong level (e.g. 'chocolate rather than cake'), meaning that the predicted outcome is relatively strong, too, and the disparity between the anticipated and alternative beliefs is very apparent

Table 7.4 Key steps in the process of a 'food–weight' behavioural experiment

- Identify a target for change in diet (as highly feared a food as possible – e.g. cake).
- Identify how large a change the patient can tolerate (e.g. one cupcake per day).
- Agree to maintain other eating, exercise, etc., rather than altering anything.
- Obtain the patient's beliefs about the impact of adding this new food (weight change).
- Ask the patient for a certainty rating about that predicted outcome (0–100% scale).
- Consider alternative belief, using psychoeducational material, etc.
- Ask the patient for a certainty rating about that alternative outcome (0–100% scale).
- Agree the behavioural change.
- Agree a time frame for that behavioural change.
- Implement the change, and see which prediction comes out as the accurate one.
- Revisit the original belief and its alternative, and their respective certainty ratings.

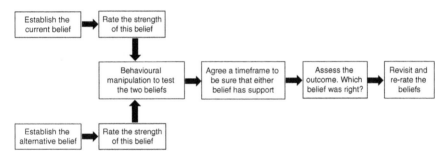

Figure 7.1 Order of tasks involved in planning a behavioural experiment.

Table 7.5 Session 3: Planning the first 'food–weight' behavioural experiment

CLINICIAN: Now that your eating is in a much more stable and normal pattern, you are far less panicked about your eating, and your bingeing and vomiting are just about completely gone. If you can keep that going until next week, it will be time to start the next phase. That next step is going to be getting you to test out your beliefs about the scary foods that I got you to list out – do they really do what you think they do to your weight, or are they far less dangerous than you believe? Of course, we couldn't do this before – it is important that we only change one thing at a time so that you can learn, and if we had tried it earlier then your anxiety would have been likely to make you want to aim for safety, by exercising more or cutting out other foods or something. So, the first step next week is going to be getting you to pick a food to add to your diet, and then see what effect you believe that will have on your weight, and to find out whether you are right or wrong in your beliefs.

Table 7.6 Session 4: Setting up the first 'food–weight' behavioural experiment

---

CLINICIAN: We agreed that you would pick a food from your feared list, so that we can find out if your beliefs about what it will do to your weight are accurate. What do you think would make a good first food to experiment with?

PATIENT: Well, chocolate is my real terror, so I can't start there. How about cake?

CLINICIAN: Before we give up on it, let's talk about chocolate, because we are going to need to do it now or later. What is your favourite kind?

PATIENT: Well, I really like dark chocolate. I can hear dark chocolate bars calling to me from the store as I go past.

CLINICIAN: 'So, if you had a single small bar of dark chocolate, that probably weighs about 50g – what do you think that would do to your weight?

PATIENT: Oh, I would put on at least half a kilo, I am sure. It's chocolate, after all.

CLINICIAN: Hmm. And if you were to eat one of those bars every day for a week?

PATIENT: That is really scary – at least 3 kg. Absolute minimum.

CLINICIAN: How certain are you about that – on a 0 to 100% scale?

PATIENT: 100%? 110%? I know that sounds silly, but I really am more that 100% certain'.

CLINICIAN: OK, so pretty definite that you would gain 3 kg in a week, then. I am not saying that you are wrong, but if we go back to those psychoeducation sheets from Session 1 and look at the number of extra calories that you would need to gain that much weight, that would be about 3000 extra calories per day for the average person, and that chocolate bar does not contain that many calories. However, everyone's calorie needs differ, and weight fluctuates a bit naturally, so it is possible that you are right. Given the calorie count in a week's worth of those chocolate bars, the books would suggest that you might gain a maximum of a quarter of a kilo if you keep your eating as it is and just add in the chocolate bars. How likely do you think *that* is on that 0-100% scale?

PATIENT: No chance at all. 0%? Minus 10%?

CLINICIAN: OK, so if you try out that change, your prediction is 100% that you will gain 3 kg, and 0% that your weight will go up by a quarter of a kilo or less. How long will you need to try that out before you know whether you are right or wrong?

PATIENT: I will know inside of a week. Maybe two weeks to be certain?

CLINICIAN: OK – that sounds like a deal. So let's find out if you are right or wrong, and give you a couple of weeks to find out. We will need to plan times when you can make that change, and get it into your diary, of course.

---

from the beginning. Having conducted our first behavioural experiment, the remaining ones become relatively straightforward and rapid. Most importantly, we aim to teach the patient the method, so that they can take responsibility for it. Our patients often continue trying out new foods to test their beliefs through into the follow-up period. Where they struggle to identify unknown or risky foods, we encourage them to go to the local supermarket and explore possible foods with which to experiment with further.

Table 7.7 Session 5: Reviewing and building on the first 'food–weight' behavioural experiment

---

CLINICIAN: OK – you were going to find out whether you are right about the effects of that extra chocolate bar per day. Did you like the chocolate?

PATIENT: It started out really scary. In fact, it was so scary that I could not eat the bar on one day. I managed it on the other days, and it got easier, and I ended up really enjoying the taste. And I kept the rest of my eating as it was the previous week – I didn't skip anything.

CLINICIAN: That is useful to know. So, we are looking at six small chocolate bars in a week. Given that you predicted a 3 kg weight gain from seven bars, what do you feel you have gained from those six bars?

PATIENT: I know it sounds silly, but still at least 3 kg – maybe even more. I am 100% certain about that. I can see it on me when I look in the mirror.

CLINICIAN: And the books would still say no more than a quarter of a kilo. Well, there is only one way to find out. Let's get you weighed.

Weighing the patient (openly):

CLINICIAN: Well, your weight is pretty much exactly where it was last week. Any comments or conclusions?

PATIENT: Well, if you are going to tell me that it is OK to eat chocolate, I am not sure how to react to that.

CLINICIAN: I'm not telling you anything – your body seems to be doing that all on its own. However, we need to decide whether you can trust this result. As mentioned last time, weight fluctuates, so it might just be a 'blip', and chocolate really is affecting your weight but we won't know for another little while.

PATIENT: I get that. So can I have another week to try it out? I could make it seven bars rather than six?

Or:

PATIENT: I get that, and if the difference hadn't been so huge I might want to give it a bit longer. However, I am pretty convinced that chocolate is not my enemy after all.

CLINICIAN: I am fine with that, so what are we going to try for the next experiment? Let's look at your list of feared foods? Hmm – fried food looks like a good one to try next, because that is pretty high up the list too. What do you think?

7.2.3.1 Troubleshooting: Errors with behavioural experiments

While the process of devising, executing, and assessing a behavioural experiment is detailed in Figure 7.1 and in Table 7.4, it is important to note that clinicians very often make errors in using behavioural experiments. This problem is not unique to eating disorders, and is seen among trainees, novice clinicians, and experienced clinicians alike. Common errors include:

- Not stressing the need to keep everything else (e.g. exercise, food intake) as stable as possible, so that one can learn the specific effects of the planned change in eating, etc.
- Lack of specificity about the predicted outcome (e.g. not asking the patient to specify how much weight will be gained if they eat the planned extra/different food).

- Not generating an alternative specific cognition to test (e.g. need to know what the patient believes is likely to happen when changing eating, but also need to know how much they believe that their weight will *not* change when they change their eating).
- Failure to get certainty ratings about each belief.
- Agreeing a level of change in eating that the patient believes will have relatively little impact (and thus failing to maximise the possible cognitive benefit from learning that they were incorrect).
- Not agreeing a time frame for reaching a conclusion (such that any short-term weight fluctuation is misinterpreted).
- Not reviewing the beliefs or their strength following the experiment.

However, the single most problematic error is when the clinician realises that a mistake has been made (often during supervision), but fails to address that point. If we make an error in teaching the patient how to do a behavioural experiment, the risk is that the patient learns the technique incorrectly, and cannot test their beliefs appropriately. It is important that the clinician should not try to cover any embarrassment about having made an error, but should address it openly and in a matter of fact way with the patient at the earliest opportunity. e.g.:

CLINICIAN: I have to apologise. After the end of the last session, I realised that when we set up that behavioural experiment, I did not ask you to predict just how much weight you thought you would gain when you changed to eating an extra bar of chocolate per day. Sorry about that. While it is great that you have eaten as planned, it could be that any change will get interpreted as evidence for or against your belief about weight. So I am going to suggest that we start again this week, and I teach you the right way to do this.

We find that our patients are very receptive to this level of openness, and it gives them a stronger chance of benefitting from the intervention, so we recommend being straightforward with the patient in this way if we have made an error in delivering a behavioural experiment.

7.2.4 Other aspects of cognitive restructuring regarding food/eating and weight

While the specific, immediate beliefs about the links between food/eating and weight change are addressed using behavioural experiments, there are some more general beliefs that require addressing in order to cover the range of eating and weight concerns that our patients experience. Such beliefs are best addressed using familiar cognitive techniques, because they are not maintained by current circumstances and behaviours. We do not use the full range of cognitive restructuring methods available, as the majority of this work is done via the behavioural experiments (above).

Table 7.8 Cognitive restructuring methods for addressing the eating/food–weight link

---

* Historical review to understanding the development of the patient's beliefs about food, eating, and weight (e.g. family experiences of acceptable and unacceptable foods; parental dietary patterns; parental criticism of weight, leaving the patient perceiving themselves as being nothing more than their weight; religious rules; aversive experiences with certain foods; teasing by others). We address those historical beliefs by developing alternative beliefs that might be more appropriate for the individual in the here and now, e.g.:

    CLINICIAN: Your parents might have left you thinking that 'No-one should ever eat between meals', but you don't live with them now, and that rule has left you feeling an urge to overeat at mealtimes and ending up feeling greedy. Let's think about whether that is a good rule for you to impose on your partner, your own children, and yourself now, or;

    CLINICIAN: So you were teased about your weight gain when you were 11. You were also the first in your class to go through puberty. Do you think that those two things could be connected? If they are and people were teasing you because you were the only one whose body was changing, then is it likely that you will experience that teasing again? Knowing a bit about your history helps us to understand why you are now overly concerned about your weight and how others might view this, but I wonder if that belongs in the past? Perhaps your concerns about your current weight fluctuations are something that you could deal with more effectively in the here and now by not starving and overeating?

* Reduction in black and white thinking (e.g. 'carbohydrates are bad'). To reduce such thinking patterns, we encourage continuum thinking, so that patients can see that it is not appropriate to treat all foods or eating patterns as 'bad'.

    CLINICIAN: Let's think about those complex carbohydrates. Right now, they are all on your list as being totally bad. So can I get you to tell me the scariest and the least scary on the list, and we will put them at the ends of this line? Then we can slot the others in between, and start to look at why the scariest ones are scary.

* Questioning the validity of current information sources (e.g. social media, magazines, diet fads, friends)

    CLINICIAN: I know that you started out with that belief that you had picked up from reading diet tips online – that no-one should eat before 6pm. It is great that you have tackled that so well in changing your eating patterns. However, I think it would be a good idea if we can use that experience to think about whether those sources of information are good ones, or why people and businesses might give out ideas that are effectively harmful. So what do you think might be the reason that so many odd bits of advice are out there?

In or around Session 6, we focus more on the individual's beliefs relating to body image, as we start to shift towards greater understanding of the maintaining behaviours that we will address in Phase 4. However, the cognitive restructuring methods used in CBT-T to address food, eating, and weight include those in Table 7.8.

7.2.5 Preparing for Phases 3 and 4

Because of the importance of adjusting therapy to the individual, we begin to prepare for the following phases, to determine whether they are necessary, and to identify appropriate targets. Therefore, during Phase 2, we aim to identify to following:

- **Phase 3** – Emotional triggers to any residual eating behaviours (e.g. restriction, bingeing, purging, exercising). This can be done through discussion of what triggered specific behaviours if they have occurred. The most common emotions that act as triggers are anxiety, anger, loneliness, and boredom, though this list is not exclusive.
- **Phase 4** – Safety behaviours that are associated with negative body image. These include avoidance, comparison, checking and 'mind-reading', all of which can be identified from observation of the patient throughout therapy, discussion with the patient at this point, and monitoring the ED-15. Again, this list is not exclusive (e.g. reassurance-seeking sometimes serves to maintain negative body image), but these are the four maintaining behaviours that are most commonly addressed in CBT-T (see Chapter 9).

7.2.6 Specific homework tasks in Phase 2

The majority of the homework tasks during this phase (see Appendix 1) are continued from previous sessions. However, there are two new tasks during this phase:

- The changes needed for the behavioural experiments outlined above, which we aim to present in written form, to remind the patient of over the coming week.
- If relevant, asking the patient to bring photos for the purposes of carrying out surveys (Chapter 9). The nature of those photos should be discussed according to the specific 'mind-reading' pattern that needs to be challenged at that stage in therapy.

Summary: Overview of behavioural experiments and cognitive restructuring in Phase 2

- This phase of CBT-T focuses particularly on the 'broken' cognitive link between eating/food and weight, as well as other maintaining cognitions.
- Manipulation of eating behaviours (e.g. eating feared foods) is used to test the feared impact on weight.
- Behavioural experiments need to follow an explicit structure, as detailed in this chapter.
- Changes in eating should involve foods that are strongly feared, as soon as possible, to maximise challenging of beliefs.
- A limited set of non-behavioural cognitive restructuring methods are used.
- Identify emotional and body image targets for Phases 3 and 4 (where present).

Chapter 8

Phase 3 – Working with emotional triggers and core beliefs

Emotional distress and negative core beliefs are widespread among people with eating disorders, and can result in the use of maladaptive eating and compensatory behaviours. Therefore, we aim to pay the necessary attention to those issues in CBT-T. However, many of those issues and beliefs are addressed by the methods used in the earlier part of CBT-T (nutritional change resulting in greater mood stability; exposure resulting in reduction in fears and negative beliefs; more positive self-esteem and mood in response to reducing bulimic behaviours). This pattern of improvement in mood and core beliefs is also well established in CBT-ED even where they are not overt targets (Raykos et al., 2013; Turner et al., 2015). In short, emotions and core beliefs respond well to CBT-ED and CBT-T, even where we do not address them directly.

Consequently, it is not always necessary to address emotional triggers and core beliefs separately. Indeed, our experience is that this is only relevant in a relatively small proportion of cases. One exception may be for people with binge-eating disorder, where a greater proportion of patients report such emotional and cognitive factors driving their binges.

Where it is necessary to address these triggers, it is often (but not always) where the individual has a history of trauma or an early emotionally invalidating environment, with the consequent development of negative core beliefs (e.g. vulnerability; defectiveness) and emotions (e.g. anxiety; anger). Therefore, this phase usually runs between Sessions 5 and 7 (in parallel with behavioural experimentation), if it is implemented at all. Emotional triggers are addressed using a combination of exposure methods and techniques derived from Dialectical Behaviour Therapy (DBT; Linehan, 1993), while core beliefs are addressed using specific approaches to attributional shifts and imagery rescripting, as appropriate. These are detailed in Section 8.2. Table 8.1 lists the broader themes that we address in this phase of CBT-T.

Table 8.1 Themes during Phase 3

- Identification and management of emotional triggers for binges and compensatory behaviours.
  - o Using exposure-based methods.
  - o Using DBT-based techniques.
- Focused work to address core beliefs relating to the emotional triggering of binges and compensatory behaviours.
  - o Challenging attributions.
  - o Imagery rescripting.

8.1 Themes in Phase 3

While some are very aware of the emotional triggers to their behaviours, other patients sometimes find this process a difficult one, feeling that there is something wrong with them because their binges appear to them to occur 'out of the blue'. Therefore, in the identification and management of emotional triggers and core beliefs, we stress that their links to the eating behaviours can be unconscious, so the first step is to bring them into awareness so that they can be challenged. We commonly use the Newton's cradle[1] analogy here (Waller et al., 2007), stressing how we can be unaware of the link between triggers (e.g. an upsetting event) and behaviours (e.g. bingeing), because of the automatic links to beliefs and emotions. This is discussed with the patient in Table 8.2.

Table 8.2 Using a Newton's cradle analogy

PATIENT: I know you say that there must be an explanation for why I still binge sometimes, but I really have no idea why I do it. I kind of assume that it is just a habit that I can't break.

CLINICIAN: I can see why it might feel that way, but let me suggest what might be going on, rather than assuming that there is nothing that we can do about it. You know what a Newton's cradle is – a line of balls on string, where you drop the first ball and the last ball pops up in response, while the ones in the middle stay still?

PATIENT: Well, yes.

CLINICIAN: The illusion with a Newton's cradle is that the balls in the middle do nothing, but actually they are carrying the impact of that first ball through to the last one. Take out the balls in the middle, and you stop the impact. Now, let's label the first ball 'experience' – something happens to you, however unrelated to eating that might be. The next ball is your 'thoughts' or 'cognitions', which are activated by the experience. Then you have your 'emotions', triggered by those cognitions. The last one is your 'behaviour', which is a result of those emotions. Making sense so far?

PATIENT: Yes – I get that. So you are saying that what I do when I binge might be started by something that I did not realise was linked at the time.

CLINICIAN: Got it. So, if we look at why you binged on that evening, what was happening that might explain what went on.

PATIENT: Well, my sister had just called to say that she couldn't babysit later that evening. Maybe I was thinking that I never let her down but she always does it to me, so maybe I was a bit angry?

CLINICIAN: OK – let's have a look at that possibility – those thoughts and emotions.

8.1.1 Identification and management of emotional triggers

Where the patient's level of eating is normalised and weight is relatively stable (or rising as planned) but the individual still uses some safety behaviours (e.g. bingeing, restriction, vomiting, exercise), we should explore whether such behaviours are being used to manage emotions. The patient is commonly unaware of any such emotion regulation, but the use of diaries and hypothesising about situation-behaviour links usually results in the patient becoming aware of their use of those behaviours to manage emotion. In some cases, that awareness is sufficient for the patient to use existing cognitive and behavioural skills to avoid using the eating behaviours in that way, e.g.:

PATIENT: After we talked about that Newton's cradle model last week, I realised that getting angry at my sister is not helping me and it's not changing her, so I asked my mum and dad to babysit instead. I was worried that they might think I was being a bit demanding, but they were great about it and even offered to have the children overnight to let me stay with my friends for longer. So now I'm not panicking that I will have to cancel my only night out at short notice. Oh, and no binges, because I am not panicking any more.

In other cases, more explicitly exposure-based methods or methods derived from DBT are appropriate for dealing with emotions such as anxiety, boredom, and anger. These are outlined in Section 8.2.

8.1.2 Addressing the core beliefs that trigger emotions resulting in eating behaviours

In a small number of cases, making the patient aware of the linkage between trigger, emotion and behaviour is not effective, and exposure (see Section 8.2.3) does not ameliorate these remaining eating behaviours. In such circumstances, we address the cognitive element of the chain, particularly negative core beliefs that commonly trigger the emotions, e.g.:

CLINICIAN: We tried the idea of delaying using bingeing after your sister called you to cancel and seeing whether you still needed to binge. However, you found that you still had that urge, so we need to go back to that Newton's cradle and look at the other ball in there – your beliefs. In particular, I think we should look at something called your 'core' beliefs – the 'who am I' sort of beliefs. For example, it could be that your sister's call triggered some long-standing thoughts about you not deserving help from other people, which you went over and over in your head. That way, while you waited for the time that we agreed, your emotions were not getting calmer because you were going over them and feeling worse. That might explain why you ended up bingeing. What do you think?.

In Section 8.2.2, we will outline how to complete specific therapeutic tasks with the patient to change attributions (e.g. "Maybe it's not me who is the problem, after all") and use imagery rescripting in order to modify those core beliefs and to reduce their impact.

8.2 Specific tasks in this phase

Table 8.3 details the specific techniques that are employed in this phase of CBT-T (other techniques used in parallel from Phase 2 are outlined in the previous chapter – see Table 7.2). As before, the order in which we use those methods is flexible (apart from the processes of using diaries and weighing the patient to challenge the 'broken' cognitive process).

8.2.1 Identifying the need to address emotional and cognitive triggers

In short, we need to exclude starvation as a possible driver of the remaining binges. This is not a matter of disbelieving the patient's account of their eating, but simply understanding how accurate they are. As indicated above, the rule of thumb is to monitor the patient's eating patterns and quantity, along with their weight.

If the patient reports eating adequately but still bingeing and their weight is stable/on track, then it is likely that their food intake/energy balance is not adequate, and they need to eat more rather than focusing on other factors. In contrast, if they report eating adequately and bingeing and their weight is rising, then that indicates that the binges are not driven by hunger/inadequate energy balance. In the latter case, we would explore potential emotional or cognitive triggers.

Table 8.3 Specific tasks in Phase 3 of CBT-T (Sessions 5–7)

These tasks are likely to be run in parallel with those in Phase 4:

- Identification of the need to address emotional and cognitive triggers of residual eating behaviours (excluding starvation).
- Use of diaries to identify emotion-driven behaviours, the relevant emotions, and underlying cognitions.
- Use exposure to the emotion where appropriate, delaying the use of the behaviours.
- DBT-based techniques for reducing emotional reactivity.
- Address core beliefs to reduce emotionally-triggered behaviours.
  - o Challenging attributions.
  - o Imagery rescripting.
- Homework.
  - o Identification of emotions and core beliefs.
  - o Exposure.
  - o Historical review.
  - o Evidence-gathering.
  - o Monitoring mood and food/eating/weight cognitions.

8.2.2 Identifying emotional and cognitive triggers

This involves a combination of methods, used in the sequence detailed in Table 8.4.

8.2.2.1 Hypothesising

As it is likely that the patient is unaware of the triggers, their ability to report them will be limited. Therefore, the clinician needs to offer the patient plausible hypotheses about what those triggers might be, e.g.:

CLINICIAN: Given that your eating is pretty much on course but you are still binge-ing and vomiting occasionally, it looks likely that you might be bingeing to block out some of your emotions or your thoughts about yourself. I wonder if you have any thoughts about what that might involve?

PATIENT: I'm not sure. I know that I feel worked up when I am about to binge and I feel a lot calmer when I have been sick, but I have no idea what goes on in between.

CLINICIAN: Well, a lot of people feel that 'worked up' feeling, but it would be good to pin it down so that we can help you to deal with in a less negative way. If you think back to the last time that it happened, do you remember any thoughts or emotions at the time?

PATIENT: Not really – no.

CLINICIAN: What was going on that time?

PATIENT: I was waiting for my partner to come home – they were late, and I was going to be late for my evening class.

CLINICIAN: Well, that gives us a couple of possibilities, I suspect. It's possible that you were anxious about whether you were going to get to your class, but it's also possible that you were getting angry at your partner. Either of those could have triggered a binge. Similarly, there could be a belief in there about being treated as worth less than other people. I am not saying that it is definitely one of those, but either might be worth looking at. I am going to give you a handout (Appendix 7) to take away about different emotions and beliefs that can trigger eating behaviours and ask you to use it to try to identify what happens for you, using an extended diary. (See Appendix 8 for diary.)

Table 8.4 Identification of potential emotional and cognitive triggers

- Hypothesising about what the relevant emotions and beliefs might be.
- Education regarding emotions and/or core beliefs.
- Diaries to identify patterns.
- Changing patterns of behaviour to reduce impact of emotions and core beliefs.

8.2.2.2 Education

Because many patients with eating disorders have difficulties in identifying emotions and the underlying core beliefs, we offer prompts so that the patient can use them to complete the diary (below) for discussion at the next session. The list that we use is contained in the handout that we give to the patient (Appendix 7), for the patient to consult when completing the extended diary (Appendix 8). However, if this is not sufficient for the individual patient, then it can be augmented with material from other CBT sources (e.g. Padesky & Greenberger, 1995; Young & Klosko, 1993).

8.2.2.3 Diary keeping

We then ask the patient to identify potential emotional and cognitive factors by asking them to record each time they get the urge to use a problem eating behaviour (e.g. bingeing). The recording of the urge is important, as it allows us to work out with the patient whether there are particular times when the patient does or does not use the behaviour, thus identifying natural coping strategies that the patient might not be aware of. We encourage the patient to use the lists of emotions and core beliefs to identify how they were feeling and thinking if they have limited awareness of those experiences. The headers in this extended diary (Appendix 8) reflect the elements in the Newton's cradle (above):

- Situation/trigger
- Possible core belief
- Possible emotion
- Outcome (eating behaviour used or not; alternative behaviours used)

8.2.2.4 Changing patterns of behaviour

These are addressed in the following sections. However, we stress to the patient that they can learn from the outcomes of those changes. In short, if working on anxiety or anger is effective in reducing the eating behaviours, then the patient can learn how to structure their life in the future to avoid the risk of later problems.

8.2.3 Use of exposure to the emotion, delaying the use of behaviours

When the emotion has been identified, we begin by using exposure with response prevention (see Chapter 5). In short, when the patient experiences the urge to use a behaviour and identifies an emotional trigger, we ask them to delay that (safety) behaviour for 30–45 minutes, stressing that they can use it then if they still wish to. We usually find that the response at the end of the delay is along the lines of: "I couldn't be bothered – I just wasn't feeling so anxious anymore".

If pure exposure (just sitting with the emotion) is too difficult, then distraction methods can be used to delay behaviours. To achieve this, we ask the patient to suggest some useful ways of delaying the safety behaviour, and we help to develop and refine these strategies, e.g.:

- "Take a bath to avoid going to get food".
- "Drive a different way home from work to avoid passing the store – you can go back later if you need to buy groceries".
- "'Go for a walk without any money to avoid buying food".
- "When you get the urge to use the behaviour, I want you to complete this very detailed diary before you do it. It looks at your urges, your beliefs about the pros and cons of doing it, what your best friend and worst enemy would tell you to do, three alternative behaviours" (of course, the aim of this task is to ensure that the patient spends so long completing the diary that the exposure has time to take effect).
- "Paint your nails, to avoid the urge to put your fingers down your throat".
- "Exercise later if you want to but make a phone call to a friend first".

8.2.4 Use of DBT-based techniques for reducing emotional reactivity

It is important to stress that this is simply a small subset of the emotional management skills that Linehan (1993) proposes. It should not be seen as using DBT per se (e.g. we do not use the 'letting go' element). These skills overlap with some of the others in this section, consisting of:

- Understanding and labelling emotions. This can include: primary emotions (the emotions experienced as a result of the trigger factors – e.g. being angry at one's colleague for not doing their part of a job); and secondary emotions (emotional reactions to the primary emotion – e.g. being anxious that others will judge one for having been angry at the colleague).
- Reducing emotional vulnerability, by changing behavioural patterns that interfere with quality of life (e.g. reducing alcohol intake; getting adequate sleep; engaging in daily activities rather than avoiding the world).
- Taking the opposite action, such as going for a walk when the urge is to hide away.

In general, these approaches can be seen as increasing emotional regulation skills, distress tolerance, and interpersonal effectiveness.

Importantly, we do not use third-wave approaches (e.g. mindfulness, acceptance and commitment, or compassion-focused therapy) as part of CBT-T, as they are not part of CBT-ED (see Chapter 1). Indeed, there is a risk that some of these approaches (e.g. mindfulness) might impair the effects of CBT – particularly exposure-based work.

8.2.5 Address core beliefs to reduce emotional triggering of behaviours

Where the behavioural methods outlined above are not effective, we address the core beliefs that underpin the emotions. This is a relatively brief process in CBT-T, compared with CBT-ED, though such beliefs might also be addressed in the relapse prevention stage and at follow-up (see Chapters 10 and 11) if they are relatively substantial.

The methods outlined here address the core beliefs that Young (1999) identifies, using cognitive-behavioural methods rather than 'schema therapy' as Young et al. (2003) present it. Most commonly, the beliefs relate to self-esteem (e.g. defectiveness; abandonment) and anxiety (e.g. mistrust; vulnerability). Our aim is not to change the beliefs themselves (that tends to happen as the individual improves in CBT-ED – e.g. Turner et al., 2016), but to change their contextualisation. In short, we aim to help the patient to identify that the beliefs made perfect sense in the context where they developed and at that time. Then we help the patient to see that the beliefs are not relevant now, and that holding on to them can be a problem in the here and now. This process has also been called 'compassionate conceptualisation' (by Christine Padesky) or 'balancing change' (by Marsha Linehan).

8.2.5.1 Attributional change

Our goal here is to help the patient to see that the belief that they have held for a long time made sense at the time, but that it no longer applies. To do this, we encourage the patient to attribute responsibility more appropriately, e.g.:

CLINICIAN: Your mother used to leave you alone and in charge of your younger brothers when you were just eight and wouldn't come back for days while she went off with her boyfriend. Given that, I don't think it is any great surprise that you grew up expecting people to abandon you, do you?

PATIENT: Well, I suppose not, but what if I did something that made her stay away? That is what I have always assumed was going on, because she told me that I was an unbearable girl to be around.

CLINICIAN: Just ask yourself – what would it take for you to do that to your children now? How bad would they have to be for you to stay away for a weekend and leave them on their own?

PATIENT: I just wouldn't. I couldn't. There is nothing that they could do or be like that would ever make me do that.

CLINICIAN: So do you think it is possible that your mother went off because she was more concerned with her boyfriend than you and your brothers? And that she told you that you were unbearable because she wanted to stop you complaining – to make you think that no-one could want to be around you?

PATIENT: Maybe – I never thought of it like that.

CLINICIAN: Well, is she different now? Or is she still not good at coping with people?

PATIENT: She is terrible – only ever wants to moan about people. I try to keep her away from my children because I don't want her doing what she always does and telling me that they are stupid and badly behaved. They aren't.

CLINICIAN: So is it possible that she abandoned you when you were young because she is not great at being a mother, rather than because you had done anything wrong? And do you think that your fear that others will abandon you now might be messing up your relationship with your partner by making you test them all the time – pushing them away to see if they run off for good?

PATIENT: That makes sense, but how could I know? Am I just being a bad person by thinking this?

CLINICIAN: Well, you could spend the next week looking for evidence. Do other people think you are bad now? Do your brothers think you were bad back then, or that you were looking after them? What do they think of your mother? How do your own children find her? What does your partner think about all that pushing away that you do, even if you are doing it to make you feel safer? Let's plan some homework.

The aim is to reduce the patient's fear of abandonment in the present by helping them to see that they were not responsible for how their mother acted, but that their current behaviour in response to that belief is having negative effects.

Following this reduction in negative attributions, it is important to consider developing more adaptive beliefs. In the following session, the patient can be encouraged to experiment with more adaptive behaviours and ways of coping in the world, and to actively notice the impact of using more adaptive behaviours, both in relation to how others respond and how it makes them feel. Again, we can use the Newton's cradle model to stress that the behaviours (e.g. bingeing) also feed back to worsen emotions and negative core beliefs (the return journey of the balls in the cradle), and we can use that to explain why reducing the maladaptive behaviours and developing more adaptive behaviours make for more positive core beliefs and emotional experiences (better self-esteem, greater confidence, and greater emotional resilience).

8.2.5.2 Imagery rescripting

This technique is addressed in detail elsewhere (e.g. Ohanian, 2002; Waller, Kennerley & Ohanian, 2007), and should be used carefully to ensure that it is effective and does not result in a negative experience for the patient (due to its focus on past trauma). We use it specifically where the patient has an identified focal trauma experience (e.g. emotional abuse, sexual abuse, observing physical violence). Imagery rescripting is used to change attributions for those trauma experiences, by allowing the patient to make sense (as an adult) of an event that they had only previously been able to see from their childhood perspective.

While imagery rescripting was initially developed for trauma victims with post-traumatic stress disorder (PTSD), it is important to remember that trauma experiences do not always result in PTSD. Imagery rescripting can be just as valuable where there is no PTSD diagnosis. We use this method where the individual has difficulty in concluding that the trauma was not their fault, and the resultant core beliefs trigger eating behaviours to escape those beliefs and the resultant emotions. However, we apply this method over a relatively short period in therapy (e.g. part of one session), to address a single event. Where the individual has an extensive trauma history, we would not attempt to address that range in CBT-T, as it is likely to need more extensive trauma work (as considered in Chapter 11).

This work requires a collaborative approach with the patient, who needs to understand the reasons for addressing such topics. Imagery rescripting differs slightly between clinical models, but we use the method outlined by Ohanian (2002). We recommend reading the examples provided by Ohanian (2002; Waller, Kennerley & Ohanian, 2007) to get a clear picture of what needs to be done here. The stages of imagery rescripting in such cases are:

- Preparation for the process, explaining the rationale for this process, and making the patient feel safe in talking about events that could be distressing to think or talk about, in their experience.
- Identify the core beliefs (e.g. mistrust) and emotions (e.g. anger) that trigger the behaviour.
- Identify the traumatic experiences that are associated with those core beliefs (e.g. having been hit repeatedly by a teacher).
- Select one or two salient examples of that trauma, which the patient remembers vividly.
- Ask the patient to visualise one event, and describe it as it was experienced at the time (using lots of sensory cues).
- Ask the patient to attribute blame for the traumatic experience (the patient will blame themselves).
- Re-run the description, but this time ask the patient to come into the scene as their adult self to defend the child at the critical point (e.g. by pulling the abuser away; threatening the abuser; shrinking the abuser), then to get rid of the abuser, and talk to the child in the scene, encouraging reattribution of responsibility/blame from the child to the abuser.
- Following the imagery rescripting session, ask the patient to attribute blame for the traumatic experience (the patient will blame the abuser).
- Monitor changes in beliefs, mood, and eating thereafter.

The change in attribution is often dramatic, and can be associated with anger on the part of the patient. We discuss that anger, stressing that it is appropriate. However, we also stress that the important thing for the patient is being able to let go of the self-blame, to be able to get on with life. So we encourage the patient not to let the anger become their only response, so that they have the space to get on with therapy and life.

8.2.6 Homework

The homework tasks specific to this phase (carried out in parallel with homework from Phases 2 and 4) follow from the techniques that we have outlined in this chapter. Several are addressed by Padesky and Greenberger (1995), Waller, Kennerley, and Ohanian (2007) and Young and Klosko (1995). The tasks include:

- Learning to identify emotions and core beliefs.
- Exposure to emotional states (e.g. "When you get the urge to binge, then I want you to use the delaying behaviour that we talked about").
- Historical review of the origins of core beliefs.
- Gathering evidence for and against the core beliefs.
- Generating more balanced alternative beliefs.
- Monitoring changes in behaviours, mood, and food/eating/weight cognitions.

Summary: Overview of working with emotional triggers and core beliefs in Phase 3

- This phase is only needed where the exposure in Phase 1 has not stopped the bulimic behaviours completely. If there are even small numbers of such behaviours, then these techniques are needed to reduce the risk of relapse.
- This phase is often run in parallel with Phase 4.
- The Newton's cradle model is a helpful way of explaining the role of emotions and core beliefs in triggering such behaviours.
- Management of emotional triggers is usually done using exposure-based methods.
- Where exposure-based methods are not effective, then some DBT skills can be used.
- Cognitive methods can be used to reduce the impact of core beliefs, usually by challenging attributions.
- Where there is a link between trauma and core beliefs that trigger bulimic behaviours, imagery rescripting can be effective.

Note

1 If you are not familiar with Newton's cradle, a quick search online should help you to visualise this and follow the analogy.

Chapter 9

Phase 4 – Working with body image

This phase usually runs between Sessions 5 and 9, usually starting during the latter part of Phase 2 (behavioural experiments). As before, this phase is not always necessary. A small number of patients have no concerns about their body image from the outset of therapy, while a larger number find that these concerns reduce across the earlier part of CBT-T. However, body image work remains relevant to most patients in CBT-T. We determine who needs this work by monitoring the patient's cognitions and behaviours. The specifics of these sessions are outlined in the protocol checklists (see Appendix 1).

As outlined earlier, we are shifting the cognitive focus from the 'broken' cognitive link (which should be relatively normalised following Phases 1 and 2) to the overvaluation of weight and shape. Each is important, as they contribute to the patient's chances of recovery and the lowering of relapse risk. Therefore, it is important to ensure that the earlier phases are completed in good time to allow for the body image work.

In keeping with CBT-ED, we focus more on the maintaining factors than on the origins of negative body image. Clearly, this is not to argue that the causation of negative body image (e.g. teasing in childhood, trauma, maturation) is trivial. However, we limit our consideration of those past events to one specific therapeutic technique that we know can be effective in addressing the consequences of some of those events – imagery rescripting for body image (Pennesi & Wade, 2018). While past events themselves cannot be modified, this approach can change the meaning and emotion ascribed to such events in the here and now, thus changing behavioural responses to this emotion. Apart from that, we focus on addressing the maintenance of negative body image through addressing safety behaviours such as body checking, comparison, and avoidance, as well as cognitive and perceptual errors (e.g. lack of knowledge regarding body function, body size misperception and mind-reading). Individuals differ in the factors that maintain their body image, so we use clinical discussion and the ED-15 to identify the targets for the individual in this phase. Finally, it is important to aim for body acceptance rather than body satisfaction, as true body satisfaction is rare among women and men.

9.1 Themes in Phase 4

Table 9.1 outlines the themes in this phase. As detailed above, these need to be tailored to the individual when techniques are being implemented.

9.1.1 Addressing overvaluation of shape

Such overvaluation is a key element to address. It is the recovery target that most patients and clinicians see as key (e.g. Emanuelli et al., 2012), and ignoring it risks the patient relapsing even if they recover in all other ways (e.g. Keel et al., 2005). However, it should not be assumed that this will be an easy phase for the patient, as it involves addressing beliefs that are particularly important to the patient and changing body-related safety behaviours that have become deeply embedded in managing their anxiety. However, that should not be allowed to stop us addressing this key symptom.

Body image has many facets (e.g. Cash & Smolak, 2012). However, the key ones that we aim to change in CBT-T are:

- Body percept – the individual's perception of their body size. Most girls and women overestimate their body size, but those with eating disorders do so to a greater degree. Men are less consistent, with most being relatively accurate, though some focus on their muscularity more. Such overestimation can be assessed relatively easily by asking the patient to show how large they believe themselves to be (e.g. indicating with their hands; drawing a perceived outline).
- Body concept – the individual's body satisfaction. Again, it is relatively common for women to experience a 'normal' level of body dissatisfaction, and more so than men. That dissatisfaction is measured using the ED-15 and measures such as the EDE-Q, as we work to reduce it to normal, functional levels (acceptance rather than satisfaction, valuing the function of the body rather than a sole focus on appearance).

Table 9.1 Themes during Phase 4

- Addressing overvaluation of shape:
  - Might not be needed at all if body image has been changing since the start of treatment.
- Limited consideration of past events, focusing on the current meaning and experience of those events.
- Target maintaining behaviours:
  - Avoidance, comparison, checking, mind-reading.
  - Identify these with the individual and monitor via ED-15 and clinical discussion.
- Implement changes, using existing CBT/CBT-ED methods:
  - Psychoeducation and corrective feedback.
  - Imagery rescripting for body image.
  - Exposure, behavioural experiments, surveys.

Both of these facets of body image are important targets and are responsive to the following interventions. Therefore, we will be monitoring those facets to determine what to target and how effective we are in this phase.

9.1.2 Origins of negative body image

There are many factors that might explain the development of negative body image, and these vary considerably across individuals (e.g. one person might dislike their body due to being teased for being the tallest in the class at the age of eight; another might have become self-conscious about their body during puberty; another might have grown up in a family where the emphasis is on appearance). Often, negative body image can develop as a combination of multiple factors, including messages from peers and family, media messages, personality traits, physical appearance, and experiences such as bullying or teasing. It can then be maintained by selecting environments that place emphasis on appearance, such as some forms of social media, peer relationships, forms of exercise, or types of work and hobbies. In short, there are many ways to arrive at a negative body image. However, even if it were possible to identify those causal factors accurately, addressing them many years after the event is not viable.

Therefore, we limit our consideration of past issues related to body image to one core technique – imagery rescripting for body image. Imagery rescripting is an approach that has been used more widely in the eating disorders (e.g. Ohanian, 2002; Waller, Kennerley, & Ohanian, 2007), but which has been developed specifically as a brief and effective approach to working with body image (Pennesi & Wade, 2018). As outlined below, this approach focuses on the current meaning and experience of those past events.

9.1.3 Targeting behaviours that maintain body image

While there is much diversity in the potential origins of negative body image but relatively few related interventions (see Section 9.1.2), there are fewer maintaining factors for negative body image but a greater number of cognitive-behavioural techniques that can be used to address those factors. The CBT-T methods relating to specific maintaining behaviours (e.g. body checking, comparison, and avoidance) are summarised in Table 9.2, alongside issues of lack of knowledge and misperception of body size. Each can be identified through clinical discussion and the use of the ED-15. Interventions for each will be addressed in Section 9.2.

9.1.4 Key maintaining behaviours in body image

Table 9.3 shows that we address four such body-related avoidant and safety behaviours, each of which has short-term benefits but long-term costs for the individual. These need to be identified and discussed with the patient, explaining the

Table 9.2 Maintenance mechanisms for negative body image to address in CBT

Maintenance mechanisms/safety behaviours	Cognitive behavioural approach
Lack of knowledge (e.g. of normal body composition; the role of fat tissue).	Education.
Misperception (e.g. overestimation of body size; experiencing difficult emotions as 'feeling fat').	Identify misperception and mechanisms (e.g. emotion) and offer corrective feedback.
Body checking (e.g. repeated self-weighing; checking one's reflection; measuring body parts, using methods such as pinching flesh).	Behavioural experiments.
Body comparison (e.g. judging one's own appearance through comparison with other people's bodies).	Behavioural experiments.
Mind-reading (e.g. assuming that one knows what the other person thinks about one's appearance, despite having no evidence for this assumption).	Surveys.
Body avoidance (e.g. avoiding one's reflection; wearing baggy clothing).	Body exposure.

Table 9.3 Intervention methods in Phase 4 of CBT-T (Sessions 6–9)

- Prioritise methods used though discussion with the patient and consideration of other tasks from earlier phases.
- Psychoeducation.
- Perceptual correction.
- Memories of past events resulting in current body shame or embarrassment addressed using imagery rescripting for body image.
- Mind-reading addressed using surveys:
  o Who should do them; what they address; creating and sharing a good survey.
- Checking and comparison addressed using behavioural experiments:
  o Cannot be used at the same time as each other or other experiments if the targets are the same (e.g. testing weight gain; anxiety reduction).
- Avoidance addressed using mirror exposure (flooding, using guided or pure exposure) or graded exposure (e.g. going out in more or less exposing clothes).
- Set homework, as per target at the time – exposure, historical review, evidence-gathering, behavioural experiment.

reasons why the patient might undertake them (short-term benefits), and why they have negative longer-term consequences, maintaining and exacerbating negative body image. The four are:

- Mind-reading – where the individual assumes that other people are thinking negatively about their body but would not say what they are thinking or even that they are thinking about it. Short-term, by not asking, the patient avoids the risk of hearing others' negative opinions. Longer term, this safety behaviour results in the patient reaching the conclusion that as there is no evidence that others are not thinking negatively about them, others must be thinking negatively about them, e.g.:

CLINICIAN: I notice from the ED-15 that you worry what other people might be thinking about the way you look. So would you tell me what you believe they are thinking?

PATIENT: I feel like I have put on loads of weight since last year, and I just know that people are thinking that I am really gross now.

CLINICIAN: Do you have any evidence that they think that? Has anyone said that, for example.

PATIENT: Well, no. I could never ask them, and no-one would ever say that sort of thing. I just know that they are thinking that when I go out.

Thus, the patient's safety behaviour ("Don't ask – they might tell me something terrible') results in a worse outcome ("I know that they think I am gross"), which fuels the use of the safety behaviour ("Now I know that they will tell me something terrible, so I can never ask").

- Body checking – where the patient checks their body repeatedly in any of a number of ways, seeking reassurance that they have not gained weight, lost muscle tone, etc. This behaviour can include mirror checking, feeling/pinching parts of the body, repeated self-weighing, trying different clothes, etc. In the short term, this checking can calm the individual (even if it is an intermittently positive experience). However, longer term it enhances focus on the body, such that the individual feels worse about their appearance, e.g.:

  CLINICIAN: In the ED-15, you say that you spend a lot of time checking your appearance. Is that right? In what ways do you check your body?

  PATIENT: Sometimes it is a bit silly. For example, when I get up, I have to try on three work suits, to see if I have got smaller or bigger than the day before. Or I find myself looking at my thighs when I sit down, to see whether they spread out on the chair. Other times, it is really problematic – I take ages to walk to work because I have to check myself in every shop window on my way. If the clothes shops were open, I would go in to check myself in the mirrors in the changing rooms. I just have to do those things, or I could never face people in case I looked awful.

  CLINICIAN: Does that work? Do you end up feeling better about your body?

  PATIENT: Maybe for five minutes, but I always end up going back and checking again, in case things have got worse and my body has got fatter.

- Body comparison – where the patient judges their own body by comparing it with other people's. This comparison can be downward (comparing with someone who is seen as less attractive, larger, etc.), which is associated with feeling better about oneself. Alternatively, it can be upward (comparing the self with someone who is seen as more attractive, smaller, etc.), which is associated with feeling worse about oneself. However, the fact that most patients feel that they are bigger and less attractive than they actually are (see below) means that the great majority of comparisons have negative outcomes for the patient. This negative outcome is made more likely by the tendency for aspirational figures to be presented as very slim and attractive, particularly on social media, e.g.:

CLINICIAN: When we first met, you said that you spend a lot of time looking at sites where you and your friends post photos, and that you end up hating yourself. Why is that?

PATIENT: Well, I always hope that I will look as good as them, and sometimes I do, but that is rare. Normally, I look at my photos and I look at theirs, and I feel really fat and ugly compared to them. It is even worse if I look at models or famous people on there, mind.

- Body avoidance – where the patient does not look at their own body and will go to extremes to ensure that they do not see themselves or let others see their bodies. This can include avoiding mirrors, wearing concealing clothes, avoiding reflective surfaces such as shop windows, etc. The short-term outcome is not feeling distressed about one's appearance, but in the longer term the lack of corrective feedback means that the patient does not learn that their body is smaller than they assume, and their anxiety enhances their fear about how much their body might have grown.

CLINICIAN: You mentioned from the beginning that the only mirrors that you have at home are covered with shawls or placed behind chairs so that you can only see your head. The ED-15 says that you are still avoiding showing or looking at your body. Why have you done all that?

PATIENT: Because I know that I look fat, whatever anyone says. So I don't want to be reminded of that all the time. I keep the mirror for my face, but definitely not my body.

CLINICIAN: So is that working to make you feel better about your body?

PATIENT: Well, it should distract me, but I know that I am now so twitchy about seeing my body that I spend all my time on alert for the possibility that I will accidentally see myself in a shop window or something. It makes me really anxious.

Having identified these cognitive and behavioural patterns, we prioritise the order of addressing the safety behaviours through discussion with the patient. This prioritisation can be facilitated by considering the relative strength of scores on the relevant ED-15 items.

9.2 Cognitive-behavioural interventions for body image

We are now in a position to implement a range of appropriate CBT methods (Table 9.3) to generate change. In all cases, we aim to teach the patient to undertake the techniques themselves, in order to reduce the overvaluation of body shape.

As before, the order in which we use those methods is flexible. However, it is important to ensure that there is no clash in predicted outcomes, and that any remaining tasks from Phases 2 and 3 running in parallel do not interfere with the potential learning outcomes of the specific body image task that we choose with the patient. For example, if a behavioural experiment addressing the outcomes of changing diet involves the patient bingeing and vomiting, then one should not run a behavioural experiment regarding body image with the same predicted outcome, as one could not determine the causality (whether bingeing and vomiting occurred or not). This need to avoid potentially conflicting outcomes means that we are more likely to use surveys earlier in the body image work.

9.2.1 Psychoeducation

We discuss any information about body image and any cognitive biases that it might be useful for the patient to be aware of. Such discussions address:

- The need for the body to include fat tissue (e.g. energy storage; insulation; organ protection), despite the common messages about body fat being 'bad' or 'undesirable'.
- The normality of weight fluctuation, meaning that any efforts to control body weight and size precisely are inevitably ineffective.
- How our body size perception is influenced by our emotions, with emotional arousal making our overestimations even larger (e.g. Proctor & Morley, 1986). Note: when addressing body misperceptions through corrective feedback, we start by asking the patient to show how big they 'feel' they are, rather than how big they 'think' they are, in order to enhance their degree of overestimation prior to testing their real size. In such cases, we ask the patient to graph their estimate of how large they are against actual weight changes, to show that their feelings about their body are not accurate (see Fairburn, 2008). Then we examine their emotional levels (e.g. rated anger, anxiety) against their perceived size, to show how emotions might be a better explanation of the patient's body size estimation.
- The biases inherent in media and social media representations of 'normal' bodies, and how viewing those representations can result in poorer body image (e.g. Hamilton & Waller, 1993) and make it inevitable that comparisons with the self will be negative.
- The role of attentional biases in ensuring that negative self-image can result in our seeking out confirmatory 'bad news' about our own bodies or in our feeling larger.
- The ways in which mirror use varies between people, with some methods (particularly over-checking and avoiding) resulting in worsening of body image.
- The psychophysics principle of the 'just noticeable difference', whereby people cannot identify comparatively small changes perceptually. For the body to increase or decrease in size, it would have to do so by 3–5% in a relatively

short period of time before we could really identify it, yet patients believe that they can detect far smaller changes. We use this information about how people function to make it clear that the patient's estimations of body size are likely to be emotionally rather than cognitively or perceptually driven.

- Examining positive aspects of one's body (e.g. parts that one likes) and positive body functions, to shift the patient's perspective and focus.

9.2.2 Correcting body misperception

We identify any body image misperception and offer corrective feedback. A key target is body size overestimation. Such overestimation is one of the factors that makes patients feel worse about their body (e.g. poorer body self-esteem; more likely to experience comparisons with others' bodies negatively). Our target is to teach the patient that their estimation of their body size might not be accurate. In order to do this, we ask the patient to estimate their body size. One method is to ask the patient to use a pair of callipers to show how big they feel their waist (or other relevant body parts) to be, and then use the same callipers to show them their real size. We use the discrepancy to illustrate to the patient how much they overestimate their body size (indeed, we find it useful to ask the patient to use the callipers to show what size their waist would have to be before they would be happy with their body, and then we are able to show the patient that this 'ideal' size that they aspire to is actually larger than their current body size). We encourage the patient to continue to estimate their body size, responding to the feedback until they learn to make more accurate estimates. Another method is to ask the patient to draw what they believe their body outline is on a large sheet of paper on the wall, and then to draw around them on the same sheet. Again, this method demonstrates a substantial level of overestimation, allowing the patient to learn from corrective feedback.

9.2.3 Use of imagery rescripting to address hurtful body memories

We have mentioned previously that there are a number of pathways to poor body image, and often there is one early memory that retains substantial emotional charge and skewing of body image away from acceptance toward body discomfort. An emerging and brief technique that we consider using in this context is imagery rescripting of a salient early experience where the person first felt ashamed or embarrassed of their body or how their body looked (Pennesi & Wade, 2018). A single, brief training session of imagery rescripting and a week's daily practice can result in appreciable increases in body acceptance and self-compassion, as well as decreases in disordered eating. The instructions for this technique are provided in Table 9.4, which can be copied and handed to the patient to undertake as a daily homework exercise following the training in the clinic session, for discussion the following week.

Table 9.4 Scripts used in the training and home implementation of imagery rescripting

Training (allow 30 minutes):

- (Part 1) Write in first person, and as it was happening in the present moment, a first or earliest memory of a personal unpleasant body experience from the past where you felt ashamed or embarrassed of your body or how you looked. Visualize it and describe it in detail.
- (Part 2) Now close your eyes and imagine (or visualize) this event, from an observer or third party perspective. Imagine that your adult self is present observing what's happening right now, watching the events unfold. Imagine that you are observing your younger self reliving the event. Please only continue once you have this event in mind. Write down what you see from an observers' perspective as if it were happening to your younger self right now. Please write in the third person (e.g. if your name is Sarah, you might write "I see Sarah in the changing room, she is trying on a pair of blue jeans ..."). Try to be descriptive and include as many details as you can, for example, where is Sarah, what is Sarah doing, who is Sarah with, how might Sarah be feeling (emotions), and what might Sarah be telling herself (thoughts).
- (Part 3) Please again think about your first or earliest memory of a personal unpleasant body experience from the past where you may have felt ashamed or embarrassed of your body or how your body looked. This time, when you close your eyes and imagine (or visualise) this event, imagine it as if it is happening to you right now, but this time your wiser and more compassionate adult self is with you and can intervene if you want her to. She can offer you compassion or provide new updated information based on what you know now. She can talk to you (or others), or do anything else that feels helpful or right in the situation. Please only continue once you have this event in mind. Please describe what you see as if it is happening to you right now but this time your adult self is with you and can intervene if you want her to. Please write in the first person (e.g. you might write "I'm in the change room, I'm trying on a pair of blue jeans ...") unless you are referring to the adult you (e.g. if your name was Sarah you might write "Adult/older Sarah said ..."). Try to be descriptive and include as many details as you can, including where you are, what you are doing, who you are with, how you are feeling (emotions), and what you are telling yourself (thoughts). Please also describe if your adult self intervenes or does anything in the situation.

Daily homework practice (allow 10 minutes per day):

- Please think about your first or earliest memory of a personal unpleasant body experience from the past where you may have felt ashamed or embarrassed of your body or how your body looked (the experience you wrote about during the session in the clinic). Now take a moment to close your eyes and imagine this event as if it is happening to you right now, but this time your wiser and more compassionate adult self is with you in the room and can intervene if you want her to. She can offer you compassion or provide new updated information based on what you know now. She can talk to you (or others), or do anything else that feels helpful or right in the situation. Please only continue once you have this event in mind. Please describe what you see as if it were happening to you right now but your adult self is with you and can intervene if you want her to. Please write in the first person (e.g. you might write "I'm in the change room, I'm trying on a pair of blue jeans ...") unless you are referring to the adult you (e.g. if your name was Sarah you might write "Adult/older Sarah said ..."). Please try to be descriptive and include as many details as you can, e.g. where you are, what you are doing, who you are with, how you are feeling, and what you are telling yourself. Please also describe if your adult self intervenes or does anything in the situation. Write down what your adult self said or did.

Source: Pennesi & Wade (2018) Reproduced courtesy of John Wiley and Sons.

9.2.4 Use of surveys to address mind-reading

If mind-reading about body image is identified as a problem, this is the aspect of body image that can usually be addressed most easily first in this phase. The rationale for this scheduling is that the surveys used are unlikely to interfere with any other aspect of treatment (unlike the behavioural experiments and exposure that are outlined in the next two sections – 9.2.5 and 9.2.6).

Surveys are used to determine whether the patient is correct in their assumption that other people have negative thoughts about their appearance, and that this belief cannot be challenged by evidence (e.g. "I know that everyone thinks I'm fat – they would just never tell me" or "They say that I look good compared to others, but I know that they are just trying to stop me worrying, and that they think I look ugly"). To address this form of belief, we use a technique adapted from CBT for social anxiety – the survey.

In working with body image, the survey usually consists of asking the individual to bring in a photo that they feel represents a key issue in their body image (e.g. size, disproportionate parts, unattractive aspects), then asking the patient to identify key questions that others should be asked. Then, those questions are taken to the relevant people (a group who the patient assumes will hold those views about them), to find out whether their views agree with or clash with what the patient believes they will say about her or him. We then use the feedback to review the patient's beliefs. Figure 9.1 details those steps.

Some clinicians find it worrying to implement a survey of this sort, fearing 'What if the patient is right, and everyone does think that they look fat/looked better when they were underweight, etc.' Our experience to date is that this does not happen. Occasionally, one person will be negative about the patient's appearance, but even then, this is an exception and can be addressed as such with the patient. The rationale for this assumption that the patient will be incorrect is as with other cognitions that we tested in Phase 2 – patients with eating disorders have extreme beliefs, which are highly unlikely to be supported by evidence. The safety behaviour (in this case – never ask other people what they are really thinking) means that the negative beliefs are maintained and accentuated, rather than reduced.

So, we use a survey when the patient uses such mind-reading, to address their beliefs about others' views of their appearance. We use a simple Socratic approach – assuming that the patient might be right before seeking evidence to challenge that belief – so that the patient does not feel that their viewpoint is being discounted. That approach is maintained throughout. For example, when the patient's beliefs are not supported in the first experiment, we do not argue

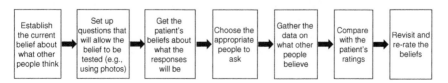

Figure 9.1 Steps in developing a body image survey.

that they were wrong. Rather, we stress that we believe that they could still be right, and that their beliefs were only not supported because of some issue in the survey, e.g.:

CLINICIAN: Well, I know that this is not the outcome that you expected, but that might just be because we picked the wrong photo/asked the wrong people/ asked the wrong questions. So how could we repeat the survey, but with a better chance of showing that you are right? Maybe we need to ask different people or use a different photo?

We use three types of survey, according to the belief being tested.

In a *simple survey*, we ask the person to bring in a photo of themselves and ask them to base their predictions of what others will say based in that photo alone. As much as possible, we make those predictions dimensional, so that the patient's extreme beliefs can be demonstrated as strongly as possible. Table 9.5 outlines such a survey.

As long as the principles above are held to, the clinician and patient can change the methodology in any way that seems suitable. For example, rather than using percentages to make predictions, body outlines (e.g. Thompson & Gray, 1995) can also be used to gain feedback regarding overall body size perception. We ask the patient to identify which body outline they feel best reflects their size (as seen in the survey photo). We then ask them to rate where they think others will rate them on the scale and the subsequent survey findings are discussed in the context of body size perception/misperception. This approach can be used alongside the techniques described in Section 9.2.2. As in the example in Table 9.5, using a very open question (e.g. "What are the first three things that you notice about the woman in this photograph?") redirects the patient away from their very narrow weight/shape focus, enabling them to grasp a bigger picture of other's thoughts, including the realisation that others see positive points about them that the patient does not see in themselves.

We use surveys with patients regardless of their body mass index, as the patient's prediction about others' beliefs is always worse than the reality of those views. However, if an overweight or obese patient is reluctant to start by considering others' views of their size, it is often useful to use surveys that address other valued aspects (e.g. the patient's belief about how others see them as "kind/ unkind" or "happy/miserable").

It is worthy of note that, unlike Cooper et al. (2004), we are happy to use our colleagues to complete such surveys. This is because we find that if a patient is going to reject the first iteration of a survey (as many do), they will do it regardless of whoever has completed it. That means that more important potential sources of opinion (e.g. family, friends) are still available for later iterations.

Following the first session, we gather survey responses (on paper, showing the photo, the questions and answers) from team members. In the next session, we bring the paper copies. We do not look at them first but bring them in as a bundle

Table 9.5 Establishing a simple survey

CLINICIAN: Your big concern is that other people see your body in a very negative way. I asked you to bring in a photo that we could ask people to comment on, to see if you are right about how they see your body. What have you brought in?

PATIENT: I have a photo that my sister took last month and sent me. I was at a cousin's wedding, and I spent the whole time thinking that people would be thinking that I was far too fat to be there – that I was an embarrassment to my cousin and my family.

CLINICIAN: What did you think that they would base that on? What parts of your body or your appearance?

PATIENT: Well, my backside obviously looks huge, and they would have seen my double chin. The worst bit is that the dress is so tight.

CLINICIAN: So let's write down some questions that you could have asked to find out if you were right or wrong. How about "Does this woman look like she should be at a wedding, given her appearance?" – that would be a yes/no answer. A better one might be: "On a one to ten scale, where one is very slim and ten is very fat, how would you rate the woman in this photo?" – so we compare what you think people will rate you as with what they do rate about you. Another one might be to ask people to say what they notice about you – something like "What are the first three things that you notice about the woman in this photograph?". Would those make sense?

PATIENT: That sounds so embarrassing – I know how negative the answers would be. But yes, it makes sense.

CLINICIAN: OK, I have written down those questions, based on this photo. So, what do you think people will say when we ask them? And let's make sure that we put some numbers on those predictions, of course.

PATIENT: Well, nearly everyone will say that I should not have been at a wedding – say 90%. On the thin-fat scale, I think I will get rated as an 8 out of 10. Definitely no-one will go below a 7, and more are likely to go up to a 10. And what will they notice first – everyone will say that the dress is too tight, so 100%. Ninety per cent will say that my backside is too big. And two thirds will say that I have a double chin.

CLINICIAN: I have written all those down, so that we can check whether you are right. So who could we ask, in this first survey?

PATIENT: Definitely no-one who I know.

CLINICIAN: OK – here is a suggestion. How about if I try it with colleagues here in the clinic, as a first go. Then we can review that next time, when you know the outcomes?

PATIENT: Well – we can try it, but I know what they will say.

---

of sheets to go through with the patient jointly, so that there is no risk that we will be tempted to screen out any potentially negative responses. Thus, the patient gets a real view of how they are seen and is not disappointed at a later point. It can be useful to keep a numerical tally of survey responses as you go along, in order to directly and immediately compare results with the patient's predictions, highlighting the size of the discrepancy. Table 9.6 demonstrates this next stage.

We repeat this process once or twice, as necessary, until the patient comes to realise that their perspective on others' beliefs is inaccurate. This can take a few weeks, but more than one survey can be run at a time, if needed. We usually find that only one or two surveys are needed, if done properly and rigorously,

Table 9.6 Reviewing the outcome of a simple survey

CLINICIAN: I have your predictions from last time, so shall we see if you were right? You started by saying that 90% of people would say that you should not have been at the wedding. However, no-one said that about you. Second, you thought that people would rate you as an eight on that thin-fat scale – and no-one would go below a seven. Actually, the mean rating was 4.5, and nobody went above a six. Nearly everyone was between three and five. Finally, you thought that most people would notice your tight dress, that they would say that you had a double chin, and that they would say that you had a large bottom. I'm not really sure that we need to worry about the specific numbers here, as nobody spotted any of those things that you thought they would be focusing on. So, what do you conclude from that?

PATIENT: Well, it's a bit of a relief, but that cannot be right. I think it's because we asked clinicians, and they are all going to be nice people, who would know what to say to stop me being upset.

CLINICIAN: You know, you might be right. So, if we can't trust people here at the clinic, who would we have to ask, so that we can see if you are right or not?

PATIENT: Well, I am not sure that I could ask my family yet, but maybe I could ask friends to get people to do it? Some people who don't know me?

CLINICIAN: Let's try that, then. Then you can be more certain that the opinions are real ones. We can use exactly the same survey, so that the results are comparable.

---

because the patient learns to implement the method if they want to do more surveys. Patients are often ingenious in setting up their own surveys, and we have had patients who have posted their survey onto social media. Even on that potentially risky platform, we have not had patients reporting that they were correct in their assumptions.

Less often, the patient suggests that it was not the people who completed the survey who were wrongly selected, but that they believe that the questions were not the right ones, or that the photos were the wrong ones to use. In that case, we return to that stance of: "You might be right, you might not. Let's try it and see". Then we try with different questions or photos, accordingly. If the patient prefers, a short video can be made using a mobile phone to give a 360-degree view.

It is also worth noting that the BMI of the patient makes no difference, as patients who are overweight or obese also benefit from this technique, whether we are asking questions about weight or other aspects of the person. For example:

CLINICIAN: Well, it is clear that you spend a lot of time worrying what other people think about you because you are overweight, because you think that that is the only thing that anyone would notice about you. Is that right?

PATIENT: Yes. There is no way that anybody could look at me without thinking how fat I am. They wouldn't notice anything else.

CLINICIAN: Well, we could find out if you are right or not. It sounds like you believe that everyone would describe you in terms of being overweight or fat. Absolutely everyone?

PATIENT: Well, at least nine out of ten people would. Maybe a couple would say something neutral or nice too, just to be polite.

CLINICIAN: That definitely sounds like a survey in the making. You think that about 90% of people would look at your photo and say that you are overweight or fat, while only 20% would say something that was nice or neutral. Is that right?

PATIENT: At least 90%, and maybe a bit below 20%. One or two out of ten.

CLINICIAN: OK – let's find out if you are right about what they think ... but we could take it further. Do you think that your weight is the *first* thing that they will comment on? For example, if we asked those people to say three things that they notice about you, how many of those people would make your weight the first think that they notice, how many would say that they notice it but not put it first, and how many would say that they had not noticed it at all?

PATIENT: At least 70% of them would notice it first. Maybe 20% would spot it later. Only 10% would not have it there at all.

CLINICIAN: That gives us a second prediction. Let's write that down, and we can see whether you are right or not.

As stated earlier, there are two other types of survey format. In an *intrapersonal survey*, we use this method to address beliefs about how the patient looks under different conditions. For example:

"Other people will think that I look so much worse than I did last year, before I put on all this weight" is a common concern among patients who have, for example, moved from an anorexic weight to a normal weight.

Alternatively, patients might say that they can only dress in particular ways, or they will be seen more negatively. In such cases, we ask patients to predict what people will say about them in each of the photos during the survey, e.g.:

PATIENT: They will say that I looked OK in that photo – say a 5 out of 10 for thinfat – but that I am gross in this current photo – 9 out of 10.

Again, we test these beliefs by asking relevant people to rate their answers to the questions that we generate and reviewing them with the patient to identify how their beliefs about what others think about the patient's body are incorrect.

The third approach is the *interpersonal survey*. Here, we use similar techniques to the intrapersonal survey, in order to address patients' beliefs about how others see them in comparison with other people. For example, the questions asked might be about 'Which of the people in this photo is more attractive?' or 'Using that 1–10 scale, would you rate these three people in terms of thinness/fatness?'. Again, the predictions made by the patient are that others will rate them far more negatively than they rate the others in the photo, and this is a prediction that we have never found to be supported by the outcome when other people are asked those questions.

9.2.5 Use of behavioural experiments to address body comparison and checking

Where body checking or body comparison are identified as maintenance mechanisms in negative body image, we address them using behavioural experiments. The key is to identify the beliefs that maintain the checking or comparison behaviour in the short term, so that they can be challenged directly. Because the experiments for testing the impact of checking and comparison usually address overlapping beliefs, we would rarely address both of these behaviours at the same time. Where both are present, we prioritise according to which is the most powerful maintaining behaviour, given both clinical discussion and the ED-15. Fortunately, the behavioural experiments for each are relatively short in duration, so they can both be addressed in this part of CBT-T, if necessary.

9.2.5.1 Body comparison

In the case of body comparison, the underlying belief to be addressed is that comparing one's appearance with that of other people is effective as a means of feeling better about one's body. As indicated earlier, that belief is highly unlikely to be supported regularly, given the tendency to make upward comparisons and the individual's own body image distortion. However, it will occasionally be supported when the patient finds a person whose appearance is less positive than their own, and this intermittent reinforcement keeps the person using body comparison, even though the behaviour results in substantial worsening of body image.

Therefore, considering the structure of behavioural experiments (Figure 7.1), the beliefs that we need to test are along the lines of:

> "Comparing my body with other people's makes me feel better about my own body and makes me feel calmer". (Initially rated 95% certain.)

versus

> "Comparing my body with other people's might occasionally make me feel better about my body for a short time, but then I end up feeling worse than before about my body and very anxious". (Initially rated 20% certain.)

Again, using that diagram, we plan a behaviour that will test the beliefs, and set a time frame for the experiment. In order to make the experiment as effective as possible in a relatively short time, we aim for substantial testing, usually over the course of a week, e.g.:

CLINICIAN: So, we have your strong belief, which is that if you compare your body with other people's it makes you feel better about yourself, but if you don't then you will feel worse about your body. And we have the alternative, which is that comparing will make you feel far worse, which you're not convinced by at all. What I would like you to do over the coming week is to test those two beliefs out, by asking you to compare yourself as often as you possibly can over the next three days, recording how you feel about your body and yourself at the end of the day. Then I want you to avoid comparison as much as possible for the next three days, and rate how you feel about your body and yourself at the end of the day. If you are right, then you should feel much better over the first part of the week, and much worse over the second part of the week. If the other belief is right, then you will feel better in the second part of the week because of not comparing yourself. Does that make sense?

PATIENT: Yes. Will that be long enough?

CLINICIAN: Well, we will have to see. We can always try it for longer if you are not sure which belief was right after a week.

At the next session, the outcome of this experiment is usually relatively dramatic. It almost always follows one of two patterns, e.g.:

CLINICIAN: So how did the comparison experiment go? We have your two beliefs written out here, and how strongly you rated them. What was the outcome of testing them as we planned?

PATIENT: OK, I get it. I thought that I was going to feel much better for the first part of the week, when I was comparing. But actually it was the other way round – completely.

CLINICIAN: So what has that done to your beliefs and how you rate them?

PATIENT: Pretty much reversed. I reckon that if I had to do it again, I would say that it is 90% certain it will make me feel worse. But I don't have to, do I?

CLINICIAN: That is entirely up to you, though you sound like you have learned something here that might make comparing yourself less appealling.

Or:

PATIENT: That was really horrible. I compared myself for about a day and a half, and realised that I felt so awful that I just stopped. I never realised before that comparing myself was so bad for me. Sorry that I didn't do all the homework, but I think I learned a good lesson. Comparing is something that makes me feel worse about my body – not better.

As with all of these body image techniques, the results of such experiments include reductions in body comparison itself (as indicated on the ED-15), as well as substantial reductions in body dissatisfaction and body size overestimation. In this case, the key learning experience for the patient is that their belief about the positive value of body comparison was incorrect. While the rated strength of this belief declines substantially, it is not often necessary to repeat or extend the body comparison experiment, as long as the original behavioural change was designed to challenge the beliefs strongly (e.g. "Compare yourself with everyone, all the time", rather than "Compare yourself with three people this week"). Therefore, CBT-T clinicians and their supervisors should not be unduly cautious in how they deliver this experiment.

If the patient is finding it difficult to understand that body comparison can be a negative behaviour, it can be useful to explain to them that the comparison is always going to be biased against themselves, because those with eating disorders are likely to overestimate their own body size but not that of others, and because our cognitive biases influence who we compare ourselves with, e.g.:

CLINICIAN: A large part of why comparing your body with another person's is bad for your body image is that thing that we talked about earlier – you overestimate your own body size, but not other people's. So if you compare yourself with someone who is just the same size as you or even bigger than you, you still think you are bigger than them. Also, you are more likely to pick what you think is the worst part of your body, and compare yourself with them.

PATIENT: So you mean that I can never win if I compare?

CLINICIAN: Not quite – you *will* win once in a while, but that makes things worse, in a rather nasty way. You look for anyone who you might look better than, and then maybe once in a while you find someone who you think fits that bill. That pattern of very occasional success – what we call 'intermittent reinforcement' – encourages you to look even harder for the next person who you look better than. So you end up comparing yourself with maybe 20 people, and you feel worse after 19 of them. So it is no surprise that you end up feeling worse about your body and yourself when you compare all the time.

One area where body comparison is particularly unhealthy is in the use of social media – where the individual is encouraged to compare themselves with others (e.g. via their ratings and 'likes') and to achieve the same levels of social esteem as other people. Again, upwards comparison, erroneous self-misperception, and attentional biases make it more likely that the patient will seek out and attend to comparison images that result in their feeling worse about themselves. Here, we ask patients to consider ways in which these influences of social media might be reduced. For example, we use the behavioural experiment structure above to test whether body comparison via social media has a positive or a negative outcome in the longer term. Social media are an important part of many people's lives, so the question is not *whether* people use it, but *how* best they can use this tool in a way that does not lead them into a 'no-win' comparison game. On occasion, patients might decide that certain sites are unhelpful and make an informed choice to stop following those media that have an unhealthy impact on their body esteem (e.g. where images are highly selected or clearly altered/airbrushed).

9.2.5.2 Body checking

These behaviour experiments are very similar to those used to address body comparison. In this case, the underlying belief to be addressed is that checking one's body is effective as a means of feeling better about one's body (e.g. stopping weight going out of control or shape changing). Such checking (e.g. using weighing scales many times per day; pinching body parts every few minutes) is associated with the belief that checking is effective at controlling weight, etc. However, we suggest that the patient consider the possibility that checking is not controlling weight, but is being used in an (ineffective) effort to control anxiety about weight and shape. That distinction provides us with two possible outcomes of body checking, which we can compare via behavioural experimentation.

As with body comparison, we use the structure of behavioural experiments in Figure 7.1 to test the existing, pathological belief against a more adaptive belief, e.g.:

"If I check myself in the mirror, it makes me feel better about my appearance and more confident". (Initially rated 100% certain.)

versus

"Checking in the mirror makes me feel less worried for a couple of minutes, but then I have to check again, and I end up feeling more worried about my appearance and not daring to go out". (Initially rated 10% certain.)

Then, as in Figure 7.1, we plan a behavioural experiment that compares those beliefs. As per that diagram, we plan a behaviour that will test the beliefs, and set a time frame for the experiment. Again, in order to make the experiment as effective as possible in a relatively short time, we aim for substantial testing, usually over the course of a week, e.g.:

CLINICIAN: What I want you to do over the coming week is to see which of those beliefs is right. So, to test that, how about if you try this – for three days, weigh yourself every time you can, and rate how it makes you feel immediately afterwards, and then at the end of the day rate how you feel about your body overall. Also, keep a note of how often you go out when you planned to. Then for the next three days, I want you not to weigh yourself at all – put the scales away or get a family member or friend to look after them. And rate how you feel about your body and record how often you went out, at the end of the day.

When we return to this topic the following week, we normally get a similar pattern of outcomes to those that we found for the comparison experiment, e.g.:

CLINICIAN: So how did your body checking experiment go? Did you do the weighing/not weighing? And what have you learned?

PATIENT: I did the whole thing. When I weighed myself lots, I realised that I sometimes felt better straight away, but by the end of the day I felt lousy about my body and I just hid away from people. But when I didn't check, I was worried at first, but I was much less bothered as the day went by, and I ended up going out to the shops once and for a drink with friends another day. I think that alternative belief was right – weighing myself lots makes me feel worse about my body and fatter. I would never have believed that.

However, body checking can involve a range of behaviours (e.g. using mirrors, scales, clothes) and can be relatively idiosyncratic (e.g. pressing a particular patch of skin to see if it wobbles), so the experiments need to be tailored to the individual. This can mean that we need to do one or more body checking experiments, e.g.:

CLINICIAN: So what could you do next about this?

PATIENT: Well, I think that I should maybe try doing another one of those checking experiments and see if I can work out whether checking myself in the mirror is good or bad for me. I am not so sure it is good now, but I think I should find out.

Of course, we aim to teach the patient the principles and the methods of behavioural experiments. Consequently, we often find that patients initiate further experiments for themselves, to address specific patterns of checking. Again, remember that these experiments can only be carried out in parallel with other experiments (e.g. changes in food intake; body comparison) if the planned outcomes do not overlap.

Again, the potential role of social media needs to be considered when understanding the possible negative effects of body checking. Many such media provide potential reinforcement about one's body via the system of ratings, messages, number of viewings/reads, and number of 'likes'. That possibility of positive reinforcement results in the individual checking very frequently, such that the likelihood of a positive event is low at any one time. Thus (as with social comparison), positive reinforcement is intermittent, while the level of negative outcomes is high. So, the patient checks social media obsessively and feels worse about their body. As before, we ask patients to consider ways in which these influences of social media might be reduced, using behavioural experiments to test whether body checking on social media results in better or worse body image over time.

9.2.6 Use of exposure to address body avoidance

Avoidance (e.g. not looking at one's body in mirrors; dressing to conceal one's body) maintains negative body image by ensuring that the existing negative body concept and percept are never challenged by reality. This pattern of avoidance means that the patient reduces their anxiety in the short term but becomes more anxious at any risk of experiencing what their body looks like (e.g. not being able to walk past shop windows).

We address this avoidance pattern using exposure with response prevention. Again, as detailed in Sections 4.13.1 and 5.1.2, we use an inhibitory learning approach to exposure, as it is faster and more effective than other approaches. As a reminder, the principles of an inhibitory learning approach are:

- Expose the patient to the maximum tolerable level of anxiety, including unpredictability.
- Focus on changes in anxiety between sessions, rather than prioritising reduction during the session (such reduction commonly occurs during the session, but is not necessary).
- Exposure should be carried out in as many settings as possible, to ensure generalisability of learning.

We also need to cope with our own concerns about being seen as a 'nasty' therapist because we are pushing our patients to experience their anxiety in order to overcome it. A consequence of this is that we need to avoid any inclination to use anxiety-reducing strategies (e.g. relaxation, mindfulness, ending early), as these will impair the effectiveness of the exposure work for reducing body image disturbance.

Most body image exposure takes place in the form of mirror exposure, using a full length mirror, and is based on flooding (full strength exposure from the beginning). It is possible to use more graded exposure for body image work in some circumstances (e.g. going out in more revealing clothing each time; going out more), but this is rarely necessary in CBT-T.

Exposure work can begin around Session 7 or 8, assuming that the patient experiences body avoidance (as discussed in session or shown in the ED-15). It is another relatively rapidly effective method, requiring most of one session, followed by homework practice, and a shorter period of time over the following session or two. As the main work with the clinician takes most of one session, it needs to be explained during the previous session, e.g.:

- Session 7 – explain the reason for and the process of exposure therapy for body image. This is usually relatively straightforward, as the patient has already undertaken exposure work in Phase 1.
- Session 8 – undertake mirror exposure for most of the session (noting initial anxiety and anxiety across the session).

- Between session homework – practice mirror exposure and any other body exposure work in multiple settings (e.g. changing rooms in clothing shops; uncovering mirrors at home).
- Session 9 – repeat the mirror exposure for part of the session (again, noting initial anxiety and anxiety across the session), stopping when the patient states that their anxiety is very low or that they are bored. This usually takes 10–20 minutes, including time to discuss the reasons that the patient now has less body image concerns or need to avoid. Review the results of this exposure work.
- Between-session homework – practice mirror exposure and any other body exposure work in multiple settings.

9.2.6.1 Preparation

Preparing the patient for exposure work (Session 7, in the example above) requires explaining to the patient that their body image remains a key target, and that you want to help them get back to a normal pattern of body acceptance. To do this, you need them to overcome their anxiety about their appearance, by using the same method that they used to overcome their fear that their weight would increase out of control in Phase 1. You then outline what will follow next week.

9.2.6.2 Core exposure work

The core exposure work (Session 8, in the example above) requires the patient to be dressed in clothes that are relatively fitted to their body, standing in front of a full-length mirror, and focusing on their reflection for 30–45 minutes. Every five minutes, we ask the patient to rate their current anxiety. That anxiety does not have to decline during the session, though it commonly does. Remember that we do not need to extend the session for the anxiety to come down, as that is not necessary for exposure to be effective (e.g. Craske et al., 2014; Reilly et al., 2017).

Evidence shows that this approach is effective regardless of BMI. However, the exposure during this session is more likely to be effective if it is relatively 'pure' (with little guidance or risk of distraction). However, it is possible to use guided exposure, where we ask the patient to describe what they see in the mirror, to be sure that they are focusing on their reflection rather than looking away. When we do use guidance, we ask the patient to use non-emotional, non-judgemental terms to describe their appearance, starting with their head, working their way down to their feet, and then describing other aspects of their bodies coming back up again. If the patient struggles to describe certain areas of their body, we can prompt with alternative less critical words (e.g. stomach viewed as 'soft' or 'rounded', rather than 'fat'), or ask the patient to describe the function of a body part (e.g. 'important for digestion'). We repeat this cycle until 30 or 40 minutes have passed. Stopping earlier in that time band is only done because of the patient's rated anxiety falling in the session.

9.2.6.3 Homework

Following the core session, we ask the patient to repeat that experience at home and elsewhere. We ask them to spend 30–40 minutes examining their reflection at least 3–4 times a week in a range of settings, stressing that more examinations in more places will be maximally effective, and with little or no clothing where appropriate. We also ask them to monitor their anxiety levels, as in the session.

9.2.6.4 Review session

In the following session, we routinely ask the patient to repeat the exposure work. However, we usually find that anxiety falls quickly, so the exposure is short-lived (if not, we ask the patient to do more homework exercises as before). However, our main aim in this session is to ensure that the patient understands how body avoidance was functioning to reduce anxiety in the short term, but worsening anxiety and negative body image in the long term. We encourage the patient to consider how they have arranged their life around this avoidance, and to plan changes (often with family members), such as having full-length mirrors on display at home, changing their wardrobe, planning holidays in hot places, etc.

As with surveys and behavioural experiments for body image disturbance, it is important to monitor changes in body image (e.g. in clinical discussion and on the ED-15) during exposure work. However, according to the case, it can also be important to consider improvements in self-esteem, anxiety, and more.

9.2.6.5 Responding to clinician anxiety about using mirror exposure

Earlier, we pointed out that body image exposure can seem like a scary prospect for both the patient and the clinician. It is important that the supervisor and clinician address the clinician's anxiety, in order to avoid worsening the patient's fear of exposure work. However, our experience is that once clinicians have delivered mirror exposure on one or two occasions and seen the benefits for the patient, they are usually far more eager to deliver it for future patients. For example, one supervisee reported back after her first use of mirror exposure with a patient:

CLINICIAN: Well, I did it. I felt really worried that the patient was going to be upset and that would never end. They did cry for the first 20 minutes but by the end of the session, the patient was so much better about her body. I know that because she told me she was so much less anxious about being in front of the mirror, but also because she agreed to do it again every evening at home and she suggested doing it twice a day at weekends. Now I want to do mirror exposure with *all* my patients.

SUPERVISOR: That is a great bit of learning for you – how our patients can learn if we are firm about trying these methods. But remember, you should only use mirror exposure if the patient has a problem with body avoidance. So target the technique on those who need it – not *all* your patients.

While encouragement from supervisors is valuable for the clinician in this learning phase, it is just as valuable to consider the changes that the patient can make towards a normal life when we help them to overcome body avoidance. Examples that we have observed are parents who could take their children swimming for the first time, adults who were able to take a holiday to hot places with their partners, people who could dress fashionably as they wished, and more. This technique is one that can result in real gains in terms of quality of life.

9.2.7 Homework tasks relating to body image

Homework is a key element of body image work, as outlined above. Thus, depending on the nature of the maintaining factor, one should stress the vital nature of that homework, to ensure that the patient ends therapy with a substantially reduced risk of relapse (Keel et al., 2005). If the target is to reduce the use of comparison or checking behaviours, then behavioural experimentation is planned in the session but executed outside of the clinic setting. The same is true of the use of surveys to reduce 'mind-reading'. In contrast, exposure to reduce body avoidance is a combination of in-session work and practice in homework, as is the imagery rescripting.

Summary: Overview of body image work in Phase 4

- Body image should be monitored throughout CBT-T, to determine whether it should be a target for specific intervention in the latter part of therapy.
- Where there are body image issues later in therapy, they should be addressed to improve recovery and reduce risk of relapse.
- Psychoeducation and body size estimation correction can be a useful start to this element of body image work.
- Different CBT-T techniques are used, according to the maintaining behaviours that the patient engages in:
  - Surveys are used to address 'mind-reading'.
  - Behavioural experiments are used where the individual uses body comparison or body checking.
  - Exposure is used where the individual avoids their own body.
  - Imagery rescripting of unpleasant past body experiences can be used where these memories continue to impact on interpretations and emotional response.
- Those techniques can be used in parallel, if their outcomes do not overlap. However, surveys normally precede behavioural experiments, and exposure is commonly the last of the three to be implemented.
- Homework is very important to ensure the optimum outcome for the patient. It should be set according to the individual patient's needs, given the nature of their cognitions and maintaining behaviours.

Chapter 10

Phase 5 – Relapse prevention

By the end of therapy, we hope to see the patient having reached a healthy point, where cognitions, emotions, and behaviours are stable and there is no diagnosable eating disorder. However, it is important that the patient maintains this change, and learns that it is something that they must work to ensure. Therefore, relapse prevention is a key element of CBT-T (rather than being an optional extra, to be done only if there happens to be time).

Relapse prevention usually takes place over Sessions 9–10, although it can be delivered earlier if the patient has made rapid progress through the other phases. It is a core element of CBT-T, as it addresses maintenance and development of the skills learned over the previous phases. We use it to set the patient up for how to use the follow-up period (Chapter 11) and beyond, based on therapy to this point.

This phase commonly overlaps with the last part of body image work in Phase 4. For example, it would be reasonable to use the first part of Session 9 to undertake some mirror exposure work (Section 9.2.4.4), then to begin the relapse prevention process in the latter part of that session (e.g. developing a therapy blueprint).

10.1 Themes in Phase 5

Three themes are addressed in this phase, as shown in Table 10.1.

Table 10.1 Themes during Phase 5

- Review progress to date:
  - o Attribution of change to the patient.
- Develop a plan to maintain progress:
  - o Use of the therapy blueprint.
  - o Planning for the follow-up sessions.
- Identify any residual comorbidity and plan for how to address it:
  - o Use of self-help approaches.
  - o Referral for therapy for other problems, if necessary.

10.1.1 Reviewing progress and attributing success to the patient

Our aim is that the patient should attribute their success to themselves, rather than to the clinician. Thus, we return to the stance that we addressed in Section 2.10 – it is a core principle of CBT-T that the patient is responsible for change, and that our job as clinicians is to coach the patient, teaching them the skills that they need to achieve that change. Here in Phase 5, we review how well they have done in taking on that role as their own therapist and stress the benefits that they have experienced as a result of their own learning and efforts.

10.1.2 Development of a plan to maintain progress

Here, we use a core CBT technique for maintaining progress in this way – the therapy blueprint. We also agree a strategy for ensuring that the blueprint is used effectively, in the form of self-monitoring and correcting any problems that arise. This blueprint becomes the basis for planning for the follow-up period, when we ask patients to have self-directed therapy sessions, using the blueprint.

10.1.3 Identify and begin to address any residual comorbidity

While CBT-T and CBT-ED each have substantial effects on comorbid psychological disorders (Table 1.6), we stressed in Section 2.8 that not all comorbidity can be dealt with in any version of CBT for eating disorders (though an effective treatment such as CBT-ED or CBT-T might make it easier to identify and target any such problems). Therefore, it is important to review whether any further therapy will be needed for other disorders. We start by considering the viability of self-help approaches, as this seems to be valued by the patients who we have worked with. Then, in the relatively rare cases where this remains necessary, we consider a referral for treatment of other problems. However, in such cases, we usually agree with the patient that any such referral should be made after the follow-up period, to give the patient the opportunity to see whether their improved functioning following CBT-T has the additional benefit of teaching them to resolve other problems.

10.2 Specific tasks in this phase

As well as maintaining any tasks from other stages (risk management, diaries, weighing, food intake, behavioural experiments, body image work), there are key tasks that facilitate the best possible end of therapy.

10.2.1 Reviewing what worked in therapy, and what did not

We go back over the course of CBT-T, and list (with the patient) what they have done over the past weeks. This includes looking at what the patient has done well, and how it was difficult but they managed it, often despite what they originally believed. It also includes looking at what did not go so well, usually adopting a stance of: "So what we can see is that when you made the changes that we agreed, it was tough, but you felt the benefits pretty quickly: when you didn't make the changes, things stayed tough, but you didn't get the benefits. Fortunately, you then made the changes, and you got those benefits – just later than it might have been".

Of course, our goal here is to overcome the learned helplessness ("I cannot make anything better") that the patient has developed following years of ineffective efforts or wishes to be different. This is done both by showing the patient that change is possible (thus developing a sense of agency) and by attributing that change to the patient rather than to the therapist or to coincidence. We stress that the patient can learn from what worked, but that they can learn just as much by being open about what did *not* work. For example, if the patient hoped that changing their eating for a week only would be enough but learned that they returned to bingeing, then it can be useful to point out that lesson, and how the patient recovered their binge-free status by going back to eating to the plan.

Table 10.2 shows an example of this approach to focusing on enhancing the patient's sense of agency and reducing the sense of helplessness that they had learned over several years of experiencing her eating disorder.

Table 10.2 Reviewing the process and outcome of therapy with the patient

---

CLINICIAN: Before we plan the next steps, I would like to quickly review your therapy so far. The first stage was when you agreed to face your fears and to be weighed. How does that seem to you now?

PATIENT: I can't really believe that I had spent so long not knowing my weight, and being so scared of it. It seemed so easy as soon as I did it the first time – I'm just glad that you were so firm about that. It feels like a different person who was so scared.

CLINICIAN: Well, I think that you should remember that it was you who decided to get on the scales. Nothing to do with me – you could just as easily have refused, and left therapy in Session 1. After that, you started eating differently – first of all, just coping with the anxiety until it faded, then testing out your beliefs about what food would do to you. How was that part of therapy?

PATIENT: That first part was really awful. I was so sure that eating meals would make me gain weight until I ballooned out. It took a lot of terrified days before I got to the point where eating seemed natural. And even more before I really believed that eating carbs would not make me binge or put on huge amounts of weight.

CLINICIAN: And yet you did both. You held onto your anxiety, and you learned that you can eat normally because you stopped all your old eating behaviours. What helped you to learn those things?

PATIENT: Sometimes it was that early psychoeducation material that you gave me, and realising that it applied to me – that told me that I am normal, and that I did what I did for very understandable reasons. The energy graph just showed me so simply – I thought I was being good by not eating, but my body needed the food. So that was why my weight didn't rocket up in therapy. And I could even understand why I binged a few weeks ago – I had missed a meal and a snack.

CLINICIAN: The best thing about this – you took all that on board, and learned what you needed to do to get better and to stay better. You even learned from that slip. And you did all that without any help.

PATIENT: I'm not sure about that – you helped me lots.

CLINICIAN: Not really – I could only teach you what might work if you tried it. You had to do all the work, and to find out what works for you as an individual. You were the therapist, because that is the only way that it could have worked so well. The same applies to the body image work you have been doing, I suspect.

PATIENT: Now that really has been scary. I have learned so much just by stopping myself from doing all that comparing and avoiding. And now that I think about it, that survey worked much better when I changed it to be more relevant to me, making it my friends who did the ratings rather than people here in the clinic.

10.2.2 Developing a therapy blueprint with the patient

The therapy blueprint is a document that we start to develop with the patient in Session 9, ask the patient to elaborate for homework, and then complete with the patient in Session 10. As with any blueprint for a building or structure, etc., the aim is to allow the patient to summarise the therapy, understand that therapy so that they can address any problems that might arise, or even repeat the therapy in the same way if necessary. Our goal is to teach the patient to identify any potential problems for the future, to maintain progress, and to troubleshoot if any unexpected problem emerges. The headers used in the blueprint are presented in Table 10.3.

It will be clear that the earlier theme continues – focusing on the patient's sense of agency. By using the 'what did I do' and 'what will I do' frameworks, we stress that the patient is the one who has made the changes so far and has responsibility for making changes into the future. In discussion, we also stress that we have no doubt that they are able to maintain their progress and make future changes.

In Session 9, we present the patient with a copy of this template (see Appendix 9 for a blank copy). We review progress (Section 10.2.1), and ask the patient to consider how they might complete the blueprint, using the headers provided. We do this so that we can troubleshoot if there are any problems in understanding that might prevent the patient from completing the homework, e.g.:

PATIENT: I think I can do most of it, but I am not sure about that one about "the signs and symptoms of a setback"?
CLINICIAN: Well, what about thinking about the things that made you feel like bingeing before? Or about the signs that your eating had gone wrong?
PATIENT: So it might be something like when I am really bored? Or when I skip breakfast to go for a run?
CLINICIAN: That sounds like a good start to me. There might be more, so think about it for homework, and let's see what you have got by next time.

While reviewing and expanding the therapy blueprint for homework, we suggest that patients should get their family and friends involved if appropriate. We stress

Table 10.3 Headers used in the therapy blueprint

- What were my problems when I was first referred?
- What did I do to change?
- What changes do I still want to make, and how will I achieve them?
- What might lead to a setback in the future?
- What will be the signs and symptoms of a setback that I can identify?
- How will I overcome the setback?
- What will I do if that doesn't work?

that these people might be able to make useful points about risks and what might be effective. Collaborating at this time is also more likely to make the patient and their loved ones collaborate over the course of the self-directed therapy sessions during the follow-up period (see Section 10.2.3).

In Session 10, we review how well the patient has done in developing this tool. We find that we rarely have to suggest fundamental changes, as the patient has normally presented a good blueprint. Any amendments are likely to be small details (e.g. *Clinician*: I notice that you have talked about bingeing as being a sign that you might need to reactivate some of your skills, but you haven't mentioned vomiting. Shall we see if there is anything that you need to add, in case that becomes an issue?). It can be reinforcing to contribute any observations of the patient's personal strengths or qualities during treatment which contributed to their success, such as their determination, commitment, or ability to take risks despite their anxiety.

At the end of the process of preparing the therapy blueprint, we aim that the patient should have a helpful tool for maintenance or their treatment gains and for future problem-solving. This blueprint is then used as the basis for planning the follow-up period, where it is used to guide self-directed therapy sessions. Table 10.4 gives an example of a completed therapy blueprint.

10.2.3 Planning self-directed therapy sessions during the follow-up period

The aim of these sessions is to ensure that the patient maintains practice and develops problem-solving skills following the ten sessions of CBT-T, to reduce the risk of relapse. We first introduce the importance of these sessions early in treatment, when explaining the structure of CBT-T. Occasionally, we also remind the patient of them later in therapy, if the topic of 'there is not enough time to do all this' comes up. However, the topic of these self-directed therapy sessions is brought up further during this relapse prevention stage, e.g.:

CLINICIAN: OK – we are on our ninth session out of ten. I want you to build up this thing called a therapy blueprint, so that you have something to remind you of what you have achieved, and what you still need to do to build on that. That blueprint is going to be your plan for how to keep the focus on life without your eating disorder. So what I am going to ask you to do is to use the blueprint to guide yourself in your therapy sessions after we stop meeting, during the follow-up period. After all, remember that you are the one who has been making all the changes – therapy doesn't have to stop just because you are not coming here. So, let's plan those home therapy sessions for after here.

Table 10.4 Example of a completed therapy blueprint

This list is for use every week in my self-directed therapy sessions, to remind myself how far I have come, what I still want to do, and how to get back on track if I have a slip.

- **What were my problems when I was first referred?**
  - o I saw myself as a fat lump, and I was terrified of gaining weight.
  - o I starved myself to try to keep in control, but I ended up bingeing and gaining even more weight.
  - o I vomited and took laxatives, and ended up fainting and wrecking my teeth.
  - o I self-harmed when I was really upset.
  - o I became obsessed with what I looked like, and how fat other people would think I was, so I never went out.
- **What did I do to change?**
  - o I read and discussed the evidence.
  - o I ate healthily – meals, not avoiding carbs or fat – and I learned how wrong my beliefs had been. My weight did not change at all.
  - o I learned to delay self-harm or vomiting when I was upset, and that I could cope without them.
  - o I spent time learning that checking my reflection actually makes me feel worse about my body.
  - o I found out that I am terrible at guessing what other people think about me.
- **What changes do I still want to make, and how will I achieve them?**
  - o Eating in public more, and trying out different foods.
  - o Being able to go on holiday somewhere hot, where there is a beach or a pool.
  - o Getting into a relationship where I am loved for who I am – not what I look like.
- **What might lead to a setback in the future?**
  - o When I get into a new relationship, if I worry that I do not look good enough for them.
  - o Spending too much time on social media.
  - o Talking about diets with my friends.
  - o Going on a crash diet if I put on weight at Christmas.
- **What will be the signs and symptoms of a setback that I can identify?**
  - o If I start skipping meals or snacks.
  - o If I start worrying that others will be judging me because of what I eat.
  - o If I go back to spending lots of time checking myself in the mirror.
- **How will I overcome the setback?**
  - o Keep having weekly reviews to see whether I am slipping back like this – using this blueprint to remind myself how horrible life was back then.
  - o Talk to my sister if I am worried that I am getting obsessed with my body and eating again.
- **What will I do if that doesn't work?**
  - o I will look back at what we did during therapy and try to do some of that from the start – eating regularly, not checking myself.
  - o I will ask for another referral for treatment, and make sure that I work at it from the start rather than being hesitant, because I know it works best if I get going straight away.

In Session 10, when we have laid out the therapy blueprint and revised it, we recommend that the patient plans their home sessions in the following way:

- Plan weekly self-directed therapy sessions, e.g.:
  CLINICIAN: I want you to plan for weekly therapy sessions for yourself over the whole of the follow-up period. Something like 30 minutes every week to go over your blueprint. Put them into your diary now, for the next three months, and if you have to change a slot then change it – don't just cancel it. Otherwise, you might end up slipping and never getting around to looking after yourself.
- Get support from friends and family, e.g.:
  CLINICIAN: It is always helpful if you can get someone else to help out with these sessions at home – either talking them through your progress and explaining it or getting their opinion or telling them about it afterwards. Is there a friend or family member who could help you in that way? Someone who you find supportive when you open up to them? If so, could you talk to them about it over the coming week, and book your home therapy sessions with them. Of course, they don't have to be at home, as you might want to have them somewhere that works for both of you, or do it over the phone or online if that works better with the person you have in mind.
- Use the blueprint to ensure that progress is maintained and developed, e.g.:
  CLINICIAN: So, at your home therapy sessions, I want you to use the blueprint as a structure. Keep reminding yourself of where you started and how you got out of it. But most importantly, I want you to check up on your progress – are you still on track to achieve your remaining goals? Are you seeing anything that might be a problem, like missing meals or worrying about your shape? If so, what are you going to do to overcome that? And remember, if you realise that your blueprint is missing something, you can always update it.
- Consider potential future changes, if necessary, e.g.:
  CLINICIAN: Let's think about 'in case' problem-solving. For example, at some point you are going to want to stop using the diaries. That is fine, as it has to happen sometime. However, if you can see problems re-emerging, then maybe getting the diaries out again would be a good idea. Any other examples that you can think of?
  PATIENT: There is one good one to think about, I suppose. If I do end up going on holiday to Greece with my sister, as we keep promising ourselves, I am going to have to eat the Greek food there or my sister will nag me for being so cautious. So maybe I should do another behavioural experiment and see if I do put on weight because of eating different foods. I think I know the answer, but if I do it soon, I can be happier about the holiday.
  CLINICIAN: That is a good example, and we need to consider how you are going to do that behavioural experiment or others – not for the detail, but how you are going to weigh yourself. If you feel ready to get the scales back from your parents, then that is good. But if you see yourself starting to check your weight more than once a week, you might need to give them back again, and just weigh yourself at your sister's to find out if your weight is or isn't changing.

PATIENT: Good point. I will give that a try. I had better update my blue-print, though.

CLINICIAN: It probably won't be the last time that you update it, but that is no bad thing, because it just means that you are learning and developing so that you are ready for anything that life throws at you.

PATIENT: What about my food diaries and getting weighed? Do I need to keep doing them?

CLINICIAN: What do you think? It really depends whether you think you need to. I suspect that you have learned not to worry about your weight going out of control, so this might be a good time to give up on both and seeing whether your weight is stable at the follow-up.

PATIENT: I see that. What I might do is to keep some blank food diaries, and if I slip or see it coming, then I will go back to using them to get back on top of my eating.

CLINICIAN: That sounds like a good plan. You can tell me about how it went when we meet at follow-up.

10.2.4 Consider any future help that might help the patient to develop further

We rarely need to consider further treatment for the eating disorder at this stage, as that decision is more commonly reached around Session 4. However, some of our patients have other issues that they want to address, and which are likely to help them to avoid relapse or to develop a better quality of life.

In a small number of cases, we consider a referral for therapy for a comorbid problem that did not change over the course of CBT-T. This might involve anxiety or depression (e.g. PTSD) or substance misuse. However, we normally suggest to the patient that they should delay taking up any such therapy until the three-month follow-up period has ended, to find out whether their greater skills in challenging their behaviour, thoughts, and emotions have enabled them to reduce this comorbidity without further therapy. We find that a number of patients benefit in this way, as they use their skills to problem-solve.

In other cases, we suggest that patients should use self-help materials to enhance their skills in any relevant domain. We stress that the patient should give as much attention to these self-help materials as they did to the CBT-T, as they now know that hard work in therapy can pay off. In Session 9, we identify any residual issues that we or the patient believe might benefit from further work and ask the patient to access the necessary resources. That might mean consulting websites that relate to eating disorders (e.g. Beat) or a wider range of disorders (e.g. CCI). Alternatively, we ask them to borrow or purchase a relevant CBT-based self-help book. Such books are usually one of the following:

- Self-esteem (Fennell, 2016).
- Anxiety (Kennerley, 2016).
- Social anxiety (Butler, 2016).

- Perfectionism (Shafran, Egan, & Wade, 2018).
- Core beliefs (Young & Klosko, 1993).

In Session 10, we review the initial reading that the patient has done and discuss how they might continue it over the three-month follow-up period, for consideration at those sessions. We also discuss whether anything has been learned that would suggest any changes to the therapy blueprint.

Box 10.1 Letter to the patient following completion of the 10 sessions of CBT-T (1)

I would like to congratulate you on completing treatment with *[Service]*. It takes a lot of courage and commitment to work through the full treatment program, so you can be proud of this achievement.

When you started treatment, you reported that you were bingeing anywhere between four to seven times a week. You were distressed at the thought of weighing yourself, engaging in driven exercise, and restricting your eating with the purpose of losing weight. You were concerned that if you ate more food it would lead to an increase in weight. The bingeing was leading to distressing consequences for you, primarily feeling depressed and not being able to leave your home or socialise with others.

Since starting treatment this year, you have succeeded in reducing the frequency of your bingeing to zero, such that you have not binged in the past month. Further, you have pushed yourself to leave home after a binge on a number of occasions and can now spend more time seeing friends, family, and engaging in the activities you enjoy. You have also managed to exercise greater self-kindness and self-compassion by increasing your eating and allowing yourself to eat 'fun' foods more frequently. Furthermore, you have observed that despite eating more, more regularly and incorporating 'fun' foods to your daily routine, you have maintained your weight for the 10-week period. You have also demonstrated to yourself that you are stronger than you think you are. Some examples of evidence for this were buying two weeks-worth of groceries, trusting yourself to be home alone without hurting yourself, and having the courage to speak to your parents about your mental health and plans for your future. You are placing less emphasis on how your weight and shape influences how you judge yourself. You have worked hard during the past 10 weeks to decrease the influence of the disordered eating in your life, and your efforts are paying off.

It is essential that you continue to work on and extend these gains that you've made. As we have discussed, bingeing has often been used as a coping mechanism to deal with difficult thoughts and emotions, so it is important for you to continue to practice your new coping strategies, and regularly reflect on the alternatives to the positive beliefs around eating using the summary card we developed in session as a reminder. I encourage you to regularly refer back to your treatment materials, such as your therapy blueprint, to remind yourself of the progress you have made with your eating, and your ongoing goals for recovery.

Over the coming weeks and months, you may experience occasional set-backs with your eating. It is important to know that this is very common, and it does not mean that you have failed, or that you are back to where you started before treatment. The best thing to do is use any such set-backs as a source of further insight, and as a reminder to go back to the skills and information you have learned during treatment. The therapy blueprint we developed together will be helpful to consult. If this does not help to resolve the problems, I encourage you to continue exploring your treatment options *[Details provided]*.

Again, I congratulate you on your hard work and successes during the treatment program, and wish you all the best for the coming months. We will review your eating together in a month.

Box 10.2 Letter to the patient following completion of the 10 sessions of CBT-T (2)

Now that you have completed treatment I thought it might be helpful to write with a summary of the therapy sessions we have had together. You first accessed treatment on *[date]* and have since attended 10 individual sessions of cognitive behavioural therapy.

When we met for your last treatment session on *[date]*, we were both pleased with the progress you have made – the frequency of your bingeing and vomiting has decreased significantly and you've been 'binge free' for five weeks now. This is a significant contrast to how things were at the start of treatment, when you were bingeing and vomiting daily. You also talked about feeling far more confident in your relationship with food and of being more appreciative of your body. This really shows the progress you have made, and how hard you have worked to use the material that we have covered and put your new skills into practise. At the start of treatment, we explored together the factors that maintain your eating disorder. We looked at your pattern of bingeing and you noticed that following a strict diet plan every day meant that you were restricting the range of foods you were allowing yourself to eat and avoiding certain foods. You were able to recognise that restricting your food intake during the day increased your vulnerability to bingeing. Given this, you spent the first few sessions normalising your meal plan. Specifically, you started following the six a day meal plan (three meals and three snacks). You noticed that although this was initially difficult due to your anxiety about gaining weight and bingeing, when you did eat regular and varied substantial meals during the day, your urges to binge lessened and you weight didn't increase uncontrollably as you had feared.

We also looked at foods which you felt safe eating and foods which you found more difficult to eat. We looked at why foods had become feared foods; most were feared because you were worried that if you ate them you would then binge and gain large amounts of weight. You tried eating bread and other foods that you'd avoided for years, and over time you learned that it was okay to eat a broader range of food. We also explored whether some of your binges were driven by emotions and we talked about other ways in which you can manage how you feel without turning to food, and you noticed that being more open with others often helps.

We spent some sessions focusing on your body image. We looked at the different habits you'd got into, such as body checking. You experimented with 'checking' and 'not checking' and from this you realised that constantly checking your body makes you feel worse about yourself. We also conducted a survey to find out whether your beliefs about what you thought others think of you were true or not. Again, you were surprised by the answers and you realised that others don't see you the way you think they do – they weren't negative or critical as you feared they would be. You also realised that others don't regard size or shape as being that important – the message seemed to be that when thinking about what they value in others, it is themes such as honesty, kindness, and humour that shine through. As we discussed, do keep building your body confidence by continuing to experiment with wearing different clothes and challenging your tendency to get into patterns of body avoidance.

In our last sessions we developed a relapse prevention plan together. You noted situations that might make a setback more likely and also listed all the strategies you can use to prevent or manage a setback. Setbacks can occur in recovery so I encourage you to continue using the skills you have learnt and look out for signs of the eating disorder re-emerging so you can address them early.

As we have reflected upon together throughout treatment, the progress you have made has all been down to your hard work and the changes that you have made – you have had the courage to face your anxieties and as a result have been able to move on significantly from your eating disorder. When we met for your last session we agreed that you have the skills you need to continue to build on your progress and to manage any 'slip-ups' if they occur in the future. We also thought it would be helpful for you to continue having 'home therapy' sessions where you would go over this material and check on your progress. You recognised the importance of keeping to three meals and three snacks a day but felt that you did not need to continue to do food diaries, which sounds like a sensible decision given the progress that you have made.

I would like to say how much I have enjoyed working with you over the last three months and I hope that you have found your treatment sessions beneficial. As we discussed, we will meet again on *[date and time]* for a one month follow-up to review your progress. If you cannot attend this appointment or need to rearrange, please contact do get in touch.

I hope things are going well, and I look forward to meeting with you again in a month.

10.2.5 Ending the final therapy session

We conclude Session 10 (or earlier, if the patient has progressed well) by emphasising how well we believe the patient has done. We repeat that we see the benefits as being attributable to the patient and encourage them to continue with their hard work. We stress that we always believed that the patient is a valuable person, who needed to learn to value themselves. We say that we will look forward to hearing how well they are progressing at the two follow-up sessions. However, we stress that if the patient is going to make a slip, it is better to do it before the first follow-up, so that they can come back and tell us how they understood the problem and (more importantly) how they solved it. Then, they are less likely to slip over the time between the first and the final follow-up.

We often provide an ending letter at the end of therapy (e.g. Box 10.1 and 10.2). Our letters at the end of follow-up are usually shorter and more practical.

**Summary: Overview of relapse prevention and
ending CBT-T sessions in Phase 5**

- This is a critical phase, as it serves to reinforce the patient's sense of agency and reduce their learned helplessness following years of having the eating disorder.
- We review progress, to remind the patient of how bad things were and how they made the key changes. This can be summarised in a letter after Session 10.
- We develop a plan to maintain that progress and to continue it (the therapy blueprint).
- We plan for the coming follow-up sessions, and develop 'self-directed therapy' plans for the patient to pursue.
- We identify any potential further therapy needs, usually addressing them via self-help methods but sometimes recommending further therapy for other disorders (after the follow-up period) .

Chapter 11

Follow-up as an active part of therapy

If they are offered at all, follow-up sessions in therapy commonly serve a relatively passive function – reviewing whether the changes achieved in therapy are maintained when therapy has ended. In CBT-T, we use the two follow-up sessions more actively, to extend the relapse prevention and problem-solving skills that were addressed in Phase 5. These follow-up sessions are conducted one month and then three months after Session 10. The evidence to date is that there is no reduction in remission and recovery rates by the end of the three-month follow-up, suggesting that this is an effective strategy.

Throughout this section, we borrow from Freeman and Dolan's (2001) very helpful expansion of the stages of change model. We introduce the patient to three key terms used in that model (Table 11.1).

Table 11.1 Three elements of the relapse process

- Prelapse
  In this stage, the patient who has recovered begins to question whether it is worthwhile to have changed and to put in the effort to staying healthy (e.g. eating regularly, and thinking about how 'things were easier' when engaging in the eating disorder behaviours (e.g. "Things weren't that bad, were they?"). At this stage, permissive cognitions are the problem, and can be addressed by: reminding the patient of how bad things really were in the past; and problem-solving to make healthier behaviours simpler to maintain.
- Lapse
  This stage is where the patient uses the problem behaviour for the first time (e.g. missing breakfast; vomiting), either due to inattention to what needed to be done or due to an active desire to be able to "do what I feel like". This behaviour is likely to recur (leading to relapse) unless the patient treats the lapse as being a key risk, requiring them to get back to what they learned in therapy.
- Relapse
  Here, the patient returns to the full pattern of their previous problem behaviours, and develops the maintaining pattern of cognitions and emotions.

11.1 Preparing the patient for the two follow-up sessions

In Session 10, we explain to the patient that we hope that the two follow-up sessions will go smoothly, with the patient simply reporting that all has gone well and that they continue to leave the eating disorder further and further behind them. However, we also state that we are aware that the patient might be afraid of slipping back into their eating disorder. Therefore, we distinguish the two follow-up sessions by stressing that if the patient is going to slip up in their thinking or behaviour, we would like that to occur between the end of the therapy and the first follow-up session, so that they can tell us what problem they experienced *and* how they solved it – stopping the prelapse becoming a lapse, or stopping the lapse becoming a relapse. Thus, we hope that the patient is better equipped to do well between the first and second follow-up, e.g.:

CLINICIAN: Your big worry is that you will have a prelapse leading to a lapse – giving yourself permission to skip a meal or to go back to using the scales. So, if that is going to happen, it would be good to get it out of the way over the next month, so that you can come back and tell me how you spotted those permissive thoughts or that first slip in your behaviour, <u>and</u> how you overcame them so that you did not slip into relapsing. Maybe going back to your diaries to remind yourself about structuring your eating, or challenging your thoughts about whether getting on the scales will be a good thing, with no costs. That way, you learn better how to cope over the longer gap before your final follow-up, and we can hope that you do not have any further slips. Then, you will be ready to finish treatment here completely, because you will be solving any problems all on your own and just getting on with life.

We also encourage the client to stretch themselves over the next month, by further tackling new steps in ongoing tasks. This can involve weighing themselves weekly at home when they have only been weighed in sessions over the previous ten weeks, adding in further challenge foods, doing further body exposure work, or working at adding in new social eating opportunities. It may also involve long-term tasks that can weaken old core beliefs and strengthen alternative core beliefs, such as continued recording of daily achievements and examples of standing up to the eating disorder, or continued work on imagery rescripting.

11.2 First follow-up: One month post-treatment

The length of both follow-up sessions varies according to what emerges, as can be seen in the lack of a detailed checklist in the protocol document (Appendix 1). Very often, they are comparatively short sessions, and we stress that this is because the patient is doing so well. In the first follow-up session, we attend to the topics in Table 11.2.

Table 11.2 Topics addressed in the first follow-up session

- Review progress.
  - Assess eating patterns and cognitions, mood, and quality of life.
  - Compare scores on the different measures with those from the beginning and end of treatment, so that the patient is aware of how far they have come.
  - Discuss ways of addressing any remaining eating, weight, and shape cognitions.
- Review use of any self-help material.
  - Consider what the patient has learned and review any misconceptions or misapplication of those techniques.
  - Assess the benefits so far of working on these other issues.
- Reinforce positive gains.
  - Stress the patient's role in making change happen.
  - Ensure that the patient maintains a healthy pattern of attribution to the self.
- Address any signs of slippage and how the patient solved the problems.
  - Permissive cognitions (prelapse).
  - Unhealthy eating behaviours (lapse).
  - If there has been any slippage (with or without a solution), stress the benefit of it having happened now, rather than between the two follow-up sessions.
- Revisit skills and problem-solve with the patient for any issue that they were not able to resolve over the past month.
- Plan for the coming two months, reviewing what the patient has coming up over that period, and considering what problems they have been more or less successful in addressing over the past month.

11.3 Second follow-up: Three months post-treatment

In the second follow-up session, we attend to some of the same topics as in the first follow-up but consider the potential need for any treatment for other disorders. As stated in Chapter 10, this is not a frequent outcome, but it is important to consider where further help is necessary. Typically, the therapist may have done some homework of their own, identifying relevant services and making contact with services to ensure that the patient is eligible. This information is then discussed with the patient and summarised in a discharge letter to the patient and their general practitioner/family physician. It is then up to the patient and general practitioner to pursue a referral to these services, and the discharge letter should be able to be used to form an adequate 'hand-over' to any other service, so that they can understand the aspects of therapy that were most effective for the patient, and the issues thought to be important to continue working on. Table 11.3 outlines the content of this session, and shows its similarities and differences to the previous follow-up session.

In keeping with the principles of CBT-T (Chapter 2), we also aim to say goodbye in a way that emphasises that we are pleased that we are unlikely to see the patient again, because they are unlikely to need further help with their eating disorder. We often provide an ending letter at the end of the follow-up period to stress how far the patient has come, though this is usually less detailed than the

Table 11.3 Topics addressed in the second follow-up session

- Review progress.
  - o Assess eating patterns and cognitions, mood, and quality of life.
  - o Compare scores on the different measures with those from the beginning and end of treatment, so that the patient is aware of how far they have come.
  - o Discuss ways of addressing any remaining eating, weight, and shape cognitions.
- Review use of self-help material.
  - o Assess the benefits so far of working on these other issues.
- Reinforce positive gains.
  - o Stress the patient's role in making change happen.
  - o Ensure that the patient maintains a healthy pattern of attribution to the self.
- Address any signs of slippage and how the patient solved the problems.
  - o Permissive cognitions (prelapse).
  - o Unhealthy eating behaviours (lapse).
- Revisit skills and problem-solve with the patient for any issue that they were not able to resolve over the past two months.
- Make a referral for treatment of other issues if needed.
  - o Ensure that there is a clear, identified issue at this stage that merits further treatment.
  - o Not simply responding to a desire on the part of the patient or the clinician to keep the patient 'in therapy' without clear purpose and focus.
- Say goodbye, stressing that you are happy for the patient to be leaving therapy with you so that they can get on with life, rather than living with their eating disorder.

letter used at the end of the 10 sessions (Tables 10.5 and 10.6), as there is less need to reinforce progress at this point, as it is more established by now.

11.4 When patients fear that they will relapse

Phase 5 addressed strategies for relapse prevention in detail. However, some patients are understandably concerned that they will experience a return of their symptoms without the ongoing support of the therapist. If it is present, this anxiety should be discussed with the patient. We explain the process in terms of the need to identify prelapses to reduce the risk of lapse, and to respond to lapses in order to avoid relapses (see Table 11.1), e.g.:

PATIENT: I know that I haven't binged or vomited for about two months, and that I am much happier with my body, but I have had a couple of weeks of not bingeing occasionally in the past, so won't it all just come back again?

CLINICIAN: In the past, when you had those gaps, did you feel good about your body? Were you able to eat so normally without panicking about it?

PATIENT: Oh no – there was nothing easy about not bingeing back then – it did not feel so natural not to binge. It was really hard work, and I felt so worried about what was happening to my body that I was always just keeping it together.

CLINICIAN: So let's think about what the real risks would be. If you worry about your eating or your weight in the future, what would be the way that you could end up turning that into a binge and feeling worse about yourself?

PATIENT: I know the answer to that one – I would go on a bit of a diet to feel less worried, and end up starving myself into another binge. I have been there quite a few times.

CLINICIAN: And then?

PATIENT: Then I worry about the effects of the binge, so I skip meals, and end up bingeing and feeling worse about my body, and I am back to bulimia and back in this chair talking to you.

CLINICIAN: And is a chair in a therapy room where you want to be?

PATIENT: Oh no. Once should be enough. I have a life to get on with.

CLINICIAN: So let's think about how you can avoid getting back into that cycle.

Consequently, it is important that the patient should be able to identify when there is any risk of relapse, so that those skills can be implemented at as early a stage as possible. Therefore, we find it useful to remind patients how to identify the risk of relapse both during Phase 5 and at each follow-up session. This approach reduces the sense of vulnerability and uncertainty that could otherwise be enhancing the patient's anxiety as the treatment comes to an end.

We outline the three stages in the relapse process for the patient (Table 11.1), stressing that it is better to deal with the prelapse than to have a lapse, and better to deal with a lapse than to experience a relapse. We also ask the patient to develop a 'flash card' of risky thoughts and behaviours, to review as part of their self-directed therapy sessions and at other times, e.g.:

CLINICIAN: So let's talk about what sort of things you might think that would mean that you were at risk of lapsing. What thoughts do you think would be risky for you?

PATIENT: Hmm. Well, the strongest one is probably "This is just hard work or boring – surely I don't have to carry on with things like eating regularly". But another one is "I wonder what I weigh – I could just have a peek". Those are the sort of thoughts that I know make it more likely that I will change how I am coping.

CLINICIAN: OK – so that is your *prelapse* pattern of thinking. Let's call those 'permissive thoughts' – they make you think that it is OK to let go of your progress and slip back to some of the old behaviours. They are always tempting, but the long-term outcome is horribly obvious. So let's put them onto a flash card – one that you can add to as you identify more thoughts that might have that effect. And if you have those thoughts and give in to them, what happens next?

PATIENT: That is when I start missing meals or jumping on the scales to check my weight.

CLINICIAN: So you move from that 'prelapse' in your thinking to starting to use your eating-disordered behaviours again. That first time that you use a behaviour, like skipping a meal or getting on the scales 'just to check', you have a *lapse*. Let's have a column on your flash card for lapse behaviours like that ... so what happens after the first time that you do those behaviours?

PATIENT: Well, normally, I would do it more and more, until I just ended back with the eating disorder.

CLINICIAN: That is the *relapse* stage. And it all started with a thought, then a behaviour, then more of the old behaviours, and feeling horrible about yourself. So, remembering your energy graphs and how you realised that your evening binge started when you skipped breakfast hours earlier ... what do you think I am going to say you need to do about your risk of relapse?

PATIENT: Well, it seems pretty obvious when you put it like that. If I don't let the behaviour happen the first time, I don't have to be a bulimic again. Don't lapse – don't relapse.

CLINICIAN: Good so far. But how do you avoid the lapse in the first place?

PATIENT: I suppose I need to change how I react to the prelapse – those permissive thoughts. When I see them, I need to challenge them. Look at the pros and cons of giving in to them, and ignore that urge to get on the scales or skip a meal.

CLINICIAN: A good plan – so let's add to that flashcard, so that when you see the prelapse or lapse signs, you are already set up to challenge them, and reduce your risk of relapsing. We can put in some of those pros and cons now, so that you are equipped to challenge the signs when you see them.

We use this formulation when discussing how to manage the follow-up period with the patient. In particular, we use it to discuss how we hope that the first follow-up session will differ from the second.

11.5 Considering the bigger picture

The end of therapy with an individual patient can be treated as the point where we move on to the next person who needs help. However, we have more learning to do. We can step back and consider the bigger picture in order to develop our skills as clinicians, and learn how an evidence-based form of CBT for eating disorders can be applied effectively in routine clinical practice, whether in a specialist service or not.

Part of that bigger picture is available through supervision, and this will be addressed in the next chapter. However, we also encourage clinicians and clinics who are adopting CBT-T to audit the impact of doing so. Such audit should initially focus on patient outcomes for the individual clinician and service. However, in IAPT, Clark et al. (2018) have shown that comparing outcomes between clinicians is beneficial for patients overall, as clinicians learn from each other and improve their own practice and effectiveness. We would advocate such transparency in the monitoring and sharing of CBT-T outcomes.

As well as considering clinical outcomes in terms of the change in eating disorder symptoms and comorbidity, it is useful to benchmark other clinical issues to determine the impact of introducing CBT-T. One of these is the applicability and sustainability of the therapy – how many patients are or are not suitable for CBT-T, how many accept the offer of CBT-T, and how many drop out or have to be taken out of the therapy? Perhaps most importantly, what does the introduction of a shorter therapy do to the patients' time on the waiting list and the risk of loss to treatment when therapy becomes available to the individual? These are questions that depend on the clinical setting, but can be answered relatively easily and usefully if considered locally.

Summary: Overview of follow-up sessions

- Follow-up sessions should be treated as an active part of relapse prevention, rather than a passive monitoring 'catch-up' opportunity.
- We ask the patient to use the period leading up to the first follow-up session to troubleshoot any problems (and to come back to report on how they got back on track if there were such problems).
- Throughout follow-up, we monitor progress on self-directed therapy sessions and on any self-help work that the patient is undertaking for other problems.
- In the second follow-up session, we consider whether any onward referral for other problems is needed.
- The end of contact with the patient should be used to reflect on what has gone well and on what could be improved for future patients.

Chapter 12

Patients' experiences of CBT-T, and the roles of clinicians and supervisors

In Chapter 1, we presented the evidence supporting CBT-T as an effective therapy for adults with non-underweight eating disorders. Following that, we have presented the protocol for CBT-T, including the principles that one needs to consider and the methods that one needs to employ in each phase. However, we have one further issue to consider – what is the experience of this therapy for the different individuals concerned? Even the most effective therapy needs to be acceptable to patients, therapists have to be willing to deliver it, and supervisors need to be happy to ensure that it is delivered appropriately and effectively. Given that CBT-T involves a substantial level of behavioural change and a firm approach by the clinician, it is important to understand how patients experience CBT-T. However, it is also important to consider what the clinician and supervisor need to bring to therapy, given that clinicians' and supervisors' own characteristics can influence how well we adhere to relatively behavioural therapy protocols (Waller & Turner, 2016).

12.1 Patients' experiences of CBT-T

Some patients have spontaneously written to us or blogged about their experiences of CBT-T. Examples are given in Table 12.1.

Such testimonials might be biased, as they come from patients who have had positive experiences. Therefore, we have asked patients for feedback on their experience of CBT-T, aiming to collect the perspectives of patients who did not complete the therapy as well as those who did. To be sure that we have a relatively comprehensive view of the experiences of those patients, we conducted a qualitative evaluation (Hoskins et al., 2019).

Themes were extracted until no new themes were being identified. Those themes are detailed below, with example quotes for each theme and sub-theme. We summarise the main themes that emerge from patients' experience of CBT-T, illustrated by quotes from those patients in order to demonstrate their positive experiences (which tell us what is working well) as well as negative ones (which tell us how we might improve CBT-T for the patient, if that can be done without compromising the effective elements of therapy).

Table 12.1 Examples of patient correspondence about the experience of CBT-T

Email from patient a year after completing CBT-T

"I'm emailing because I never thanked you enough for how much you helped me overcome my eating disorder last year. I am so grateful. I honestly don't think I would be where I am today without going through treatment with you. I am doing really well and it feels amazing! I am still referring back to things we went through in treatment and following the eating structure we established but I rarely spend more than 5 minutes thinking about food now. I've become a lot more 'present' in life and have changed jobs, I'm working in ******** and coaching ********. I've decided on ****** for uni, and I've recently started ******** which I love. Overall, I am so much happier and more optimistic about life and I know how to deal with and move on from the 'bad days'. I can't express how thankful I am!"

Email from a patient immediately after the first follow-up appointment

"Thank you so much for everything, I am so proud of myself and how far I have come, of course it couldn't have been done without you the psychologist with all of the knowledge behind this specific disorder. It feels like I have lifted such a heavy weight off my shoulders, I can now go back to living life like I was before the eating disorder took its hold on me. I couldn't be happier! I left the session today feeling the best I have ever felt in years (I almost cried tears of happiness). I look forward to the final appointment".

Email from a patient some time after the end of CBT-T and the follow-up appointments

"I'm emailing because I wanted to say thank you. I don't think I could convey with words how much I appreciate what you did for me. Since CBT finished I have remained in remission, significantly improved my own perception of myself, and am much happier overall. The empathy, compassion, and respect you employed is something I hope to be able to do with my own patients one day. Thank you for helping me regain my life back, thank you for helping me realise that I still had some sense of worth outside of my illness. I will be giving a talk ********. I wouldn't currently be doing this if it wasn't for you. Instead I would be sitting in the audience, internally imploding, and feeling very alone. Just me and my negative thoughts. Now I will be standing up and discussing the importance of awareness, of tackling stigmas, and sharing my own experience. So I email you today because you were so fundamental to my experience in mental health, it was overwhelmingly positive in retrospect and I want express how thankful I am. I hope … you continue to help clients like you did for me. You helped me gain my life back and for that I will be forever grateful".

(All correspondence has been edited to ensure anonymity.)

The first theme was the *therapeutic relationship*, where patients described therapists in the following ways:

"[Therapist] was very approachable, understanding and helpful".

"She was really good at re-affirming her advice at every meeting until it sunk in".

"I never felt judged or like I was wasting the clinic's time and she was really understanding and encouraging".

They stressed feeling comfortable in therapy and not feeling alone:

> "Regular sessions helped me to develop a relationship and trust to my therapist".

> "All the therapists were fantastic and I felt comfortable talking to them".

> "Just having someone to talk to about my issues helped me so much as I didn't feel I could speak to family and friends".

It was particularly noteworthy that patients valued the firm empathy stance, to the point where one even stated that the CBT-T could have been firmer (the only critique on this topic):

> "She was firm about my eating plan which I needed but also kind and caring".

> "I was in a safe space where I could be honest. But she encouraged me to push myself and question my boundaries and worries head on".

> "Maybe could have been a bit firmer".

The second theme related to the *nature of CBT-T*, including issues such as timing, personalisation, the need for personal effort, and the structure of therapy. Patient experiences relating to personal effort and the structure of CBT-T were generally positive:

> "I had to go away and actually make the changes happen myself".

> "We agreed on goals and worked together to come up with something achievable and realistic".

> "[Therapist] always understood my reasons for feeling the way I did about certain situations and encouraged me to overcome them by carrying out experiments".

Whereas the experiences relating to the timing of therapy and personalisation were more mixed:

> "Some things I found more difficult and it took me longer to do hence we were pushed for time when it came to body image which is the area I struggled with the most".

> "Weekly sessions helped me break down week by week goals and allowed me to stay in touch with my therapist".

> "Ideas on how to achieve my goals which were specific to my life rather than general goals. Discussing my specific schedule and behaviours and how to best move forwards".

> "Felt it could be a bit more tailored to each person's needs".

The third theme related to CBT-T being seen as *challenging but beneficial*, as illustrated by the following quotes. These indicated how sticking with the tasks set had been worthwhile, as the patient found that their initial scepticism was not supported:

"Challenging but effective in reducing my behaviours".

"The first couple of weeks were HARD because I needed to make immediate changes straightaway. But ultimately this was a good thing".

"The mirror thing was hard but it was worth doing".

"The start was hard getting the meal structure in and types of food I was afraid of. One week was hard when I gained weight but went back the next".

"At first, I struggled with having to be weighed each week but eventually it became routine and I became much more relaxed about the situation".

"I felt quite irritated and cross in the beginning, I felt I was being told to eat more which didn't help me but I did understand it was to establish a sensible eating pattern which worked in the end, probably all part of my healing process".

The fourth theme related to *ending therapy*. Patients focused particularly on the outcome of CBT-T and what came next:

"I found it extremely helpful. It made me think more about what I was doing and why in a common sense way. This allowed me to put the past behind me".

"Allowed me to move forward to an eating disorder-free life".

"CBT has actually changed my behaviour and thought process for the better".

"It showed me I could rise to the challenge and make progress".

"[Therapist] gave me tips on how to carry on with 'home-therapy' which allows me to carry on tackling this eating disorder confidently on my own".

The final theme was about the overall experience of CBT-T, where patients stressed comparison with previous therapies, as well as giving their own overall judgement of CBT-T. Here, the appraisal of CBT-T was strongly positive across all patients who responded:

"The only previous therapy I had was counselling and I didn't find dwelling on horrible past events helpful at all. CBT-T focused on the present and the future which gave me a much more positive outlook on the situation".

"I think it went better this time [compared to previous therapy]. I was eating regularly in less time and we got to the root of why my eating was not ideal".

"So different to before. Rather than looking at what I am doing wrong it was straight into doing things the right way".

"The previous therapy didn't focus on food diaries etc. but more on the possible root causes. I found [CBT] more helpful and with a better initial outcome".

"A wholly positive experience".

To summarise, patients' experiences of CBT-T to date have been broadly positive, in the same way as for other evidence-based therapies (Hoskins et al., 2019). None of these therapies are universally effective, and none are without any negative perceptions. However, CBT-T's perceived effectiveness and acceptability do not seem to suffer as a result of its shorter nature, and the firmness and level of challenge were regarded as positives of the therapy. We recommend that clinicians should be open with patients from the outset about all of these characteristics of CBT-T when explaining it, to enable them to make an informed choice about undertaking therapy. To assist in this, we include a brief patient guide to CBT-T (Appendix 4), which addresses such patient experiences, as well as details of the therapy.

12.2 The clinician's role in the delivery of CBT-T

The clinicians who have delivered CBT-T to date include qualified clinicians (from a range of professions), graduate psychology assistants, and doctoral students. They have differed in experience levels, with some having extensive experience of CBT-ED, some with experience of delivering CBT for other disorders, but more having no previous experience of delivering CBT or working with eating disorders at all.

Our experience has been that all of these diverse clinicians can and do get positive results with CBT-T. Most deliver the therapy well from the beginning, following the protocol appropriately and getting good results. However, some clinicians take time to engage in the best delivery of CBT-T, usually where their prior experience of delivering other therapies (including longer versions of CBT-ED) has not involved the degree of structure involved in this therapy or has had a different focus. This pattern appears to be similar to that seen in eating disorder clinicians more broadly, as the majority state that they do not normally adhere to a single model (e.g. Tobin et al., 2007). The other factor is the clinician's own level of trait anxiety, which is equally a problem in other treatments for eating disorders and in therapies for other disorders (e.g. Mulkens et al., 2018; Waller & Turner, 2016). For some such clinicians, whilst the change in approach initially felt unusual or uncomfortable, their confidence and belief in the delivery of CBT-T grew as they saw their patients progressing. We find uniformly that clinicians report that they are amazed at how well the firm empathy approach was accepted by patients and how well it worked.

Based on our experience when teaching and supervising clinicians to deliver CBT-T, we have a simple list of dos and don'ts that can guide them to be more effective (Table 12.2). Key elements are the monitoring of progress, focusing on

Table 12.2 Tips for clinicians: Enhancing CBT-T delivery

Do

- Use the protocol and checklist, in an appropriately patient-centred, flexible way.
- Use supervision to discuss case material.
- Monitor progress and outcomes, to demonstrate that the therapy is working.
- Talk to patients about the experience of CBT-T, particularly in the early and later stages.
- Share experiences with colleagues, to enhance problem-solving.
- Consider training in CBT-T, to supplement this manual (the therapy delivered in the evidence base outlined above was delivered by clinicians without a formal therapy qualification, but with 1–2 days of training and regular supervision).

Don't

- Bring in elements from other therapy models that we find appealing, when they do not fit with the CBT-T protocol (or with CBT-ED in general – NICE, 2017). Sometimes, these are therapeutic elements that work more or less well in other therapies, but which occupy time and effort that should be focused on the CBT-T protocol elements (e.g. prioritising the development of the working alliance). At other times, they are elements that are likely to hinder the CBT-T approach (e.g. the introduction of relaxation or mindfulness-based work to make anxiety more tolerable, thus impairing the effects of exposure).
- Let our own anxiety and intolerance of uncertainty influence our delivery of CBT-T. Clinician anxiety can reduce our willingness to be firm and to push for the necessary change, particularly in terms of exposure. Among other methods, clinicians themselves might need to undertake exposure themselves (e.g. to learn that their feared outcomes for their patients do not come true).
- Focus on any need to please the patient in the short term.
- Try to make the therapy more empathic by reducing how firmly it is delivered.

the core tasks of the protocol rather than extraneous therapeutic techniques, and a willingness to be firm about the tasks of therapy, rather than over-emphasising empathy.

12.3 Supervising clinicians in the delivery of CBT-T

Supervision is a very active, patient-centred approach in the delivery of CBT-T. Whereas most models of psychotherapy supervision rarely mention patient outcomes explicitly (Simpson-Southward et al., 2018), we stress that clinicians should always be aware of how their patients are progressing in such objective terms. Supervision should also match the pace of expected change in the patient, which is why we recommend weekly supervision. This does not prevent us from being interested in the clinician's experience of therapy and their professional and skills development, but it is important to prioritise the patient's progress and outcomes. Therefore, we ask the clinician to prepare a written agenda where patient progress, stuck points, or risk are prioritised, and where other issues are addressed later in the supervision meeting.

This supervision agenda is similar to the agenda set in the CBT-T protocol for most sessions. The clinician's agenda-setting needs to focus on ensuring that key material is addressed, with professional and experiential issues appearing later in the supervision session. There are other such parallels with the CBT-T protocol, due to the way that both the therapy and supervision are focused on skills development and implementation.

For example, it is also important that we address clinicians' own therapy-interfering behaviours. As noted above, the tendency of some clinicians to drift off-protocol and to respond to their own anxiety by not pushing for change is stronger when first delivering CBT-T. That is not to suggest that this drift is intentional, but it still reduces the patient's chances of recovery. Therefore, it is critical that we address such therapy-interfering behaviours by the clinician. We can think of the supervisory relationship as one that mirrors the therapeutic relationship between clinician and patient (Bordin, 1979) – it needs to involve collaborative agreement on goals and tasks, as well as the relational bond that supervisors and clinicians often focus on. Given the supervisor's need to teach clinicians how to enhance patient outcomes by applying the protocol and the fact that some clinicians take time to learn how to overcome their natural anxiety and to become appropriately firm, this means that the supervisor and clinician will not always be on the same page about how to deliver therapy. Consequently, as with the clinician-patient relationship, the supervisor-clinician relationship is not always going to be smooth. We normally address this with the supervisee from the beginning, stressing that the goal of both supervisor and clinician needs to be the best outcomes for our patients, and that we can accept if the supervisee is angry at us sometimes, as long as they learn.

Of course, this approach will be familiar from Chapter 2, where we stressed that it does not matter if the patient dislikes the clinician at times, as long as they improve. The supervisor-supervisee relationship is about change and the development of skills, as much as the clinician-patient relationship. In each case, firm empathy is a necessary principle for us to follow. Taking that principle one step further, a very rare outcome is that the supervisee fails to prepare for supervision adequately. For example, the clinician might not have asked the patient to undertake the actions recommended by the protocol (e.g. changing eating; keeping diaries). Alternatively, the clinician might not have prepared the necessary information, such as patient progress relative to the previous week. In such rare cases, we let the clinician know that supervision is going to be very limited on this occasion, due to having little that we can usefully discuss in the time available. If the problem in supervision continues, it is even possible to end the supervision session as soon as it has become clear that there is no useful way in which we can continue – a five-minute supervision.

However, there is one other issue to consider, where the clinician and patient might both be negatively affected by the supervisor's own cognitions and emotions. Supervisors in psychotherapy are not perfect. Two pieces of evidence in particular need to be considered. First, just as clinicians overrate their own abilities (e.g. Walfish et al., 2012), supervisors also overrate their supervisees' abilities (Denhaag et al., 2012). Second, while we have identified that anxious clinicians are poor at delivering some key CBT skills, it is also important to know that anxious supervisors are less demanding of both anxious patients and clinicians, setting different therapy directions and targets (Simpson-Southward et al., 2018). The combination of an anxious supervisor and anxious clinician does not bode well for the patient's chances of getting the best therapy that they could in CBT-T. Therefore, we recommend that supervisors of CBT-T should ensure that their supervision practice is reviewed regularly (supervision for the supervisor).

Finally, how should the supervisor determine whether the clinician is doing well, and how should we respond if they are not? We focus first on patient outcomes – is the clinician getting good clinical outcomes, as shown by changes in eating pathology, behaviours, and body image (and monitored across clinical caseload over extended periods to ensure that outcomes are not dropping)? If they are not, then we move our focus to adherence – is the clinician delivering the core techniques of CBT-T, while adhering to its principles (examined through monitoring the use of the checklist, listening to tapes of sessions, or observing the clinician delivering therapy)? If the clinician is not adherent, then we consider whether the therapist is competent to deliver CBT-T – do they

Table 12.3 Tips for supervisors: Enhancing CBT-T delivery

- It is important that clinicians present all cases, so supervision should be delivered on a one-to-one basis, whether the supervisor is a senior clinician or a peer.
- Group discussion of cases and team outcomes is good practice, as our supervisees can learn, understand the value of adhering to the protocol, and deliver better outcomes.
- Discuss every patient, every time.
- Start with anything that is life-threatening or therapy-interfering.
- Make it clear if the supervisee is underprepared.
  o Use a five-minute supervision session, if necessary to re-focus the clinician.
- Patient outcomes are the key index of how well the supervisee is doing.
- Other issues can be addressed as appropriate.
  o Training needs; experience of being a clinician; compared with previous supervision.
- Set tasks for the coming week to keep the clinician and patient on track.
- Do not let our own anxiety or uncertainty influence how we manage our supervisee.
- Focus on the patient getting the best deal – it does not matter whether the clinician likes the supervisor early on – that can come later.
- Consider the level at which the clinician is operating.
  o Always monitor progress with the supervisee (outcomes).
  o Monitor technique implementation (adherence).
  o Regularly review clinician's development – outcomes; confidence (competence).

know the principles and tasks of the therapy. If not, then we consider further training as a priority.

We would argue that these principles are not ones that should be limited to CBT-T, as many therapies would benefit from supervision that was structured and delivered in this way. Studies showing that supervision is effective in enhancing patient outcomes (rather than clinician satisfaction in isolation) tend to adhere to some of these principles (e.g. Öst et al., 2012). Table 12.3 provides tips for CBT-T supervisors.

Conclusions

In developing CBT-T, we wanted to provide an effective treatment for the great majority of adults with eating disorders, and one that would be widely accessible. CBT-T is a structured application of the effective parts of CBT for eating disorders combined with a firm empathy approach. The evidence that we have generated allows us to conclude that CBT-T can lead to life-changing experiences for our patients. We encourage the reader to implement this approach to treating eating disorders, seeing how it might be implemented by clinicians and services. We believe that this development will help more patients to recover and to do so more quickly, and that this faster outcome will allow clinicians and services to reduce waiting times so that more patients can be treated. The improvement in health and quality of life for sufferers and for their loved ones promises to be substantial.

We close with two comments from our patients, taken from the qualitative evaluation, above.

First:

> "I really appreciate all your time and effort and can't thank you enough for helping me".

We would like all clinicians to hear that more often, and CBT-T is a way of making that more likely.

Second:

> "I just wish it was available to more people".

This manual makes CBT-T available to many more people. Over to you.

CBT-T protocol (version 3)

CBT-T checklist

Patient name: _____

Date of birth: _____

Patient gender: Female / Male

ID Number: _____

Therapist name:_____

Date of first appointment:_____

<u>Diagnosis at start of treatment, and symptoms that lead to that diagnosis:</u>

<u>Comorbid conditions</u>

<u>History of treatment for eating disorder</u>

Symptom record (all behaviours per week)

Week	Weight (kg)	Objective binges	Vomiting	Laxatives used
1				
2				
3				
4				
5				
6				
7				
8				
9				
10				
FU1 (1 month)				
FU2 (3 months)				

© Copyright: Waller, Turner, Tatham, Mountford & Wade (2019).

Session 1: Agenda/Task checklist

- Introduce yourself to the patient, and ask a little about them (what they do, family, etc.).
- Patient to complete ED-15.
  - o Explain that this will be weekly, and you want them to do it every week just prior to the session (in the waiting room).
  - o Check that all items are completed.
- Acculturation to the therapy.
  - o Review past therapy experience.
  - o Identify the lack of evidence-based work (whatever the therapy was called).
  - o Explain the 'firm empathy' stance.
    - o There will be anxiety about change, but that is necessary.
  - o Patient acts as their own therapist: you are the coach.
  - o Brief and focused, four sessions in the first instance, extending to ten if the patient is making changes.
  - o No desire to waste the patient's time and make them think that they cannot succeed in therapy.
- Review current eating.
  - o Ask about the last 24 hours (especially if the patient is vague).
  - o Ask about the last episode of bingeing/purging.
- Explain the model (using diagrams where helpful).
  - o Focus on maintenance (here and now) rather than history of problem.
  - o Change in behaviours and biology/nutrition to improve emotions, cognitions, and behaviours (food as medicine rather than a threat).
  - o Vital to learn that the best predictor of weight is going to be what is eaten.
  - o Non-negotiables – staying safe; attendance on time; diaries and other homework; dieting for weight loss during treatment for bulimia nervosa; being weighed (be prepared to explain each).
- Outline the course of therapy
  - o Phase 1 (Sessions 1–4): Learning and changing eating (psychoeducation; exposure).
  - o Phase 2 (Sessions 3–6): Challenging beliefs about eating, food and weight (cognitive restructuring; behavioural experiments).
  - o Phase 3 (Sessions 5–7): Addressing emotional triggers (exposure; cognitive restructuring).
  - o Phase 4 (Sessions 5–9): Body image work (surveys; exposure).
  - o Phase 5 (Sessions 9–10): Relapse prevention (therapy blueprint).
- Determine core symptoms (and record them in the relevant slots).
  - o Get weight estimate and certainty rating, and record them.
  - o Weighing and taking height (done by clinician – not by self-report).
  - o Reported weekly frequency of objective binges, vomiting, laxative use, etc.).

- Provide relevant psychoeducation handouts for discussion in Session 2.
  o   Include healthy eating plan.
- Identify possible reasons for bulimic behaviours and weight change.
  o   Long gaps in intake (particularly carbohydrate gaps) leading to craving.
  o   Low carbohydrate intake resulting in unstable mood.
  o   Discuss how a sensation of fullness can be due to anxiety (locate stomach).
- Plan initial dietary change for homework, and predicted weight gain.
  o   Aim for structure before content.
  o   Stress importance of generating anxiety so that the patient can learn, but not run away.
- Agree next appointment.
- Set homework.
  o   Questionnaire pack 1 (EDE-Q, GAD-7, PHQ-9, WAI-SR).
  o   ED-15 (do while waiting for the next appointment).
  o   Read handouts.
  o   Get a folder to hold diaries.
  o   Standard food diary.
  o   Change intake according to need (including any need to gain weight).
      o   Structure – add breakfast; three meals; two or three snacks.
      o   Content – carbohydrate; calorie content into meals and snacks (rather than binges).
- End session – ask patient to rate confidence in this approach, and suitability for them

Session 1 record: DATE _____

Tick the items that you have addressed with the patient on the facing list as you progress.

Check that all items are ticked (or marked N/A if not applicable).

Symptoms			Frequency of behaviours		
Weight	_____	kg	Objective binges	_____	per week
Height	_____	m	Subjective binges	_____	per week
BMI	_____		Vomiting	_____	per week
Anticipated weight change	_____	kg	Laxatives (episodes)	_____	per week

Ways in which the patient would like to change using therapy

Problems with non-negotiables (e.g. weighing; urge to lose weight), and how they were addressed

Summary of problems identified in dietary intake that might trigger binges

Homework tasks set

Handouts provided: Starvation/Bingeing/Vomiting/Laxatives/Other: _____
Changes to eating planned

Patient's ratings
Anticipated impact of that eating change on weight over the next week(s)
Gain = _____ kg ; Loss = _____ kg; Confidence rating = _____ %
Patient's confidence in this approach (0–100%) _____ %
Patient's rating of the suitability of this approach for them (0–100%) _____ %

Date and time of next appointment _____

Session 2: Agenda/Task checklist

- Welcome back.
- Retrieve questionnaire pack and ED-15.
  - ○ Check that all items are completed.
- Review homework.
  - ○ All done?
- Address any life-threatening or therapy-interfering behaviours (e.g. self-harm; missed appointment; late arrival).
  - ○ Responsibility for solving these given to the patient, where appropriate.
- Ask patient about experience of Session 1 and any contrast with previous therapies.
- Patient agenda items and questions from last time?
  - ○ Give ten minutes to these, after the diaries and weighing.
- Review what the patient learned from the handouts.
  - ○ Any others needed? Give to patient.
- Review food diaries.
  - ○ If these have not been done, then weigh the patient and end the session.
  - ○ Identify changes from previous eating patterns.
  - ○ Identify and note core symptoms (teaching patient to mark bulimic behaviours, if not done).
- Congratulate patient on any positive changes in eating pattern and symptom reduction; problem solve any slippage.
- Add to chart of bulimic behaviours.
- Using the diary, identify one or more episodes of objective binge-eating where there is clear linkage to low/inappropriate food intake (if no binges took place, then look at high-risk situations).
  - ○ Work with the patient on identifying the risk factors, stressing the low food intake/carbohydrate gap.
  - ○ Acknowledge other possible reasons (e.g. mood, alcohol), but focusing on the starvation factor for now.
- Stress the likelihood that the patient will have taken in about 1200 kcal if they have binged, even if they vomited (and that laxatives will have done even less).
- Weighing process.
  1. Ask regarding believed change in weight from last time (and certainty rating).
  2. Remind the patient about weight fluctuations, so not yet sure about patterns.
  3. Weigh the patient.
  4. Chart the actual and anticipated weight change (copy for the patient).
  5. Review patient's beliefs relative to actual change, but stressing that it is too still too early to draw conclusions.
- Patient's agenda items.
- From the diary, start to identify the foods that the patient finds 'safe' and 'feared'.

- Plan next dietary change for homework, as per health eating plan.
  - o   Maintain/develop structure.
  - o   Shift towards better content if appropriate (especially planned carbohydrates).
  - o   Predict what these changes will do (likely weight gain, more binges, etc., and certainty ratings).
- Agree next appointment.
  - o   Stress that you will be reviewing for progress weekly.
- Set homework.
  - o   ED-15 (do while waiting for the next appointment).
  - o   Read any additional handouts.
  - o   Standard food diary.
  - o   Change intake according to need (including any need to gain weight).
  - o   Prepare a list of 'feared' and 'safe' foods.
- End session.

Session 2 record: DATE _____

Tick the items that you have addressed with the patient on the facing list as you progress.

Check that all items are ticked (or marked N/A if not applicable).

Symptoms		Frequency of behaviours	
Weight	_____ kg	Objective binges	_____ per week
BMI	_____	Subjective binges	_____ per week
		Vomiting	_____ per week
Anticipated weight change	_____ kg	Laxatives (episodes)	_____ per week

Problems with non-negotiables (e.g. homework; attendance), and how they were addressed

Summary of problems identified in dietary intake that trigger binges/urges to binge

Patient agenda items

Homework tasks set

Additional handouts provided

Changes to eating planned

Patient's ratings

Anticipated impact of that eating change on weight over the next week(s)

Gain = _____ kg ; Loss = _____ kg; Confidence rating = _____ %

Date and time of next appointment _____

Session 3: Agenda/Task checklist

- Retrieve ED-15.
  - o   Check that all items are completed.
- Review homework.
  - o   All done?
- Address any life-threatening or therapy-interfering behaviours (e.g. self-harm; missed appointment; late arrival).
  - o   Responsibility for solving these given to the patient, where appropriate.
- Ask patient about experience of Session 2.
- Patient agenda items and questions from last time?
  - o   Give ten minutes to these, after the diaries and weighing.
- Review food diaries.
  - o   If these have not been done, then weigh the patient and end the session.
  - o   Identify changes from previous eating patterns.
  - o   Identify and note core symptoms.
- Congratulate patient on any positive changes in eating pattern and symptom reduction; problem solve any slippage.
- Add to the chart of patient bulimic behaviours.
- Weighing process.
  1. Ask re believed change in weight from last time (and certainty rating).
  2. Remind the patient about weight fluctuations, so not yet sure about patterns.
  3. Weigh the patient.
  4. Chart the actual and anticipated weight change (copy for the patient).
  5. Review patient's beliefs relative to actual change, but stressing that it is too still too early to draw conclusions.
- Patient's agenda items.
- Using the diary, identify one or more episodes of objective binge-eating where there is clear linkage to low/inappropriate food intake (if no binges took place, then look at high-risk situations).
  - o   Work with the patient on identifying the risk factors, stressing the low food intake/carbohydrate gap.
  - o   Acknowledge other possible reasons (e.g. mood, alcohol), but focusing on the starvation factor for now.
- Review what the patient learned from the additional handouts (if applicable).
- Review the safe and feared foods.
  - o   Explore any evidence that the feared foods have been a problem in the past.
  - o   Instead, have they become 'binge foods' and hence feared?

- Plan next dietary change for homework.
    - Content and structure.
- Agree next appointment.
    - Stress that you will be reviewing for progress weekly.
    - Remind that next time is the big review point.
- Set homework.
    - ED-15 (do while waiting for the next appointment).
    - Standard food diary.
    - Change intake according to need (including any need to gain weight).
- End session.

Session 3 record: DATE _____

Tick the items that you have addressed with the patient on the facing list as you progress.
Check that all items are ticked (or marked N/A if not applicable).

Symptoms			Frequency of behaviours		
Weight	_____ kg		Objective binges	_____	per week
BMI	_____		Subjective binges	_____	per week
			Vomiting	_____	per week
Anticipated weight change	_____ kg		Laxatives (episodes)	_____	per week

Problems with non-negotiables (e.g. homework; attendance), and how they were addressed

Summary of problems identified in dietary intake that trigger binges/urges to binge

Patient agenda items

Homework tasks set
Changes to eating planned
Other

Patient's ratings
Anticipated impact of that eating change on weight over the next week(s)
Gain = _____ kg; Loss = _____ kg; Confidence rating = _____ %

Date and time of next appointment _____

Session 4: Agenda/Task checklist

- Retrieve ED-15.
  - o   Check that all items are completed.
- Review homework.
  - o   All done?.
- Address any life-threatening or therapy-interfering behaviours (e.g. self-harm; missed appointment; late arrival).
- Ask patient about experience of Session 3.
- Patient agenda items and questions from last time?
  - o   Give ten minutes to these, after the diaries and weighing.
- Review food diaries.
  - o   If these have not been done, then weigh the patient and end the session.
  - o   Identify changes from previous eating patterns.
  - o   Identify and note core symptoms.
- Congratulate patient on any positive changes in eating pattern and symptom reduction; problem solve any slippage.
- Add to the chart of patient bulimic behaviours.
- Weighing process.
  1. Ask re believed change in weight from last time (and certainty rating).
  2. Remind the patient that this is week 4, and that you will be looking at their average (median) weight over the period so far, as a baseline.
  3. Weigh the patient.
  4. Chart the actual and anticipated weight change (copy for the patient).
  5. Review patient's beliefs relative to actual change, but stressing that it is too still too early to draw conclusions.
- Ask regarding believed change in weight from last time (and certainty rating).
- Chart the actual and anticipated weight change (copy for the patient).
- Review patient's beliefs relative to actual change, but stressing that it is too still too early to draw conclusions.
- Review progress to date.
  - o   Use the behavioural and weight charts to stress benefits to date.
  - o   Congratulate on positive change in terms of dietary structure and content, bulimic behaviours, and challenging fears about weight gain.
  - o   Stress need to work on remaining symptoms.
  - o   If no change has been made, then offer to end now, and if the patient wants to continue then contract for only two more sessions unless there is progress over that time.
- Patient's agenda items.

- Using the diary, identify one or more episodes of objective binge-eating where there is clear linkage to low/inappropriate food intake (if no binges took place, then look at high-risk situations).
  - o   Work with the patient on identifying the risk factors, stressing the low food intake/carbohydrate gap.
  - o   Acknowledge other possible reasons (e.g. mood, alcohol), but focusing on the starvation factor for now.
- Cognitive challenges.
  - o   Set up a behavioural experiment with trying a feared food (two weeks).
  - o   Clarify belief and alternative belief, and time frame for testing them out.
- Agree next appointment.
  - o   Stress that you will be maintaining the review to ensure progress.
- Set homework.
  - o   ED-15 (do while waiting for the next appointment).
  - o   Questionnaire pack 2 (EDE-Q, GAD-7, PHQ-9; WAI-SR).
  - o   Standard food diary plus record of trigger-core belief-emotion-behaviour links.
  - o   Change intake according to need (including any need to gain weight).
  - o   Food-related behavioural experiment.
- End session.

Session 4 record: DATE _____

Tick the items that you have addressed with the patient on the facing list as you progress.

Check that all items are ticked (or marked N/A if not applicable).

Symptoms		Frequency of behaviours		
Weight	_____ kg	Objective binges	_____	per week
BMI	_____	Subjective binges	_____	per week
		Vomiting	_____	per week
Anticipated weight change	_____ kg	Laxatives (episodes)	_____	per week

Problems with non-negotiables (e.g. homework; attendance), and how they were addressed

Summary of problems identified in dietary intake that trigger binges/urges to binge

Patient agenda items

Homework tasks set
Behavioural experiment
Other

Patient's ratings
Anticipated impact of that eating change on weight over the next week(s)

Gain = _____ kg; Loss = _____ kg; Confidence rating = _____ %

Date and time of next appointment _____

Session 5: Agenda/Task checklist

- Retrieve ED-15 and Session 4 questionnaire pack.
  - o   Check that all items are completed.
  - o   Eyeball EDE-Q for change in pattern of cognitions since Session 1.
- Review homework.
  - o   All done?.
- Address any life-threatening or therapy-interfering behaviours.
  - o   Remind any 'slow to start change' patients that they have one more before ending.
- Ask patient about experience of Session 4.
  - o   Stress that any changes are attributable to the patient's hard work.
  - o   The same applies to the following six sessions.
  - o   Plan is now to work on those beliefs about food, weight, and shape, as necessary (based on current beliefs, rather than past ones).
  - o   Have to keep going with eating changes to make that work.
- Patient agenda items and questions from last time?
  - o   Give ten minutes to these, after the diaries and weighing.
- Review food diaries.
  - o   Identify changes from previous eating patterns.
  - o   Identify and note core symptoms.
- Congratulate patient on any positive changes in eating pattern and symptom reduction; problem solve any slippage.
- Add to the chart of patient bulimic behaviours.
- Weighing process.
  1. Ask regarding believed change in weight from last time (and certainty rating).
  2. Weigh the patient.
  3. Chart the actual and anticipated weight change (copy for the patient).
  4. Review patient's beliefs relative to actual change.
- Patient's agenda items.
- Review bulimic behaviours.
  - o   Address any remaining starvation-related issues.
  - o   Focus on emotional basis for remaining binge-purge behaviours, using new record.
  - o   Explain exposure work for purging behaviours.
- Review behavioural experiment.
  - o   Check outcome against predicted outcome.
  - o   Maintain as planned (two more weeks).
- Cognitive challenges.
  - o   Identify remaining cognitive concerns regarding eating, weight, and shape.
  - o   Historical review of eating and weight concerns.
  - o   Consider evidence for and against those beliefs in the here and now.

- Begin body image work with cognitive challenges.
    o Historical review of body image concerns, considering evidence for and against those beliefs in the here and now.
    o Psychoeducation regarding body image.
    o Challenge misperception.
    o Imagery rescripting for body image.
    o Identify body-related behaviours that maintain the body image.
- Agree next appointment.
    o Plan to move further on body image concerns, but need to maintain eating and weight work.
- Set homework.
    o ED-15 (do while waiting for the next appointment).
    o Standard food diary plus record of trigger-core belief-emotion-behaviour links.
    o Change intake according to need (including any need to gain weight).
    o Maintain/develop food-related behavioural experiment.
    o Review of evidence for beliefs.
    o Exposure work for purging behaviours.
    o Bring in photos if needed for surveys.
- End session.

Session 5 record: DATE _____

Tick the items that you have addressed with the patient on the facing list as you progress.
Check that all items are ticked (or marked N/A if not applicable).

Symptoms		Frequency of behaviours	
Weight	_____ kg	Objective binges	_____ per week
BMI	_____	Subjective binges	_____ per week
		Vomiting	_____ per week
Anticipated weight change	_____ kg	Laxatives (episodes)	_____ per week

Problems with non-negotiables (e.g. homework; attendance), and how they were addressed

Summary of problems identified in dietary intake that trigger binges/urges to binge

Patient agenda items

Homework tasks set
Maintain behavioural experiment
Cognitive challenges regarding eating and weight
Exposure work for purging behaviours

Patient's ratings
Anticipated impact of that eating change on weight over the next week(s)
Gain = _____ kg; Loss = _____ kg; Confidence rating = _____ %

Date and time of next appointment _____

Session 6: Agenda/Task checklist

- Retrieve ED-15.
  - o Check that all items are completed.
- Review homework.
  - o All done?
- Address any life-threatening or therapy-interfering behaviours.
  - o If no progress so far in therapy, stop here.
- Ask patient about experience of Session 5.
- Patient agenda items and questions from last time?
  - o Give ten minutes to these, after the diaries and weighing.
- Review food diaries.
  - o Identify changes from previous eating patterns.
  - o Identify and note core symptoms.
- Congratulate patient on any positive changes in eating pattern and symptom reduction; problem solve any slippage.
- Add to the chart of patient bulimic behaviours.
- Ask regarding believed change in weight from last time (and certainty rating).
- Weighing process.
  1. Ask regarding believed change in weight from last time (and certainty rating).
  2. Weigh the patient.
  3. Chart the actual and anticipated weight change (copy for the patient).
  4. Review patient's beliefs relative to actual change.
- Review bulimic behaviours.
  - o Focus on emotional basis for remaining binge-purge behaviours.
  - o Review the impact of exposure work for purging behaviours.
- Review behavioural experiment.
  - o Check outcome against predicted outcome.
  - o Review beliefs.
  - o Either maintain for two more weeks or plan new two-week experiment.
- Continue body image work, beginning on behavioural change targets.
  - o Begin to address behavioural targets, as selected in Session 5.
  - o Avoidance – mirror exposure.
  - o Others' opinions – survey.
  - o Checking or comparison – behavioural experiments).
- Agree next appointment.
- Set homework.
  - o ED-15 (do while waiting for the next appointment).
  - o Basic food diary.
  - o Change intake according to need (including any need to gain weight).
  - o Start new food-related behavioural experiment (if needed).
  - o Addressing body image.
  - o Exposure work for purging behaviours.
- End session.

Session 6 record: DATE _____

Tick the items that you have addressed with the patient on the facing list as you progress.

Check that all items are ticked (or marked N/A if not applicable).

Symptoms			Frequency of behaviours		
Weight	_____ kg		Objective binges	_____	per week
BMI	_____		Subjective binges	_____	per week
			Vomiting	_____	per week
Anticipated weight change	_____ kg		Laxatives (episodes)	_____	per week

Problems with non-negotiables (e.g. homework; attendance), and how they were addressed

Summary of problems identified in dietary intake that trigger binges/urges to binge

Patient agenda items

Homework tasks set
Maintain/start new behavioural experiment
Cognitive challenges re eating and weight
Exposure work for purging behaviours
Bring in photos for surveys, if appropriate

Patient's ratings
Anticipated impact of that eating change on weight over the next week(s)
Gain = _____ kg; Loss = _____ kg; Confidence rating = _____ %

Date and time of next appointment _____

Session 7: Agenda/Task checklist

- Retrieve ED-15.
  - o   Check that all items are completed.
- Review homework.
  - o   All done?.
  - o   Ask patient to maintain it.
- Address any life-threatening or therapy-interfering behaviours.
- Review diary, chart behaviours, weigh patient (usual procedure), chart weight.
  - o   Stress what needs to be done over the next week, given skills learned already.
- According to patient body image need:
  - o   Mirror exposure.
  - o   Survey.
  - o   Behavioural experiments around body checking or comparison.
- Agree next appointment.
- Set homework.
  - o   ED-15 and WAI-SR (do while waiting for the next appointment).
  - o   Standard food diary plus record of trigger-core belief-emotion-behaviour links.
  - o   Change intake according to need (including any need to gain weight).
  - o   Maintain behavioural experiment (last week).
  - o   Exposure work for purging behaviours.
  - o   Repeat/extend body image work, as appropriate to maintaining factors.
    - o   Exposure at home (recorded).
    - o   Survey carried out by clinician.
    - o   Behavioural experiments.
- End session.

Session 7 record: DATE _____

Tick the items that you have addressed with the patient on the facing list as you progress.
Check that all items are ticked (or marked N/A if not applicable).

Symptoms			Frequency of behaviours		
Weight	_____ kg		Objective binges	_____	per week
BMI	_____		Subjective binges	_____	per week
			Vomiting	_____	per week
Anticipated weight change	_____ kg		Laxatives (episodes)	_____	per week

Problems with non-negotiables (e.g. homework; attendance), and how they were addressed

Summary of problems identified that trigger purging

Body image approach used:
Exposure / Survey / Behavioural Experiment

Homework tasks set
Maintain behavioural experiment
Exposure work for purging behaviours
Body image work to be carried out

Patient's ratings
Anticipated impact of that eating change on weight over the next week(s)
Gain = _____ kg; Loss = _____ kg; Confidence rating = _____ %

Date and time of next appointment _____

Session 8: Agenda/Task checklist

- Retrieve ED-15.
  - o Check that all items are completed.
- Review homework.
  - o All done?.
- Address any life-threatening or therapy-interfering behaviours.
- Review diary, chart behaviours, weigh patient (usual procedure), chart weight.
  - o Stress what needs to be done over the next week, given skills learned already.
- Revisit body image work from last time.
  - o Mirror exposure – listen to home tape of exposure, identify problems; repeat in session, stress earlier reduction in anxiety.
  - o Survey – review outcomes, and repeat/renew as necessary (different target; different respondents).
  - o Checking/comparison – review behavioural experiments, repeat/extend/ test alternative hypothesis.
- Review outcome of behavioural experiment(s).
  - o Review cognitive impact.
- Agree next appointment.
  - o Plan for relapse prevention and follow-up.
- Set homework.
  - o ED-15 (do while waiting for the next appointment).
  - o Standard food diary plus record of trigger-core belief-emotion-behaviour links.
  - o Maintain behavioural experiment (last week).
  - o Exposure work for purging behaviours.
  - o Repeat/extend body image work, as appropriate to maintaining factors.
    - o Exposure at home (recorded).
    - o Survey carried out by clinician or patient.
    - o Behavioural experiments.
- End session.

Session 8 record: DATE _____

Tick the items that you have addressed with the patient on the facing list as you progress.
Check that all items are ticked (or marked N/A if not applicable).

Symptoms		Frequency of behaviours		
Weight	_____ kg	Objective binges	_____	per week
BMI	_____	Subjective binges	_____	per week
		Vomiting	_____	per week
Anticipated weight change	_____ kg	Laxatives (episodes)	_____	per week

Problems with non-negotiables (e.g. homework; attendance), and how they were addressed

Summary of outcomes from behavioural experiments

Body image approach used:
Exposure / Survey / Behavioural Experiment

Homework tasks set
Exposure work for purging behaviours
Body image work to be carried out

Patient's ratings
Anticipated impact of that eating change on weight over the next week(s)
Gain = _____ kg; Loss = _____ kg; Confidence rating = _____ %

Date and time of next appointment _____

Session 9: Agenda/Task checklist

- Retrieve ED-15.
  - o Check that all items are completed.
- Review homework.
  - o All done?
- Address any life-threatening or therapy-interfering behaviours.
- Review diary, chart behaviours, weigh patient (usual procedure), chart weight.
  - o Stress what needs to be done over the next week, given skills learned already.
- Review what helped to reduce bingeing and purging.
  - o Or what got in the way.
- Revisit body image work from last time.
  - o Mirror exposure – listen to home tape of exposure, identify problems; repeat in session, stress earlier reduction in anxiety.
  - o Survey – review outcomes, and repeat/renew as necessary (different target; different respondents).
  - o Checking/comparison – review behavioural experiments, repeat/extend/ test alternative hypothesis.
- Relapse prevention plan.
  - o Therapy blueprint (start in the session, but getting the patient to generate it as much as possible).
  - o Include the 'what got in the way' elements.
  - o Identify prelapses/permissive cognitions.
  - o Plan life changes and dietary maintenance.
  - o No weight loss plans for the next three months, to ensure stability.
  - o Plan 'home therapy' sessions (weekly; get others involved?).
- Agree next appointment.
- Set homework.
  - o Questionnaire pack 3 (EDE-Q, GAD-7, PHQ-9, WAI-SR) to complete just before next session.
  - o ED-15 (do while waiting for the next appointment).
  - o Standard food diary plus record of trigger-core belief-emotion-behaviour links Repeat/extend body image work, as appropriate to maintaining factors.
    - o Exposure at home (recorded).
    - o Survey carried out by patient.
    - o Behavioural experiments.
  - o Complete therapy blueprint.
- End session.

Session 9 record: DATE _____

Tick the items that you have addressed with the patient on the facing list as you progress.

Check that all items are ticked (or marked N/A if not applicable).

Symptoms			Frequency of behaviours		
Weight	_____ kg		Objective binges	_____	per week
BMI	_____		Subjective binges	_____	per week
			Vomiting	_____	per week
Anticipated weight change	_____ kg		Laxatives (episodes)	_____	per week

Problems with non-negotiables (e.g. homework; attendance), and how they were addressed

Summary of what helped with reducing bingeing and purging

Body image approach used:
Exposure/Survey/Behavioural Experiment

Homework tasks set
Body image work to be carried out

Preparing therapy blueprint

Patient's ratings
Anticipated impact of that eating change on weight over the next week(s)

Gain = _____ kg; Loss = _____ kg; Confidence rating = _____ %

Date and time of next appointment _____

REMEMBER TO HAND OVER THE END OF THERAPY QUESTIONNAIRES

Session 10: Agenda/Task checklist

- Retrieve ED-15 and questionnaire pack 3.
  - o   Check that all items are completed.
- Address any life-threatening or therapy-interfering behaviours.
- Review diary, chart behaviours, weigh patient (usual procedure), chart weight.
- Review beliefs about weight being related to eating.
- Revisit body image work from last time.
  - o   What worked?
- Review all changes across therapy.
  - o   Congratulations for a job well done.
  - o   Stress patient's responsibility for changes made to date, to enhance sense of agency.
  - o   Same for any remaining changes that are needed.
- Relapse prevention plan.
  - o   Finalise therapy blueprint.
  - o   Stress importance of maintaining behavioural changes, challenging beliefs, and identifying and responding to prelapses.
  - o   No weight loss plans for the next three months, to ensure stability.
  - o   Schedule of 'home therapy' sessions.
- Plan one-month follow-up.
  - o   Give ED-15 and EDE-Q (to complete just before next session).
- End session.

Session 10 record: DATE _____

Tick the items that you have addressed with the patient on the facing list as you progress.
Check that all items are ticked (or marked N/A if not applicable).

Symptoms		Frequency of behaviours		
Weight	_____ kg	Objective binges	_____	per week
BMI	_____	Subjective binges	_____	per week
		Vomiting	_____	per week
Anticipated weight change	_____ kg	Laxatives (episodes)	_____	per week

Problems with non-negotiables (e.g. homework; attendance), and how they were addressed

Summary of what helped overall (stressing patient's role)

Content of therapy blueprint (attach a copy of the final version)

Date and time of next appointment _____

Follow-up 1 – One month: DATE _____

Symptoms			Frequency of behaviours over past month		
Weight	_____	kg	Objective binges	_____	per week
BMI	_____		Subjective binges	_____	per week
			Vomiting	_____	per week
Anticipated weight change	_____	kg	Laxatives (episodes)	_____	per week

Collect measures

Review use of therapy blueprint

Troubleshooting

Homework
• Individualise to address any slippage/development.

Plan final follow-up in (two months).
• Give ED-15, WAI-SR, and EDE-Q (to complete just before final session).
• End session.

Follow-up 2 – Three months: DATE _____

Symptoms			Frequency of behaviours over past month		
Weight	_____ kg		Objective binges	_____	per week
BMI	_____		Subjective binges	_____	per week
			Vomiting	_____	per week
Anticipated weight change	_____ kg		Laxatives (episodes)	_____	per week

Collect measures

Review use of therapy blueprint

Troubleshooting

Review progress overall
- Stress the patient's contribution and ability to maintain change

Say goodbye

<u>Therapy Blueprint</u>

1. **What were my problems when I was first referred?**

2. **What did I do to change?**

3. **What changes do I still want to make and how will I achieve that?**

4. **What might lead to a setback in the future?**

5. **What will be the symptoms of a setback?**

6. **How will I overcome the setback?**

7. **What if that doesn't work?**

Basic food diary

Food and drink diary

Day:_____

Date:_____

Please keep a record of everything that you eat and drink, noting the time and the context.

If you binge, please put a 'B' against the food that you ate.

If you vomit or take laxatives, please mark the diary with a 'V' or an 'L'

Time	Food and liquids consumed • Type and amount • Including alcohol	Context (Where was I? Who was about? What was I doing?)

ED-15 questionnaire and scoring key*

This questionnaire considers your eating attitudes and behaviours over the last week. Please complete this measure by ticking the appropriate answers for all items.

	Over the past week, how often have I:	Not at all	Rarely	Occasionally	Sometimes	Often	Most of the time	All the time
1	Worried about losing control over my eating	0	1	2	3	4	5	6
2	Avoided activities or people because of the way I look	0	1	2	3	4	5	6
3	Been preoccupied with thoughts of food and eating	0	1	2	3	4	5	6
4	Compared my body negatively with others'	0	1	2	3	4	5	6
5	Avoided looking at my body (e.g. in mirrors; wearing baggy clothes) because of the way it makes me feel	0	1	2	3	4	5	6
6	Felt distressed about my weight	0	1	2	3	4	5	6
7	Checked my body to reassure myself about my appearance (e.g. weighing myself; using mirrors)	0	1	2	3	4	5	6
8	Followed strict rules about my eating	0	1	2	3	4	5	6
9	Felt distressed about my body shape	0	1	2	3	4	5	6
10	Worried that other people were judging me as a person because of my weight and appearance	0	1	2	3	4	5	6

* *Source:* Tatham, M., Turner, H., Mountford, V. A., Tritt, A., Dyas, R., & Waller G. (2015). Development, psychometric properties and preliminary clinical validation of a brief, session-by-session measure of eating disorder cognitions and behaviours: The ED-15. *International Journal of Eating Disorders*, *48*, 1005–1115. Reproduced courtesy of Wiley & Sons.

If you have never used any of the following behaviours, please respond with N/A.

For those that you have used, over the past week, how many times have you:	*Number of times*
a	Binged (felt out of control of your eating, and eaten far more than a person normally would at one go)	
b	Vomited to control your weight (whether you had to make yourself sick or not) *	
Finally, on how many days in the past week have you:	*Number of days*
c	Used laxatives to control your weight or shape	
d	Restricted or dieted in order to control your weight	
e	Exercised hard in order to control your weight	

* *i.e. Using your fingers or medicines to make yourself sick, or vomiting without such aids.*

ED-15 scoring key

- All items are positively scored from 0–6.
- The ED-15 includes two attitudinal subscales, scored as follows:
  - Weight & Shape Concerns = mean of items 2, 4, 5, 6, 9, and 10 (add the six scores and divide by six)
  - Eating Concerns = mean of items 1, 3, 7 and 8 (add the four scores and – divide by four)
- The overall attitudinal score is the mean of the scores on all ten items (total the 10 items and divide by 10).
- Up to one item can be missed from either scale, and the item mean can be corrected accordingly. If more are missing, then the scores are invalid.

Information sheet for patients and their families and friends

CBT-T: Brief therapy for eating disorders
Information sheet for patients and their families and friends

So you have an eating disorder, and you want to overcome it.

If you are reading this, it is likely that you have an eating disorder or you are affected by someone in your life who has an eating disorder. Whether you are reading this leaflet because it is you who has the problem or a loved one, the information below should help you to understand what is involved.

Cognitive-behavioural therapy (CBT) is a psychotherapeutic approach to eating disorders that has a strong evidence base. There are different forms of effective CBT for eating disorders, which are similar in lots of ways. This leaflet is to explain one specific form of CBT, known as CBT-T (where the 'T' stands for 'ten sessions'), because it might be useful to help you overcome your eating disorder.

Who does CBT-T help?

The evidence shows that CBT-T is suitable for adults who have eating disorders other than anorexia nervosa. If you are under 18 or if you have a diagnosis of anorexia nervosa, then other evidence-based options are available. However, CBT-T is effective for women and men who are at a near-healthy weight or above.

What is CBT-T?

CBT-T is a time-limited, focused therapy, which is ten sessions long (followed by two follow-up sessions). It starts by addressing your safety, then aims to help you change your eating, your beliefs about food, and your body image. It should also help you to reduce any anxiety and other emotional concerns.

What will I need to do to get well?

When you undertake CBT-T, you will learn that a lot of the changes that are needed mean changing your behaviour – your eating, your body-related behaviours, your response to your emotions. These will help you to learn to overcome your fears about eating and your body. In the sessions, we will work at helping you to make changes early on, as that is so important in helping you to change overall. You will also need to work at recovery between sessions, as homework is a key element in helping you to learn to get well and stay well.

CBT-T involves several phases in treatment:

- Getting into a regular, healthy, eating routine and tackling your anxiety.
- Changing your beliefs about food.
- Learning to tackle the emotions that can drive eating problems.
- Normalising your body image.
- Making sure that you stay well.

As no two people are the same in their eating, CBT-T should be applied flexibly, based on your own needs.

We will also be monitoring your behaviours, weight, beliefs, emotions and body image on a regular basis, so that we can make sure that we are on the right track.

"What can I do to help my loved one?"

If you are reading this because you are a family member, a friend, or a partner, you can play a valuable role in:

- Suggesting to the patient that they have a problem, if they seem unaware or unwilling to think about it.
- Supporting the patient in seeking help, especially in accessing evidence-based treatment.
- Talking to the patient about their treatment sessions, if they are happy to do so, to help them to learn fully and try things out with your support (e.g. eating new foods).
- Joining them in their homework and in their 'therapy at home' sessions, where appropriate.

Two important points for everyone to remember

First, and most importantly, don't beat yourself up over how you got here, especially as the eating problem might be have been around for a very long time. Eating disorders have lots of potential causes, and we don't fully understand them all. There is no point in worrying about how you or your loved one developed the eating disorder. Focus on the process of getting well in the present, so that life can go more positively for everyone.

Second, you might have other concerns alongside your eating disorder, such as low self-esteem, anxiety, or perfectionism. A lot of such problems are likely to be reduced substantially when you undertake CBT-T for your eating disorder. However, if such problems continue by the end of therapy, we might recommend that you get hold of a good self-help guide to try out during the follow-up period and beyond. The ones that we commonly recommend are:

- self-esteem (Fennell, 2016)
- anxiety (Kennerley, 2014)
- social anxiety (Butler, 2016)
- perfectionism (Shafran, Egan & Wade, 2018)
- core beliefs (Young & Klosko, 1993)

The references for these are provided at the end of this handout, in case you want to consult any of them as therapy goes along.

Will CBT-T work for me or my loved one?

CBT-T is as effective as other forms of CBT for most people with eating disorders, and is more effective than some other therapies. However, it is hard work for all concerned. While we cannot guarantee that you will recover, we know that if you engage fully with CBT-T then you have the best possible chance of a full recovery and being able to get on with your life. We think that the hard work is worth it.

However, there is no opinion about a therapy that is better than the opinion of someone who has received it, so please consider the following quotes about the experience of CBT-T from patients who have undertaken it, so that you know what the experience and benefits are like:

- I never felt judged or like I was wasting the clinic's time, and the [therapist] was really understanding and encouraging.
- Made me feel like I was in a safe space where I could be honest.

- She was firm about my eating plan, which I needed, but also kind and caring.
- I was able to tackle personal demons and allow myself to get better.
- CBT-T focused on the present and the future, which gave me a much more positive outlook on the situation.
- Challenging but effective in reducing my behaviours.
- Best therapy I have received – didn't feel judged.
- I honestly believe I would be heading down a dark road if I had not got the help when I did.
- Allowed me to move forward to an eating disorder-free life.

Now it is your turn.

Glenn Waller
Hannah M. Turner
Madeleine Tatham
Victoria A. Mountford
Tracey D. Wade

Self-help books

Butler, G. (2016). *Overcoming social anxiety and shyness: A self-help guide using cognitive behavioural techniques* (2nd ed.). London, UK: Robinson.

Fennell, M. (2016). *Overcoming low self-esteem: A self-help guide using cognitive behavioural techniques* (2nd ed.). London, UK: Robinson.

Kennerley, H. (2016). *Overcoming anxiety: A self-help guide using cognitive behavioural techniques* (2nd ed.). London, UK: Robinson.

Shafran, R., Egan, S., & Wade, T. (2018). *Overcoming perfectionism: A self-help guide using cognitive behavioural techniques* (2nd ed.). London, UK: Robinson.

Young, J. E., & Klosko, J. S. (1993). *Reinventing your life.* New York, NY: Plume Publishers.

The REAL Food Guide for CBT-T Clinicians

Basic Food and Eating Training for Eating Disorders

Susan Hart & Caitlin McMaster

The REAL Food Guide (*Recovery from EAting disorders for Life*) is a framework that uses core principles of nutrition, with consideration of the beliefs and misinformation that are frequently endorsed by individuals with eating disorders. It is a pictorial tool based on the best evidence to date bringing practical information together in one place[1]. It is designed for all clinicians who work with clients with eating disorders, who require basic knowledge on food and eating, in order to identify distortions and therefore effectively provide intervention[2]. It is not intended to teach clinicians who are not dietitians to provide detailed nutrition intervention, write meal plans, undertake nutritional assessment, or be an alternative to seeing a dietitian. Rather, it is a framework that summarises key messages on food and eating, tailored to the needs, and concerns of eating disorder clients. Using a standardised framework for talking about food and eating allows all clinicians working in a team to be consistent, as well as delivering a clearer and more tailored message than current public health nutrition messages.[1]

Additionally, the guidance provided on food and eating for clients by the REAL Food Guide is nutritionally adequate.[1] This means that the meal plans for weight maintenance and weight regain, if followed, will provide enough protein, carbohydrate and fat, essential vitamins, and minerals to meet *most* individuals' needs. There are exceptions to this, as individuals may have preferences, dislikes, or nutritional needs meaning they require more or less food on their day-to-day meal plan, particularly if they exercise, are tall, or just because it is the way their body is designed (Table A.1).

Table A.1 Meal plan (including number of servings of each food group) for weight maintenance

	Recommended servings	*Sample food choices*
BREAKFAST Before 9 am	1 carbohydrate serving 1 calcium serving 1 fruit serving 1 fluid	1 bowl cereal 1 cup milk/tub yoghurt Fresh fruit/fruit cup/juice Tea/coffee
AM SNACK	1 fruit serving 1 calcium serving 1 fluid	1 apple 1 tub yoghurt/2 slices cheese Tea/coffee/water
LUNCH Between 12 and 2 pm	1 carbohydrate serving 1 protein serving 1 fat/oil serving 2 vegetable servings 1 fluid	2 slices bread 1 chicken breast 1 tablespoon avocado Grated carrot, & lettuce 1 cup water
PM SNACK	1 fun food 1 fluid	1 piece carrot cake Tea/coffee/water
DINNER Between 6 and 8 pm	1 carbohydrate serving 1 protein serving 1 fat/oil serving 2 vegetable servings 1 fluid	1 cup cooked rice 3/4 cup beef mince 1 teaspoon sesame oil Onion, capsicum, & beans 1 cup water
SUPPER	1 fruit serving 1 calcium serving 1 fluid	6 dried apricot halves/banana 1 cup hot chocolate Tea/coffee/water

When should I refer my client to a dietitian?

Evidence-based practice recommends the inclusion of nutrition and dietetic assessment, education, and intervention as part of the multidisciplinary management of clients with eating disorders.[3,4] Dietitians help patients define dietary problems and plan solutions to these dietary challenges.[5] However, in real life there may be barriers to accessing dietetic treatment such as availability and affordability of care; waiting times for services; a perception that patients may not benefit from dietetic input or implement nutrition changes; or patient's willingness to attend dietetic services.[6,7] It is ideal that any clinician working with clients with eating disorders has access to a dietitian to be able to discuss cases and clients' nutritional issues as well as to refer patients to when necessary.[8]

Indications for referral to a dietitian may include clients with the following presentations:

- Pregnancy or breastfeeding.
- A co-morbid medical diagnosis that impacts on food intake e.g. type 1 diabetes mellitus; gastrointestinal conditions such as Crohn's disease; food

allergies or intolerances (including Coeliac disease); cystic fibrosis; and kidney disease to name a few.

- Taking medication that impacts on nutritional needs, appetite, or weight e.g. anti-psychotic medications.
- Losing weight or unable to gain weight if they are underweight. 'Underweight' does not refer only to clients with a BMI below 20 but may also include clients who have lost a large amount of weight rapidly and exhibit symptoms of malnutrition and medical instability despite their BMI being above 20.
- Ongoing intake of a limited range of foods throughout treatment.
- Avoidance of other necessary skills and behaviours associated with eating such as grocery shopping, preparing, and cooking food.

USING THE REAL FOOD GUIDE

The REAL Food Guide recommends *eating mechanically* (in addition to regular eating as is considered best practice[8,9]) when a client commences treatment for an eating disorder. Although clients often experience difficulty in eating regularly and mechanically, establishing structure with eating is a key component of achieving nutritionally adequate eating patterns and forms the scaffold for recovery from an eating disorder. Eating mechanically refers to:

- Planning eating episodes.
- Relying on external cues to regulate eating such as a meal plan or setting an alarm.
- Acknowledging internal cues of eating such as hunger and fullness signals but not acting on them.

The bottom layer of the REAL Food Guide Pyramid depicts five core food groups (fruit, vegetables, carbohydrate, protein, calcium foods), and fluid.[1] There are three additional layers providing recommendations on the inclusion of fats and oils, fun foods and social eating, and diet foods and fillers. The recommended number of servings per day is an estimate of the minimum number of servings required each day for an adult older than 18 years to achieve nutrient requirements. It is a starting point, and some individuals on weight maintenance or regain may require more servings than is recommended below. The authors define weight regain meal plan as being suitable for those individuals with a Body Mass Index less than 20 kg/m^2 (Figure A.1).

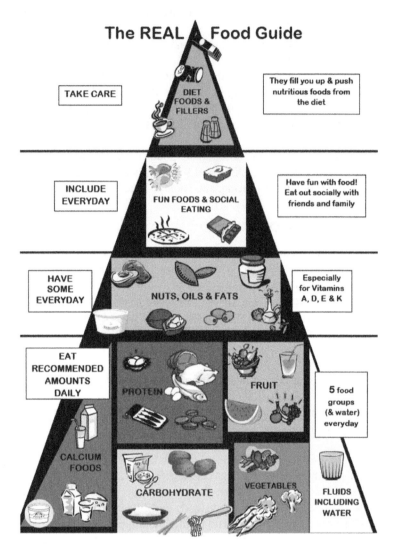

Figure A.1 REAL Food Guide.

Calcium Foods

This food group refers to foods that are rich sources of calcium such as dairy products and calcium enriched soy products. There is no recommendation to choose fat modified products such as low fat milk or diet yoghurt, typical of many other nutrition guides.

Most of the body's calcium is stored in the bones and teeth with a small amount needed for blood clotting, muscle functioning, nerve conduction, and fluid balance. Having adequate dietary calcium to build strong healthy bones before middle age is the best way to prevent osteoporosis. Because of restrictive eating behaviors, eating disorder clients severely compromise their chance of achieving peak bone mass, and as a result, often experience early onset of osteoporosis (or brittle bones).[10] Therefore, obtaining an adequate amount of dietary calcium is a key message and nutritional target for eating disorder clients. Avoiding or removing calcium rich foods from the diet also means compromising adequate intake of many nutrients essential for good health such as protein, vitamins (A, E, B12, and riboflavin), and other minerals (phosphorus, magnesium, potassium, and zinc).

For clients who choose not to have dairy products, calcium-*fortified* soy-milk is the best option. *Fortification* means vitamins and minerals are added to the product to improve its nutrient content. It is essential for clients to take care with alternatives sources of calcium (i.e. rice, almond, coconut, and oat milk) as many have limited nutritional value. None of these non-dairy alternatives have any naturally occurring calcium, are low in energy and protein, and require fortification to be nutritionally equivalent to dairy or calcium fortified soy products.

Recommended servings of calcium foods per day
Weight maintenance = 3 servings
Weight regain = 4 servings
One serving size of calcium food
1 cup flavoured milk
1 ¼ cups plain, unflavoured milk
1 ½ cups plain, unflavoured soy milk
2 slices of cheese (each slice is size of your palm)
½ cup grated cheese
½ cup custard
1 cup flavoured yoghurt
1 cup plain, unflavoured yoghurt

It is important to note that 'Calcium foods' refer to standard, whole varieties and NOT modified versions such as 'light' or 'skim' milk. It is important to clarify with your client precisely what type of calcium food they are having. To demonstrate why this is important, it is necessary to have almost 2 cups of 'light' milk or 2 and a quarter cups of 'skim' milk to provide the same nutritional value as one serving of standard milk.

Protein Foods

Protein is an essential *macro*nutrient from food required to transport vitamins and minerals around the body, to provide the building blocks (amino acids) for growth and repair of body tissue, and to provide energy. Protein rich foods also provide iron, zinc, vitamin B12, and omega-3 essential fatty acids.

Many eating disorder clients choose a vegetarian diet because they believe it is a 'healthier' way of eating.[11] It is possible to have a balanced vegetarian or meat containing diet, however a nutritious vegetarian diet is not one where meat has been excluded and nothing else has been added in its place. It is important that alternative sources of nutrients found in meat, in particular iron and zinc, are replaced. A well-planned vegetarian diet can meet the nutritional requirements of patients needing to maintain or gain weight. However, one of the main differences of a vegetarian diet is that the iron found in vegetarian protein sources (such as legumes) is not well absorbed by the body. Adding a vitamin C source to meals containing non-meat sources of iron can increase absorption[12] and is an important food message for eating disorder clients. Some examples of this in practice are adding fruit or a glass of juice to breakfast cereal or a serving of leafy greens with lentils to a main meal. Additionally, *polyphenols* from tea and coffee reduce the absorption of iron,[12] so it is best if clients following a vegetarian diet avoid drinking tea and coffee with lunch and dinner when they will be consuming vegetarian protein sources that contain iron.

The REAL Food Guide recommends a variety of animal and vegetarian protein foods each day, one serving at lunch and one at dinner. A simple method for achieving balanced meals at lunch and at dinner is to use the Thirds Rule (See Figure A.2). This means that on an average size dinner plate, one third of the plate should be filled by carbohydrate foods, one third filled by protein foods, and one third filled by vegetables. For most people with eating disorders, this usually means increasing the quantity of protein and carbohydrate but reducing the amount of vegetables that are on the plate. At first glance it may appear as though a client is eating a large amount of food, but often the meal will not contain adequate amounts of carbohydrate and protein.

Recommended servings of protein foods per day
Weight maintenance = 2 servings
Weight regain = 2 servings
One serving of protein food

Animal protein sources	Vegetarian protein sources	Vegan protein sources
Palm size portion of chicken	2 slices of cheese (each slice size of your palm)	I cup chopped tofu
¾ cup beef mince		¾ cup baked beans
Palm size portion of steak	½ cup grated cheese	I cup legumes (e.g.
½ cup canned salmon, drained	½ cup ricotta cheese	chickpeas, kidney beans)
	3 eggs	I full handful of almonds
¾ cup canned tuna, drained		2 tablespoons tahini
Piece of white fish the size of whole hand		1/3 cup hummus
		2 tablespoons peanut butter

Analysis of vegan meal plans for both weight maintenance and weight regain demonstrate that it is feasible to achieve nutritional adequacy with a vegan diet.[1] When working with eating disorder clients in an outpatient setting, negotiating meeting nutritional requirements with a vegan-style meal plan may be appropriate when considered on a case-by-case basis, but it is not recommended as a standard treatment. While there may be genuine ethical reasons for choosing a vegan diet,

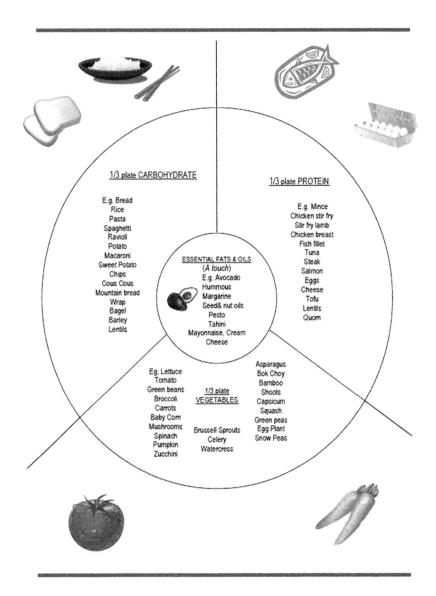

Figure A.2   Thirds rule for lunch and dinner meals.

continued endorsement of such a diet involves restricted food choices, dichoto-mous thinking about food, hyper-vigilance about ingredient lists on food labels and limitations on social eating such as avoiding restaurants or food prepared by others because of uncertainty about the ingredients used. Currently there is a lack of research as to whether adhering to such a strict diet is helpful or harmful, and it is unclear how this would impact on recovery from both a nutritional, and psychological, point of view. Until the relationship between endorsement of a vegan eating pattern and recovery from an eating disorder is better understood, a vegan meal pattern for routine use in the treatment of eating disorders is not recommended.[1] As a treatment principle, clients who choose a limited number of foods should be encouraged to broaden their choices, and this applies for those who have limited their protein intake by following a vegan diet (Figure A.2).

Carbohydrate Foods

This core food group refers to foods that contain the macronutrient carbohydrate such as grains, cereal, rice, and some starchy vegetables such as potatoes. It is recommended that a variety of whole grains and carbohydrate foods are included at each meal to achieve an adequate intake of energy, fibre, thiamine, folate, and iodine. 'Variety' means choosing more than one food from this group over an average day. For example, a carbohydrate choice at lunch might be two slices of bread and at dinner it could be 1 cup of cooked pasta. Additionally, variety over the week may mean one night is rice as the carbohydrate of choice at dinner, one night it is potato, and one night is spaghetti. A meal plan that has poor or low variety would be having rice every night of the week. When introducing a meal plan the initial goal may be to include any source of carbohydrate at dinner. As treatment progresses, the goal may be to have a variety of choices as eating patterns improve. The REAL Food Guide recommends that carbohydrate is included at breakfast (e.g. cereal and/or toast), lunch (e.g. sandwich or wrap), and at dinner (e.g. rice, pasta, potato). It is also included as a snack option at least once per day. The amount of carbohydrate that is required is proportional to the amount of physical activity undertaken and if weight gain is required. Clients that are physically active will require a greater intake of carbohydrate to meet their energy and nutritional requirements than clients who are relatively inactive.

During digestion, carbohydrate foods are digested and broken down into glucose and absorbed into the bloodstream. Carbohydrate is needed for the body to function effectively, to provide fuel for the muscles and brain, and to stabilize blood glucose levels in the blood. The brain struggles to use any fuel other than glucose to meet its energy demands. Inadequate carbohydrate intake can lead to tiredness, fatigue, dizziness, irritability, and low blood glucose levels. The effects of low blood glucose include blurred vision, difficulty concentrating, hunger, sweating, weakness, light-headedness, and confusion.

As a result of malnutrition, eating disorder clients often have no glycogen (the stored form of glucose) in their muscles and liver. When starting to eat more regularly and increasing the amount of carbohydrate in their diet, clients will store some glucose in the liver and muscles as glycogen, which is packaged up with water. This may result in increases in weight of a few kilograms at the beginning of treatment, which often occur in a short space of time and do not align with the client's eating. This initial increase in weight is perceived as catastrophic for clients with eating disorders whose worst beliefs appear to be confirmed, that they will gain large amounts of weight by consuming even small amounts of food. An explanation of the role of carbohydrate and how it is stored by the body is useful at this time.

Recommended servings of carbohydrate (meals) per day
Weight maintenance = 3 servings
Weight regain = 4 servings
One serving of carbohydrate (meals)

Breakfast	**Lunch and Dinner**
½ cup muesli/granola	2 slices bread
I cup cereal flakes	I bread roll
I cup bran cereal	2 dinner sized bread rolls
I cup cooked oatmeal/porridge	I cup cooked pasta
2 slices bread	I cup cooked rice
2 slices raisin/fruit toast	I cup cooked quinoa
I ½ cups puffed cereal (e.g. Rice Bubbles)	I ½ cups cooked thick noodles
	I cup sweet corn
	I potato (size of a fist)

Recommended servings of carbohydrate (snack) per day
Weight maintenance = I serving
Weight regain = 2 servings
One serving of carbohydrate (snack)
I muesli bar
4 cups popcorn
I crumpet + I teaspoon spread
I slice bread + I teaspoon spread
I slice raisin/fruit toast + I teaspoon spread
16 rice crackers
6 plain crackers (no spread)
3 large or 4 small crackers + I teaspoon spread

Fruit

The REAL Food Guide recommends a variety of different fruits of different colour are chosen each day to provide potassium, dietary fibre, vitamin C, and other beneficial antioxidants. It is ideal to include fruit in different forms such as tinned, juiced and dried fruits, which are just as nutritious as fresh fruit. On a weight maintenance meal plan, two pieces of fruit are recommended. For weight regain four servings are recommended, with two of these servings coming from fruit juice, added to lunch and dinner instead of having a glass of water. As a rule of thumb having more servings of fruit than this is not recommended as it can be filling, and pushes other foods from the diet, affecting the overall nutrient balance of the diet.

Recommended servings of fruit per day
Weight maintenance = 2 servings
Weight regain = 4 servings
One serving of fruit
1 orange
1 apple
1 pear
1 small or ½ large banana
¾ cup grapes
1 cup cherries
2 kiwi fruit
2 mandarins
3 plums
1 cup blueberries
2 cups strawberries*
2 tablespoons raisins or sultanas
6 dried apricot halves
1 cup tinned fruit, drained
1 cup fruit juice
Include strawberries only occasionally as the large portion can contribute to feeling full

Vegetables

It is recommended that clients choose a variety of vegetables of different colours to provide vitamin C, folate, potassium, beta-carotene and dietary fibre. It is important clients do not to eat vegetables in excessive quantities as they are filling and push other nutritious food groups such as carbohydrate, fats, and protein foods from the diet.

Recommended servings of vegetables per day
Weight maintenance = 4 servings
Weight regain = 4 servings
One serving of vegetables
½ cup raw mushrooms
1 cup mixed salad
½ cup cooked peas
1 cup cherry tomatoes
1 fist sized tomato
1 piece of cucumber the length of an index finger
½ capsicum
1 piece of carrot the length of an index finger

Fluid

Water is included as a core food group to emphasise that adequate hydration is an important component of daily nutritional requirements.[1] Research has shown that eating disorder clients' fluid or drink choices are often related to eating disorder beliefs (for example, fluid is used as a weight control method by suppressing appetite or to aid vomiting[13]). Disordered fluid intake is observed in the majority of eating disorder clients with most (54%) drinking excessively, and some (28%) drinking restrictively.[14] Some clients will restrict fluid intake to the extent that they put themselves at risk of dehydration. Other clients drink large quantities of fluid to stop feelings of hunger, and to distract from the thought of food and eating. Individuals who are underweight tend to drink large amounts of caffeinated beverages such as coffee, tea, and/or diet soft drinks.[14] As a general rule, kidneys will excrete any fluid in excess of requirements, however it is possible to become water overloaded. Although this is rare it has been reported in eating disorder clients[15] and individuals who drink too much in a short space of time.

It is important for fluids and drinks to be incorporated into meal plans in a structured way similarly to the way that food is planned. The REAL Food Guide recommends that clients:

- Include at least one cup of fluid and no more than two cups at every meal and snack each day (*fluid includes milk, flavoured milky drinks, juice, tea and coffee*).
- Do not drink continuously from large bottles, which may encourage excessive intake.
- Do not drink fluid rapidly before the start of the meal.
- Do not drink to suppress appetite *i.e. if hungry, do not choose diet soft drink, tea or coffee instead of eating.*
- Drink fluids during or at the end of a meal if they are struggling with feeling full during meals and snacks.
- Do not drink excessively when vomiting and engaging in the behaviour of 'flushing'.
- Are conscious of the importance of drinking adequate fluid to replace fluid losses from excessive exercise or from purging behaviours.

Recommended amount of fluid
Weight maintenance or regain = 1 to 2 cups of fluid at each meal and snack
(1 cup = 250 mL)
The following drinks count towards fluid intake
Water
Juice
Tea and coffee
Soft drink
Milk based drinks
Mineral water
Iced tea

Nuts, Oils, and Fats

The second layer of the REAL Food Guide describes 'Nuts, Oils and Fats' to communicate that a healthy balanced diet includes adequate amounts of dietary fats and oils and foods that contain them each day.[1] Foods containing essential fatty acids such as nuts, seeds, olives, unsaturated fats and oils (i.e. sunflower, olive and sesame oil) are essential for good health and it is recommended that one third of the total energy of the food eaten each day comes from dietary fat and oils.[16] Fat-soluble vitamins are also provided by this food group, including vitamin A (for eyesight and healthy skin), vitamin D (for strong bones and teeth and the absorption of calcium and phosphate), vitamin E (a component of cell membranes), and vitamin K (involved in blood clotting). Low dietary intake of these vitamins and deficiencies of essential fatty acids have been documented in clients with eating disorders[17,18] (Table A.2).

As demonstrated by dietary modeling and nutritional analysis[1] there are three important steps, which should be recommended to eating disorder clients (regardless of whether they are required to gain weight or not) to achieve nutritional adequacy:

1   Include full fat or whole dairy and calcium rich foods, as clients will be unlikely to meet their energy requirements if they choose skimmed or low fat varieties.

Table A.2 Meal plan (including number of servings of each food group) for weight regain

	Recommended servings	Sample food choices
BREAKFAST Before 9 am	2 carbohydrate servings 1 fat/oil serving 1 calcium serving 1 fruit serving 1 fluid	1 bowl cereal 2 slices bread + spread 1 cup milk/tub yoghurt Fresh fruit/fruit cup/juice Tea/coffee
AM SNACK	1 carbohydrate snack 1 calcium serving 1 fluid	Muesli bar or 16 rice crackers 1 tub yoghurt/2 slices cheese Tea/coffee/water
LUNCH Between 12 and 2 pm	1 carbohydrate serving 1 protein serving 1 fat/oil serving 1 vegetable serving 2 fruit serving	2 slices bread 1 chicken breast 1 tablespoon avocado Grated carrot, & lettuce 1 orange 1 cup juice
PM SNACK	1 fun food 1 calcium serving 1 fluid	1 piece carrot cake 1 glass flavoured milk Tea/coffee/water
DINNER Between 6 and 8 pm	1 carbohydrate serving 1 protein serving 1 fat/oil serving 1 vegetable serving 1 fruit serving	1 cup cooked rice 3/4 cup beef mince 1 teaspoon sesame oil Onion, capsicum, & beans 1 cup juice
SUPPER	1 fruit serving 1 calcium serving 1 fluid	6 dried apricot halves/banana 1 cup hot chocolate Tea/coffee/water

2   Include a spread or a source of fat/oil at each main meal.

Include a fun food once per day (see below for details on this food group).

Recommended servings of nuts, oils, and fats per day
Weight maintenance = 2 servings
Weight regain = 4 servings
One serving of nuts, oils, and fats
1 teaspoon olive oil
2 teaspoon butter or margarine
2 teaspoon peanut butter
3 teaspoon cream cheese
1 tablespoon avocado
1 tablespoon hummus
5 whole olives
2 tablespoon almonds or 6 almonds

Fun Foods and Social Eating

The third layer of the pyramid is for foods consumed when eating out or eating socially with others. These foods are included to assist with meeting energy requirements and to challenge clients' beliefs that these foods should be avoided or removed from the diet for good health.[1] It is also clinically important from a dietary and psychological perspective to include higher energy foods.

Clients with eating disorders tend to isolate themselves socially because of their eating behaviour, and their anxiety related to eating in a social situation. For example, they often perceive that people are looking at them when they eat or making judgments about what they are eating. To avoid the anxiety associated with eating these foods, clients may avoid eating with their family; eat alone or in their bedroom; avoid social occasions such as birthdays; or avoid eating out in restaurants. This behaviour maintains dietary restriction and results in further social isolation.

Eating out and eating in social situations is recommended so that clients practice skills that enable them to spend time with family and friends and participate in social activities that involve food, eating in a manner similar to others at a social event, and expanding eating experiences. Some experts recommend targeting eating related anxiety by exposure to feared eating situations. These situations engage the client in challenging rather than avoiding their food fears, and provide an opportunity to experience habituation of anxiety and the disconfirmation of the feared consequence.[19]

The REAL Food Guide recommends eating out and having social eating occasions at least two times per week. Social eating can be a daunting and challenging experience for someone with an eating disorder and there are many eating situations that cause anxiety and stress such as banquets, shared meals with several dishes on the table, celebrations like Christmas, cocktail parties with finger foods, and ordering from a menu where the portion size and ingredients are not listed.

These situations are difficult for clients with eating disorders as they are often concerned about:

- Others' impressions of their eating.
- Difficulty monitoring how much is eaten.
- Difficulty controlling portion size.
- Pressure to engage in social interaction.
- Ingredients used in the meal.
- Seeing food on display.
- Food hygiene issues and.
- Spending money on food.

Recommended servings of fun foods per day
Weight maintenance = 1 serving
Weight regain = 1 serving
One serving of fun food
3 rich chocolate biscuits
4 chocolate coated biscuits
3 cream biscuits
4 wafer biscuits
5 plain sweet biscuits
1 medium chocolate bar (50–60g)
1/3 cup lollies or sweets
1 single serving bag crisps (50g)
1 cupcake (bottom fits neatly into ½ cup)
1 muffin (bottom fits neatly into ½ cup)
1 palm sized piece of cake

Diet Foods and Fillers

The top layer of the REAL Food Guide depicts low energy foods, which are commonly used by eating disorder clients as a method of suppressing appetite and restricting energy for weight loss.[1,20] Examples of the use of diet foods and fillers includes filling up on low energy foods, excessive use of artificial sweeteners, excessive quantities of fruit and vegetables, intake of low calorie drinks such as water and diet soft drinks, and excessive intake of tea and coffee.[14,21-23] From a nutrition standpoint, these foods become problematic when they make up a significant proportion of a client's daily intake as they replace or push out more nutritious foods from the diet. They may also keep clients focused on dietary rules and restricting food, and the inclusion of diet foods and fillers is also counterproductive for weight restoration in clients who need to regain weight.[1] The recommendation is not necessarily to eliminate these foods but to 'be careful' in regard to how they might affect overall dietary intake.

Another group of foods that fit in this category are foods with a 'health halo'. These are foods where a significant health benefit is attributed to the food making it more desirable as a food choice[24] e.g. choosing almond milk over dairy milk; or choosing 'organic' foods.

Diet foods and fillers include
Diet drinks and soft drink (e.g. diet cola, artificially sweetened beverages)
Foods labelled as 'diet'
Artificial sweeteners
Artificially sweetened beverages
Chewing gum
Sugar free sweets
Fat or energy modified foods
Excessive servings of fruits (especially lower calorie fruits such as strawberries)
Excessive servings of vegetables
Excessive use of sauces (e.g. sweet chilli sauce, tomato sauce)
Excessive use of salt and pepper

Sample Meal Plans

A nutritionally adequate meal plan will usually be more food than clients with an eating disorder have allowed themselves to eat, and initially they may doubt that this is an appropriate amount of food. Other barriers reported by clients to following a meal plan include:

- It being too time consuming.
- Feeling that the whole day revolves around food with less time for non-food activities.
- It costs too much money.
- It's inconvenient to stop other activities to plan, purchase, and prepare food and.
- Initially, there is an increase in distress when following a meal plan and a perception that they feel worse not better by having a meal plan.

Notes

1. Hart S, Marnane C, McMaster C, Thomas A. Development of the Recovery from Eating Disorders for Life. Food Guide (REAL Food Guide) – A food pyramid for adults with an eating disorder. *Journal of Eating Disorders* 2018;6:6 https://doi.org /10.1186/s40337-018-0192-4
2. Cordery H, Waller G. Nutritional knowledge of health care professionals working in the eating disorders. *European Eating Disorders Review* 2016;14:462–7.
3. Ozier AD, Henry BW. Position of the American dietetic association: Nutrition intervention in the treatment of eating disorders. *Journal of the American Dietetic Association* 2011;111(8):1236–41.
4. Hay P, Chinn D, Forbes D, Madden S, Newton R, Sugenor L, Touyz S, Ward W. Royal Australian and New Zealand College of Psychiatrists clinical practice guidelines for the treatment of eating disorders. *Australian and New Zealand Journal of Psychiatry* 2014;48(11):1–62.
5. Holli BB, Calabrese RJ, O'Sullivan-Maillet J. *Communication and Education Skills for Dietetics Professionals*. 4th Edition. Lippincott, Williams and Wilkins: London, 2003.

6. Innes NT, Clough BA, Casey LM. Assessing treatment barriers in eating disorders: A systematic review. *Eating Disorders* 2017;25(1): 1–21. DOI: 10.1080/10640266.2016.1207455

7. Cant RP, Pomeroy SEM. General practitioners' decision to refer patients to dietitians: Insight into the clinical reasoning process. *Australian Journal of Primary Health* 2010;16:147–53.

8. Waller G, Cordery H, Corstorphine E, Hinrichsen H, Lawson R, Mountford V, Russell K. *Cognitive Behavioral Therapy for Eating Disorders: A Comprehensive Treatment Guide* 1st Edition. Cambridge: Cambridge University Press, 2007.

9. Fairburn CG. *Cognitive Behavior Therapy and Eating Disorders*. New York, NY: Guilford Publications, 2008.

10. Jagielska G, Przedlacki J, Bartoszewicz Z, Racicka E. Bone mineralization disorders as a complication of anorexia nervosa- etiology, prevalence, course and treatment. *Psychiatria Polska* 2016;50(3):509–20.

11. Zuromski KL, Witte TK, Smith AR, Goodwin N, Bodell LP, Bartlett M, Siegfried N. Increased prevalence of vegetarianism among women with eating pathology. *Eating Behaviors* 2015;19:24–7.

12. Ahmad Fuzi SF, Koller D, Bruggraber S, Pereira DIA, Dainty JR, Mushtaq S. A 1-h time interval between a meal containing iron and consumption of tea attenuates the inhibitory effects on iron absorption: A controlled trial in a cohort of healthy UK women using a stable iron isotope. *American Journal Clinical Nutrition* 2017;106:1413–21.

13. Hart S, Abraham S, Franklin RC, Russell J. The reasons why eating disorder patients drink. *European Eating Disorder Review* 2011;19(2):121–8. doi: 10.1002/erv.1051.

14. Hart S, Abraham S, Luscombe G, Russell J. Fluid intake in patients with eating disorders. *International Journal of Eating Disorders* 2005;38:55–9.

15. Santanso P, Sala A, Favaro A. Water Intoxication in anorexia nervosa: A case report. *International Journal of Eating Disorders* 1998 Dec;24(4):439–42.

16. Nutrient Reference Values for Australia and New Zealand. *National Health and Medical Research Council, Australian Government.* https://www.nrv.gov.au.

17. Chiurazzi C, Cioffi I, De Caprio C, De Filippo E, Marra M, Sammarco R, Di Guglielmo ML, Contaldo F, Pasanisi F. Adequacy of nutrient intake in women with restrictive anorexia nervosa. *Nutrition.* 2017;38:80–4.

18. Allen KL, Mori TA, Beilin L, Byrne SM, Hickling S, Oddy WH. Dietary intake in population-based adolescents: Support for a relationship between eating disorder symptoms, low fatty acid intake and depressive symptoms. *Journal of Human Nutrition and Dietetics* 2013;26:459–69.

19. Steinglass J, Albano AM, Simpson HB, Schebendach J, Attia E. Fear of food as a treatment target: Exposure and response prevention for anorexia nervosa in an open series. *International Journal of Eating Disorders* 2012;45(4):615–21.

20. Santiago A, Zimmerman J, Feinstein R, Fisher M. Diet quality of adolescents with eating disorders. *International Journal of Adolescent Medical Health* 2017; https://doi.org/10. 1515/ijamh-2017-0033.

21. Burgalassi A, Ramacciotti CE, Bianchi M, Coli E, Polese L, Bondi E, Massimetti G, Dell'osso L. Caffeine consumption among eating disorder patients: epidemiology, motivations, and potential of abuse. *Eating and Weight Disorders* 2009;14(4):e212–18.

22. Brown TA, Keel PK. What contributes to excessive diet soda intake in eating disorders: Appetitive drive, weight concerns, or both? *Eat Disorders* 2013;21(3): 265–74.

23. Schebendach J, Klein DA, Mayer LES, Attia E, Devlin MJ, Foltin RW, Walsh BT. Assessment of the motivation to use artificial sweetener among individuals with an eating disorder. *Appetite* 2017;109:131–6.
24. Schuldt JP, Muller D, Schwarz N. The "Fair Trade" effect: Health halos from social ethics claims. *Social Psychological and Personality Science* 2012;3(5):581–9

Questionnaires to give to the patient at each session

In addition to the clinical measures taken throughout therapy (e.g. weight, frequency of bulimic behaviours), we use a number of questionnaires to monitor progress.

The questionnaire measures outlined below are ones that have been used in developing the evidence for CBT-T, and we recommend their use clinically. They are useful and valid regardless of diagnosis. They divide into those questionnaires that we regard as critical for clinical purposes, and those that are clinically helpful.

Critical measures to use

Minimum dataset:

- Eating attitudes (ED-15 and EDE-Q).
- Anxiety and depression (DASS *or* GAD-7 and PHQ-9).

We also recommend using the Working Alliance Inventory (WAI-SR).

When to use each measure

The schedule that we recommend for using these measures is as outlined below. This pattern allows us to:

- Monitor change in eating cognitions and behaviours, discuss them with the patient, and respond to them on a weekly basis (ED-15).
- Summarise change in eating characteristics to denote early progress (Session 4), outcome (Session 10), and maintenance (Follow-ups) (EDE-Q).
- Monitor changes in key comorbidity levels (anxiety and depression) (DASS or GAD-7 and PHQ-9).
- Monitor the nature of the working alliance with the patient (remembering that the patient's view of the alliance has greater validity than the clinician's view) (WAI-SR).

Session	Weekly change in eating attitudes (ED-15)	Longer term change in eating attitudes (EDE-Q)	Anxiety (DASS or GAD-7)	Depression (DASS or PHQ-9)
1	✓	✓	✓	✓
2	✓			
3	✓			
4	✓	✓	✓	✓
5	✓			
6	✓			
7	✓			
8	✓			
9	✓			
10*	✓	✓	✓	✓
FU 1 month	✓	✓		
FU 3 month	✓	✓		

* Given after Session 9, to be completed just before Session 10.

Availability of measures in minimum dataset.

ED-15 – this measure is provided in Appendix 3 of this book.

- The scoring key is also in Appendix 3.
- Please note that the ED-15 is copyrighted, but has approval for non-commercial use.
- Reference: Tatham, M., Turner, H., Mountford, V. A., Tritt, A., Dyas, R., & Waller G. (2015). Development, psychometric properties and preliminary clinical validation of a brief, session-by-session measure of eating disorder cognitions and behaviors: The ED-15. *International Journal of Eating Disorders*, *48*, 1005–1115.

EDE-Q (version 6) is downloadable from the CREDO website (http://www.credo-oxford.com/7.2.html).

- Please note that the EDE-Q is copyrighted, but has approval for non-commercial use.
- Reference: Fairburn, C. G. (2008). *Cognitive Behavior Therapy and Eating Disorders*. New York, NY: Guilford Press.

DASS is downloadable from http://www2.psy.unsw.edu.au/dass/down.htm

- The scoring key is available from the same site.
- Please note that the DASS is copyrighted, but has approval for non-commercial use.

- Reference: Lovibond, P. F., & Lovibond, S. H. (1995). The structure of negative emotional states: Comparison of the Depression Anxiety Stress Scales (DASS) with the Beck Depression and Anxiety Inventories. *Behaviour Research and Therapy, 33*, 335–343.

GAD-7 and **PHQ-9** can be downloaded from a variety of locations, such as https://www.plu.edu/counseling/wp-content/uploads/sites/148/2015/03/phqgad.pdf, which also shows the scoring key.

- Both are free to use.
- Reference: Kroenke, K., & Spitzer, R. L. (2002). The PHQ-9: A new depression diagnostic and severity measure. *Psychiatric Annals, 32,* 509–521.
- Reference: Spitzer, R. L., Kroenke, K., Williams, J. B. W., & Löwe, B. (2006). A brief measure for assessing generalized anxiety disorder: the GAD-7. *Archives of Internal Medicine, 166,* 1092–1097.

Patient handout on emotions and beliefs that can trigger eating behaviours

Emotions and beliefs that can trigger eating behaviours

Sometimes, people are uncomfortable with their thoughts and feelings, and do not know how to deal with them. That can be because they were brought up in a way that did not encourage them to experience or express how they felt, and do not feel safe or able to talk about their thoughts and feelings now.

That difficulty can lead people to find other ways of coping with their feelings. Those ways include:

- bingeing and vomiting to block out emotions and thoughts
- restricting, taking laxatives, and exercising compulsively to avoid feeling those emotions and thoughts in the first place

These are avoidant and safety behaviours, which we already talked about earlier in this treatment. As before, such behaviours make you feel calmer in the short term, but worse in the longer term. For example, bingeing can make you feel 'zoned out' when you were feeling angry or worried, but then you end up feeling more worried or ashamed after the binge.

The diary that you are going to keep asks you to identify the feelings and thoughts that might drive your eating behaviour. You need to do this when you first get the urge to use the behaviour, so that you can challenge your thoughts and feelings at the time. That gives you a chance to choose whether you use the eating behaviour or not.

When first completing the diary, there are two columns where you might find it hard to identify what is going on – your thoughts and your feelings. The reason that these are hard is that your eating behaviours stop you thinking the thoughts or feeling the feelings, so you find it hard to see patterns the next time round. The thoughts that are most likely to trigger binges are what are called 'core beliefs' – beliefs about who we are and how we routinely interact with the world.

Therefore, this table is a list of the type of thoughts/'core beliefs' and feelings/ emotions that often trigger eating behaviours, to help you pick out the beliefs and emotions that you could enter into your diary, until you are used to spotting them yourself. Use it when you feel like using the behaviour, rather than waiting until afterwards. Most are negative in their content, though very occasionally people use eating behaviours when they cannot manage an extremely positive emotion. If you identify other thoughts or emotions that relate to you personally, please add them to the list, as that will help you to recognise your own patterns.

Core belief/thoughts

Vulnerable
(fear of harm or loss)

Defectiveness
(lack of worth/self-esteem, and belief that others see us the same way)

Mistrust
(belief that others are not trustworthy and will do us harm)

Abandonment
(fear that others will abandon us, or will disappear and let us down when we need them)

Emotional deprivation
(belief that no-one will be there to support or care for us)

Social isolation
(belief that we are never going to have others who want to be around us or who we can rely on)

Failure
(belief that one is unable to succeed in tasks, relationships, etc.)

Dependence
(belief that one cannot succeed or get by without other people to support us)

Poor self-control
(belief that one cannot control one's behaviour)

Perfectionism
(belief that one must always do one's best, and even that is not good enough)

Emotional inhibition
(belief that emotions are not safe things to experience or express)

Emotions

Angry
(at others; at yourself)

Anxious
(about what is going to happen)

Lonely
(wishing that you were not alone)

Guilty
(feeling that you have done something wrong)

Ashamed
(worried that other are judging you negatively because of something that you have done)

Sad or depressed
(feeling you have lost something or someone)

Disgusted
(appalled at a situation and how others have acted or the fear of contamination)

Happy
(feeling extremely excited and aroused)

Extended food diary, assessing triggers to behaviours

Diary of potential triggers to using unhealthy eating behaviours

Day:_____ Date: _____

Every time you feel like overeating, bingeing, taking laxatives, restricting, being sick, etc., please complete this diary.

Then decide whether you want to use that behaviour, and make a note of the outcome.

Look at what you can learn, before going into your next therapy session

Time	What did I last eat? When?	Context/ trigger (Where was I? Who was about? What was I doing?)	What eating behaviour(s) did I feel like using?	What thoughts/ core beliefs can you identify that might be relevant?	What emotions are you experiencing that you might be trying to block out?	What do I want to do? (safety behaviour) What am I going to do, having thought about why?

Template for therapy blueprint

Therapy blueprint

Please complete this template document as well as you can before the final session of CBT-T. Then, you can discuss it with your clinician in that last session and make any amendments that would be useful.

When completing the blueprint, think about what worked for you in therapy, as well as anything that did not work well. Remember, the goal is to remind yourself in the future about what you have learned from therapy, so that you can make sure that you maintain your progress over the follow-up period and far beyond.

It might help if you imagine yourself now, giving advice to yourself a few months ago, when you were starting CBT-T. What would your advice be then, and how can you make sure that you keep taking that advice into the future.

1. What were my problems when I was first referred?

2. What did I do to change?

3. What changes do I still want to make and how will I achieve that?

4. What might lead to a setback in the future?

5. What will be the symptoms of a setback?

6. How will I overcome the setback?

7. What if that doesn't work?

References

Addis, M. E., & Krasnow, A. D. (2000). A national survey of practicing psychologists' attitudes towards psychotherapy treatment manuals. *Journal of Consulting and Clinical Psychology, 68,* 331–339.

Addis, M. E., & Waltz, J. (2002). Implicit and untested assumptions about the role of psychotherapy treatment manuals in evidence-based mental health practice. *Clinical Psychology: Science and Practice, 9,* 421–424.

Allen, K. L., O'Hara, C. B., Bartholdy, S., Renwick, B., Keyes, A., Lose, A., Kenyon, M., DeJong, H., Broadbent, H., Loomes, R., McClelland, J., Serpell, L., Richards, L., Johnson-Sabine, E., Boughton, N., Whitehead, L., Treasure, J., Wade, T., & Schmidt, U. (2016). Written case formulations in the treatment of anorexia nervosa: Evidence for therapeutic benefits. *International Journal of Eating Disorders, 49,* 874–882.

Beat (2015). *The costs of eating disorders social, health and economic impacts.* London, UK: PriceWaterhouseCoopers.

Becker, C. B. & Waller, G. (2016). The use of exposure-based strategies in treating eating disorders. In T. Wade (Ed.). *Encyclopaedia of eating and feeding disorders.* New York, NY: Springer.

Beintner, I., & Jacobi, C. (2018). Are we overdosing treatment? Secondary findings from a study following women with bulimia nervosa after inpatient treatment. *International Journal of Eating Disorders, 51,* 899–905.

Bell, C., Waller, G., Shafran, R., & Delgadillo, J. (2017). Is there an optimal length of psychological treatment for eating disorder pathology? *International Journal of Eating Disorders, 50,* 687–692.

Bennett-Levy, J., Butler, G., Fennell, M., Hackmann, A., Mueller, M., & Westbrook, D. (Eds). (2004) *Oxford guide to behavioural experiments in cognitive therapy.* Oxford, UK: Oxford University Press.

Bordin, E. S. (1979). The generalizability of the psychoanalytic concept of the working alliance. *Psychotherapy: Theory, Research and Practice, 16,* 252–260.

Bulik, C. M., Sullivan, P. F., Carter, F. A., McIntosh, V. V., & Joyce, P. R. (1998). The role of exposure with response prevention in the cognitive-behavioural therapy for bulimia nervosa. *Psychological Medicine, 28,* 611–623.

Butler, G. (2016). *Overcoming social anxiety and shyness: A self-help guide using cognitive behavioural techniques* (2nd ed.). London, UK: Robinson.

Byrne, S. M., Fursland, A., Allen, K. L., & Watson, H. (2011). The effectiveness of enhanced cognitive behavioural therapy for eating disorders: an open trial. *Behaviour Research and Therapy, 49,* 219–226.

Calugi, S., El Ghoch, M, & Dalle Grave, R. (2016). Intensive enhanced cognitive behavioural therapy for severe and enduring anorexia nervosa: A longitudinal outcome study. *Behaviour Research and Therapy, 89*, 41–48.

Cash, T. F., & Smolak, L. (Eds.) (2012). *Body image: A handbook of science, practice and prevention*. New York, NY: Guilford.

Clark, D. M. (2018). Realizing the mass public benefit of evidence-based psychological therapies: The IAPT program. *Annual Review of Clinical Psychology, 14*, 159–183.

Clark, D. M., Canvin, L., Green, J., Layard, R., Pilling, S., & Janecka, M. (2018). Transparency about the outcomes of mental health services (IAPT approach): An analysis of public data. *The Lancet, 391*, 679–686

Cooper, M. J., Whitehead, L., & Boughton, N. (2004). Eating disorders. In J. Bennett-Levy, G. Butler, M. Fennell, A. Hackmann, M. Mueller, & D. Westbrook (Eds.). *Oxford guide to behavioural experiments in cognitive therapy* (pp. 267–286). Oxford, UK: Oxford University Press.

Cowdrey, N. D. & Waller, G. (2015). Are we really delivering evidence-based treatments for eating disorders? How eating-disordered patients describe their experience of cognitive behavioural therapy. *Behaviour Research and Therapy, 75*, 72–77.

Craske, M. G., Treanor, M., Conway, C. C., Zbozinek, T., & Vervliet, B. (2014). Maximizing exposure therapy: An inhibitory learning approach. *Behaviour Research and Therapy, 58*, 10–23.

Cukrowicz, K. C., Timmons, K. A., Sawyer, K., Caron, K. M., Gummelt, H. D., & Joiner Jr, T. E. (2011). Improved treatment outcome associated with the shift to empirically supported treatments in an outpatient clinic is maintained over a ten-year period. *Professional Psychology: Research and Practice, 42*, 145–152.

Delgadillo, J., McMillan, D., Lucock, M., Leach, C., Ali, S., & Gilbody, S. (2014). Early changes, attrition, and dose–response in low intensity psychological interventions. *British Journal of Clinical Psychology, 53*, 114–130

Dennhag, I., Gibbons, M. B., Barber, J. P., Gallop, R., & Crits-Christoph, P. (2012). Do supervisors and independent judges agree on evaluations of therapist adherence and competence in the treatment of cocaine dependence? *Psychotherapy Research, 22*, 720–730.

Dray, J., & Wade, T. D. (2012). Is the transtheoretical model and motivational interviewing approach applicable to the treatment of eating disorders? A review. *Clinical Psychology Review, 32*, 558–565.

Emanuelli, F., Waller, G., Jones-Chester, M, & Ostuzzi, R. (2012). Recovery from disordered eating: Sufferers' and clinicians' perspectives. *European Eating Disorders Review, 20*, 363–372.

Fairburn, C. G. (2008). *Cognitive behavior therapy and eating disorders*. New York, NY: Guilford Press.

Fairburn, C. G., & Cooper, Z. (2011). Therapist competence, therapy quality, and therapist training. *Behaviour Research and Therapy, 49*, 373–378.

Fairburn, C. G., Cooper, Z., Doll, H. A., O'Connor, M. E., Bohn, K., Hawker, D. M., Wales, J. A., & Palmer, R. L. (2009). Transdiagnostic cognitive-behavioral therapy for patients with eating disorders: A two-site trial with 60-week follow-up. *American Journal of Psychiatry, 166*, 311–319.

Fairburn, C. G., & Harrison, P. J. (2003). Eating disorders. *Lancet, 361*, 407–416

Fairburn, C. G., Norman, P.A., Welch, S. L., O'Connor, M. E., Doll, H. A., & Peveler, R. C. (1995). A prospective study of outcome in bulimia nervosa and the long-term effects of three psychological treatments. *Archives of General Psychiatry, 52*, 304–312.

Fennell, M. (2016). *Overcoming low self-esteem: A self-help guide using cognitive behavioural techniques* (2nd ed.). London, UK: Robinson.

Forbush, K. T., Richardson, J., & Bohrer, B. K. (2015). Clinicians' practices regarding blind versus open weighing among patients with eating disorders. *International Journal of Eating Disorders, 48*, 905–911.

Freeman, A., & Dolan, M. (2001). Revisiting Prochaska and DiClemente's Stages of Change theory: An expansion and specification to aid in treatment planning and outcome evaluation. *Cognitive and Behavioral Practice, 8*, 224–234.

Gawande A. (2011). *The checklist manifesto: How to get things right.* London, UK: Profile.

Geller, J., & Srikameswaran, S. (2006). Treatment non-negotiables: Why we need them and how to make them work. *European Eating Disorders Review, 14*, 212–217.

Graves, T. A., Tabri, N., Thompson-Brenner, H., Franko, D. L., Eddy, K. T., Bourion-Bedes, S., Brown, A., Constantino, M. J., Flückiger, C., Forsberg, S., Hildebrandt, T., Isserlin, L., Couturier, J., Paulsson Karlsson, G., Mander, J., Teufel, M., Mitchell, J. E., Crosby, R. D., Prestano, C., Satir, D. A., Simpson, S., Sly, R., Lacey, J. H., Stiles-Shields, C., Tasca, G. A., Waller, G., Zaitsoff, S. L., Rienecke, R., Le Grange, D., & Thomas, J. J. (2017). A meta-analysis of the relation between therapeutic alliance and treatment outcome in eating disorders. *International Journal of Eating Disorders, 50*, 323–340.

Grove, W. M., Zald, D. H., Lebow, B. S., Snitz, B. E., & Nelson, C. (2000). Clinical versus mechanical prediction: A meta-analysis. *Psychological Assessment, 12*, 19–30.

Hamilton, K., & Waller, G. (1993). Media influences on body size estimation in anorexia and bulimia: An experimental study. *British Journal of Psychiatry, 162*, 837–840.

Hoskins, J. I., Blood, L., Stokes, H. R., Tatham, M., Waller, G., & Turner, H. (2019). Patients' experiences of brief cognitive behavioural therapy (CBT-T) for eating disorders: A qualitative investigation. *International Journal of Eating Disorders.* doi: 10.1002/eat.23039.

Institute of Medicine (2001). *Crossing the quality chasm: A new health system for the 21st century.* Washington, DC: National Academy Press.

Karačić, M., Wales, J. A., Arcelus, J., Palmer, R. L., Cooper, Z., & Fairburn, C. G. (2011). Changes in alcohol intake in response to transdiagnostic cognitive behaviour therapy for eating disorders. *Behaviour Research and Therapy, 49*, 573–577.

Keel, P. K., Dorer, D. J., Franko, D. L., Jackson, S. C., & Herzog, D. B. (2005). Postremission predictors of relapse in women with eating disorders. *American Journal of Psychiatry, 162*, 2263–2268.

Kennerley, H. (2016). *Overcoming anxiety: A self-help guide using cognitive behavioural techniques* (2nd ed.). London, UK: Robinson.

Knott, S., Woodward, D., Hoefkens, A., & Limbert, C. (2015). Cognitive behaviour therapy for bulimia nervosa and eating disorders not otherwise specified: translation from randomized controlled trial to a clinical setting. *Behavioural and Cognitive Psychotherapy, 43*, 641–654.

Kuyken, W. (2006) Evidence-based case formulation: Is the emperor clothed? In N.Tarrier (Ed.). *Case formulation in cognitive behaviour therapy: The treatment of challenging and complex cases* (pp. 12–35). London, UK: Routledge.

Lambert, M. J., Harmon, C., Slade, K., Whipple, J. L., & Hawkins, E. J. (2005). Providing feedback to psychotherapists on their patients' progress: Clinical results and practice suggestions. *Journal of Clinical Psychology, 61*, 165–174.

Lambert, M. J., Whipple, J. L., Vermeersch, D. A., Smart, D. W., Hawkins, E. J., Nielsen, S. L., & Goates, M. (2002). Enhancing psychotherapy outcomes via providing feedback on client progress: A replication. *Clinical Psychology and Psychotherapy, 9*, 91–103.

Linardon, J., & Brennan, L. (2017). The effects of cognitive-behavioral therapy for eating disorders on quality of life: A meta-analysis. *International Journal of Eating Disorders, 50*, 715–730.

Linardon, J., Wade, T. D., de la Piedad Garcia, X., & Brennan, L. (2017). The efficacy of cognitive-behavioral therapy for eating disorders: A systematic review and meta-analysis. *Journal of Consulting and Clinical Psychology, 85*, 1080–1094.

Linehan, M. M. (1993). *Cognitive behavioral treatment of borderline personality disorder.* New York, NY: Guilford.

Meehl, P. E. (1973). Why I do not attend case conferences. In P. E. Meehl: *Psychodiagnosis: Selected papers* (pp. 225–302). Minneapolis, MN: University of Minnesota Press.

Moore, E., Turner, H., Tatham, M., Whitty, E., Wood, F., Blood, L., Davies, H., Stokes, H. R., Russell, R., Hoskins, J., & Waller, G. (under consideration). Cognitive-behavioural therapy for non-underweight eating disorders: What constitutes meaningful clinical change in eating attitudes? *Behaviour Research and Therapy.*

Mulkens, S., de Vos, C., de Graaff, A., & Waller, G. (2018). To deliver or not to deliver cognitive behavioral therapy for eating disorders: Replication and extension of our understanding of why therapists fail to do what they should do. *Behaviour Research and Therapy, 106*, 57–63.

National Institute for Health and Care Excellence (2017). *Eating disorders: Recognition and treatment.* London, UK: National Institute for Health and Care Excellence.

Ohanian, V. (2002). Imagery rescripting within cognitive behaviour therapy for bulimia nervosa: An illustrative case report. *International Journal of Eating Disorders, 30*, 352–357.

Öst, L.-G., Karlstedt, A., & Widén, S. (2012). The effects of cognitive behavior therapy delivered by students in a psychologist training program: An effectiveness study. *Behavior Therapy, 43*, 160–173.

Öst, L.-G., & Ollendick, T. H. (2017). Brief, intensive and concentrated cognitive behavioral treatments for anxiety disorders in children: A systematic review and meta-analysis. *Behaviour Research and Therapy, 97*, 134–145.

Padesky, C. A., & Greenberger, D. (1995). *Clinician's guide to mind over mood.* New York, NY: Guilford.

Pellizzer, M., Waller, G., & Wade, T. D. (in press). Ten-session cognitive behaviour therapy for eating disorders: Outcomes from a pragmatic pilot study of Australian non-underweight patients. *Clinical Psychologist.*doi:10.1111/cp.12170

Pennesi, J. L., & Wade, T.D. (2018). Imagery rescripting and cognitive dissonance: A randomized controlled trial of two brief online interventions for women at risk of developing an eating disorder. *International Journal of Eating Disorders, 51*, 439–448.

Proctor, L., & Morley, S. (1986). ''Demand characteristics'' in body size estimation in anorexia nervosa. *British Journal of Psychiatry, 149*, 113–118.

Raykos, B. C., Erceg-Hurn, D., Fursland, A., McEvoy, P. M., & Waller, G. (2018). Severe and enduring anorexia nervosa? Illness severity and duration are unrelated to outcomes from cognitive behaviour therapy. *Journal of Consulting and Clinical Psychology, 86*, 702–709.

Raykos, B. C., Watson, H. J., Fursland, A., Byrne, S. M., & Nathan, P. (2013). Prognostic value of rapid response to enhanced cognitive behavioral therapy in a routine clinic sample of eating disorder outpatients. *International Journal of Eating Disorders, 46*, 764–770.

Reilly, E. R., Anderson, L. M., Gorrell, S., Schaumberg, K., & Anderson, D. A. (2017). Expanding exposure-based interventions for eating disorders. *International Journal of Eating Disorders*, *50*, 1137–1141.

Rose, C., & Waller, G. (2017). Cognitive-behavioral therapy for eating disorders in primary care settings: Does it work, and does a greater dose make it more effective? *International Journal of Eating Disorders*, *50*, 1305–1355.

Roth, A., & Fonagy, P. (2005). *What works for whom? A critical review of psychotherapy research*. London, UK: Guilford.

Royal College of Psychiatrists (2011). *National audit of psychological therapies for anxiety and depression, national report 2011*. London, UK: Royal College of Psychiatrists.

Royal College of Psychiatrists (2013). *Report of the second round of the National Audit of Psychological Therapies (NAPT) 2013*. London, UK: Healthcare Quality Improvement Partnership.

Shafran, R., Egan, S., & Wade, T. (2018). *Overcoming perfectionism: A self-help guide using cognitive behavioural techniques* (2nd ed.). London, UK: Robinson.

Signorini, R., Sheffield, J., Rhodes, N., Fleming, C., & Ward, W. (2018). The effectiveness of enhanced cognitive behavioural therapy (CBT-E): A naturalistic study within an out-patient eating disorder service. *Behavioural and Cognitive Psychotherapy*, *46*, 21–34.

Simpson-Southward, C., Waller, G., & Hardy, G. (2017). How do we know what makes for "best practice" in clinical supervision for psychological therapists? A content analysis of supervisory models and approaches. *Clinical Psychology and Psychotherapy*, *24*, 1228–1245.

Simpson-Southward, C., Waller, G., & Hardy, G. (2018). Supervisor practice when guiding therapists working with depression: The impact of supervisor and patient characteristics. *The Cognitive Behavioural Therapist*, *11*, 1–13.

Tatham, M., Turner, H., Mountford, V. A., Tritt, A., Dyas, R., & Waller G. (2015). Development, psychometric properties and preliminary clinical validation of a brief, session-by-session measure of eating disorder cognitions and behaviors: The ED-15. *International Journal of Eating Disorders*, *48*, 1005–1115.

Thompson, M. A., & Gray, J. J. (1995). Development and validation of a new body-image assessment scale. *Journal of Personality Assessment*, *64*, 258–269.

Tobin, D. L., Banker, J. D., Weisberg, L., & Bowers, W. (2007). I know what you did last summer (and it was not CBT): A factor analytic model of international psychotherapeutic practice in the eating disorders. *International Journal of Eating Disorders*, *40*, 754–757.

Turner, H., Marshall, E., Stopa, L., & Waller, G. (2015). Cognitive-behavioural therapy for outpatients with eating disorders: Effectiveness for a transdiagnostic group in a routine clinical setting. *Behaviour Research and Therapy*, *68*, 70–75.

Turner, H., Marshall, E., Wood, F., Stopa, L., & Waller, G. (2016). CBT for eating disorders: The impact of early changes in eating pathology on later changes in personality pathology, anxiety and depression. *Behaviour Research and Therapy*, *77*, 1–6.

Turner, H., Tatham, M., Lant, M., Mountford, V. A., & Waller, G. (2014). Clinicians' concerns about delivering cognitive-behavioural therapy for eating disorders. *Behaviour Research and Therapy*, *57*, 38–42.

Vall, E., & Wade, T. D. (2015). Predictors of treatment outcome in individuals with eating disorders: A systematic review and meta-analysis. *International Journal of Eating Disorders*, *48*, 946–971.

Walfish, S., McAlister, B., O'Donnel, P., & Lambert M. (2012). An investigation of self-assessment bias in mental health providers. *Psychological Reports*, *110*, 1–6.

Waller, G. (2012). The myths of motivation: Time for a fresh look at some received wisdom in the eating disorders? *International Journal of Eating Disorders*, *45*, 1–16.

Waller, G. (2016). The functional analytic model of anorexia nervosa and bulimia nervosa. In T. Wade (Ed.). *Encyclopaedia of eating and feeding disorders*. New York, NY: Springer

Waller, G., Cordery, H., Corstorphine, E., Hinrichsen, H., Lawson, R., Mountford, V., & Russell, K. (2007). *Cognitive-behavioral therapy for the eating disorders: A comprehensive treatment guide*. Cambridge, UK: Cambridge University Press.

Waller, G., Evans, J., & Pugh, M. (2013). Food for thought: A pilot study of the pros and cons of changing eating patterns within cognitive-behavioural therapy for the eating disorders. *Behaviour Research and Therapy*, *51*, 519–525.

Waller, G., Gray, E., Hinrichsen, H., Mountford, V., Lawson, R., & Patient, E. (2014). Cognitive-behavioral therapy for bulimia nervosa and atypical bulimic nervosa: effectiveness in clinical settings. *International Journal of Eating Disorders*, *47*, 13–17.

Waller, G., Kennerley, H., & Ohanian, V. (2007). Schema-focused cognitive behavioral therapy with eating disorders. In L. P. Riso, P. L. du Toit, D. J. Stein, & J. E. Young (Eds.). *Cognitive schemas and core beliefs in psychiatric disorders: A scientist-practitioner guide.* (pp. 139–175). New York, NY: American Psychological Association.

Waller G., & Mountford, V. (2015). Weighing patients within cognitive-behavioural therapy for eating disorders: how, when and why. *Behaviour Research and Therapy*, *70*, 1–10.

Waller, G., Mountford, V., Lawson, R., Gray, E., Cordery, H., & Hinrichsen, H. (2010). *Beating your eating disorder: A cognitive-behavioral self-help guide for sufferers and their carers*. Cambridge, UK: Cambridge University Press.

Waller, G., Mountford, V. A., Tatham, M., Turner, H., Gabriel, C., & Webber, R. (2013). Attitudes towards psychotherapy manuals among clinicians treating eating disorders. *Behaviour Research and Therapy*, *51*, 840–844.

Waller, G., Stringer, H., & Meyer, C. (2012). What cognitive behavioral techniques do therapists report using when delivering cognitive behavioral therapy for the eating disorders? *Journal of Consulting and Clinical Psychology*, *80*, 171–175.

Waller, G., Tatham, M., Turner, H., Mountford, V. A., Bennetts, A., Bramwell, K., Dodd. J., Ingram, L. (2018). A 10-session cognitive-behavioral therapy (CBT-T) for eating disorders: Outcomes from a case series of non-underweight adult patients. *International Journal of Eating Disorders*, *51*, 262–269.

Waller, G., & Turner, H. (2016). Therapist drift redux: Why well-meaning clinicians fail to deliver evidence-based therapy, and how to get back on track. *Behaviour Research and Therapy*, *77*, 129–137.

Wilson, G. T., Fairburn, C. G., & Agras, W. S. (1997). Cognitive behavioral therapy for bulimia nervosa. In D. M. Garner, & P. E. Garfinkel (Eds.). *Handbook of treatment for eating disorders* (pp. 67–93). New York, NY: Guilford.

Young, J. E., & Klosko, J. S. (1993). *Reinventing your life*. New York, NY: Plume Publishers.

Young, J. E. (1999). *Cognitive therapy for personality disorders: a schema-focused approach*, 3rd Ed. Sarasota, FL: Professional Resource Press.

Young, J. E., Klosko, J. S., & Weishaar, M. E. (2003). *Schema therapy: A practitioner's guide*. New York, NY: Guilford.

Index

Numbers in **bold** denote tables, numbers in *italics* denote figures.

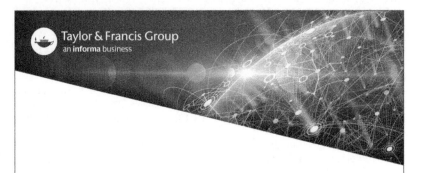